In the Heart of
Ozark Mountain Country

A Popular History of
Stone and Taney Counties,
including Branson, Missouri

———————

White Oak Press
P.O. Box 188
Reeds Spring, MO 65737

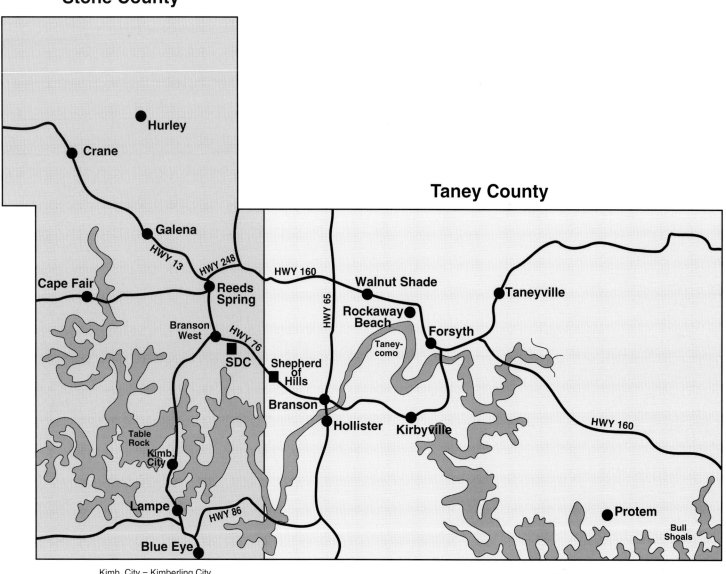

Stone County

Taney County

- Hurley
- Crane
- Galena
- HWY 13
- HWY 248
- Cape Fair
- Reeds Spring
- HWY 160
- Walnut Shade
- Taneyville
- HWY 65
- Rockaway Beach
- Forsyth
- Branson West
- HWY 76
- Taney-como
- SDC
- Shepherd of Hills
- Branson
- Hollister
- Kirbyville
- HWY 160
- Table Rock
- Kimb. City
- Lampe
- HWY 86
- Protem
- Bull Shoals
- Blue Eye

Kimb. City = Kimberling City
SDC = Silver Dollar City

Map created by Joanna Reuter

mouie-Deliuerance

ACKNOWLEDGEMENTS

General Editor:

Frank Reuter

Contributors:

Kathleen Van Buskirk   Fern Angus   Mary Hartman
James D. Lancaster, Jr.   Robert McGill   Frank Reuter
Charlie Farmer   Jane Fitzgerald   Tom Aley
Ellen Gray Massey   Edith McCall   Robert Wiley
Fern Nance Shumate   Viola Hartman

Illustrations:

Many of the photographs in this book are from the collection of Chloe LaRue of Reeds Spring. Fortunately, Chloe retrieved them from the belongings of Doctor Shumate of Reeds Spring when he passed away several years ago, or the photographs might have been lost forever. Many of these fine old photographs were taken by the Hall Photo Co. Whenever possible, we have credited the contributors of photographs. A few photographs have been used extensively over the years in regional publications and their origin is impossible to ascertain.

The line drawings are the creative efforts of Dana and Jessie Christofferson, area residents who attend the College of the Ozarks.

Technical Assistance:

John Neimeyer

Cover:

Concept by Karlene McGill, design by Annette Oatman. Photos of Peter Engler and musical instruments (from Mountain Music Shop) by Denise McGill, cabin courtesy of Shepherd of the Hills, church courtesy of Silver Dollar City.

Special Thank You:

Karlene McGill and David Dugan

Thank You:

Many others have also assisted with the book by consenting to interviews, reading drafts, or otherwise adding to our understanding of the Ozarks. Their contributions have been incalculable. Thank you Pansy Albers, Ruth Asher, Cathryn Babbit, Stephen Babbit, John Baltes, Blanche Cary, Tonya Chambers, Betty Clark, Howard Claybough, Ron Conn, Charlene Cox, Dan Davis, Robert Emerson, Jack England, Peter Engler, Rockwell Fletcher, Henry Gugel, Jr., Jessie May Hackett, Mary Scott Hair, Bill Ellen Hall, Walter Hammers, Ken Hay, Alden Hembree, Peter Herschend, Lois Holman, Nelson Holt, Paul Jaenicke, Donna Lonchar, Bill Mabe, Jim Mabe, Lyle Mabe, Douglas Mahnkey, Marilyn Mathis, Clint Maxwell, R. Layne Morrill, Linda Myers-Phinney, John Neimeyer, Dr. Lyle Owen, Ruth and Clarence Parkey, Noel Perkins, Walker Powell, Raeanne Presley, Lisa Rau, Mary Reuter, Noona Robertson, Jessie Taneyhill Rozell, David Sample, Ardis Stewart, Maggie Hensley Stuart, Shoji Tabuchi, Ott Teague, Rita Thomas, I. M. Thompson, Juanita Thompson, Lester Vining, Georgia Ware, Kim Whaley, Spike and Darnell White, Boxcar Willie, and Carnation Wing.

Source Materials:

Because this text is a popular history, we have avoided utilizing extensive footnotes. The contributors have relied upon and would like to acknowledge the following publications, books, and organizations:

Publications:

The Ozarks Mountaineer, White River Valley Historical Quarterly, Branson Echo, White River Leader, Branson Beacon-Leader, Taney County Republican, Springfield News-Leader, Branson Daily News, Stone County Oracle, College of the Ozarks Visitor, Lyons Memorial Library—College of the Ozarks, Taneyhills Community Library—Branson, Vital Signs—Skaggs Community Hospital.

Books:

Elmo Ingenthron, *Land of Taney, Borderland Rebellions, Indians of the Ozarks Plateau*
Ronald L. Martin, *Marvel Cave*
Harold Bell Wright, *To My Sons*
John Keever Ross, *Old Matt's View of It—1913*
Stone County Historical Society, *History of Stone County Missouri*
Margaret M. Lucas, *The Ozark Canners and Freezers Association Progress Report*
Lucile Folse Aly, *John G. Neihardt*
Unpublished autobiography of Rose O'Neill
Robert Liebert, *Osage Life and Legends*
John Joseph Mathews, *The Osages*
Helen and Townsend Godsey, *Flight of the Phoenix*
Postal Inspection Service Bulletin—Spring 1977

Organizations:

Skaggs Community Hospital Staff and Volunteers, Empire District Electric Company, U.S. Army Corps of Engineers

In the Heart of Ozark Mountain Country:
A Popular History of Stone and Taney Counties,
Including Branson, Missouri

Copyright © 1992 by White Oak Press

Library of Congress Cataloging-in-Publication Number 92-080599

ISBN 0-935069-04-6

10 9 8 7 6 5 4 3 2
Printed in USA

White Oak Press
P.O. Box 188
Reeds Spring, MO 65737

In the Heart of

OZARK MOUNTAIN COUNTRY

A Popular History of Stone and Taney Counties including Branson, Missouri

Contents

Introduction

A billboard on the approach to Silver Dollar City announces, "You've got a great past ahead of you," a statement which helps explain what lures so many tourists to Ozark Mountain Country. Here in the hills, life still seems to be a little simpler than elsewhere. The visitor to Ozark Mountain Country can expect family entertainment: a theme park centered on the traditional values and crafts of the last century, an outdoor drama which promotes ideals which seem to have been lost in the rush of modern life, and music which is country oriented. Add to this the beauty of the countryside and the chance to fish or boat on the lakes, and the Branson area offers an ideal family vacation.

Yet in the midst of all the crowds which now visit the area, the flavor of the past is often lost. Many visitors never really get to know what life in the Ozarks was once like—or still is like off the beaten path. The purpose of this book, then, is to record the history of Taney and Stone Counties, Missouri, in popular form, both for the local population and to enrich the experience of the tourist.

In the broadest possible terms, we hope to capture the flavor of Ozark life, both past and present, and to give the reader a taste for what makes the area unique. For Ozark Mountain Country does have a distinct culture and way of life, one which continues to lure many in-migrants to the area.

Unlike most history books, this text will be organized in reverse chronological order, its first section dealing with the present economic success of the area—the entertainment industry. Then we will strip away the bright lights and traffic jams and plunge back through time—to the taming of the White River with Table Rock Lake Dam and the subsequent change in the character of the area (Section II), to the lifestyles of early settlers and the development of the culture of the Ozarks (Section III), to the violence of the Civil War era and its aftermath (Section IV), and to the Indian past (Section V). A final section of local community histories rounds out the book.

The contributors to the book are experienced local historians and writers, familiar with the area and its character. Though the book is a popular history, every effort has been made to ensure that information is both correct and representative of Ozark life.

Frank Reuter

A Cabin in the Ozarks

A Cabin in the Ozarks
Is the happiest place I know
When the frogs begin to sing
And the March winds start to blow.
When the dogwood trees are shining
On the hills in robes of white
Then my old reel gets to whining
For 'tis now the bluegills bite.

A cabin the Ozarks
In the summer's dreamy haze
Is where I love to linger
Loitering through the quiet days;
Now the cornfields are enticing
All the squirrels for miles around,
And I take my old gun with me
Where the frisky folks are found.

When the Autumn winds are shifting
And the hills in glory glow
And the wild ducks start their drifting
And the foxhounds chanting go,
Wild grapes, nuts, pawpaws, persimmons
Hang in Nature's festal hall—
O a cabin in the Ozarks
Is the finest in the fall.

This cabin in the Ozarks
Has a fireplace deep and wide;
A pot a-stew on the hearth
And my old dog by my side;
I can see a big wild turkey
In a white oak on the hill,
Where the frosty ridge is sparkling
In the moonlight cold and still,
And I think I'll stop my wanderings
For this spot that I have found
In the blue-hazed Ozark mountains
Is just right the whole year round.

Mary Elizabeth Mahnkey

Section I
The Entertainment Industry

As Branson and the lakes area gains national attention for drawing to its stages large numbers of the nation's most popular and enduring country and western stars, it is easy to forget that the area did not become a magnet for country music celebrities overnight. The entertainment industry is here because of a long and involved history. Fishing, originally in the White and James Rivers and then in the lakes, caving in Marble Cave, and visitors' interest in the setting of a best selling novel all contributed to a gradual increase in the area's tourism. In this section, therefore, we explore the histories of Silver Dollar City, the Shepherd of the Hills, and Country Music Boulevard—the three most visited tourist attractions in the region. Since the modern entertainment industry has stimulated a revival of crafts, we also offer an essay on the role local promoters have played in rejuvenating the country's almost lost art of woodcarving.

Mary Herschend with sons Jack and Pete, originators and owners of Silver Dollar City, during the early days of the theme park. (Photo courtesy of Silver Dollar City)

Silver Dollar City

When I was a boy, our family had a favorite outing. Once or twice every summer, in the late 1950's, we would attend Sunday school but "skip" church and, instead, pile into the family's old grey Studebaker to make the one and a half hour trek into the hills of Stone County. Our first stop was always the park at the Shepherd of the Hills attraction where we would eat a picnic lunch mother had prepared. The second stop was at the dam which was under construction on the White River just west of Branson, a project which, when finished, created Table Rock Lake. On one trip, soon after the dam was completed, we discovered a new, small, craft-oriented tourist village called Silver Dollar City.

Once discovered, this village became a regular stop on our outings. We would park, walk across the highway, and take the path up the hill and across the swinging bridge to Main Street, eagerly anticipating the entertainment that we knew would be waiting for us.

On every visit the Hatfields and McCoys renewed their bitter and boisterous feud for us. They called each other names, hurled bitter accusations, and took shotgun blasts at one another. So realistic was their rivalry that, on my first visit, I was quite relieved to see the same participants return an hour later to continue the fracas.

Adventures surrounded us. The rides at that time were on real stage coaches drawn by spirited horses that responded to the yells of the wiry, energetic stagedrivers. The aroma of country food wafted through the air. And, at the end of Main Street, a gentle blacksmith with a full beard hammered out a horseshoe on his anvil while telling people about his craft. Nearby, a basketmaker wove white oak strips into a basket. I vividly remember, too, a craftsman who stood next to a full-size Conestoga wagon and explained about the lumber and techniques necessary to construct such a sturdy transporter. The wheels of the wagon were taller than my head.

That huge wagon astounded me. Indeed, I was mesmerized by the entire visit. Even then, I wished that the excursion into the past could be more than just a Sunday outing. I wanted that past to be an everyday part of my world.

Origins—The Cave

In the years since my childhood visits, Silver Dollar City has developed into one of the most successful theme parks in the United States. Little did I realize, as a boy, that the history of the park began a full decade before our first family visit. In fact, as a child, I did not realize that the history of the city began not above ground, but as an outgrowth of Marvel Cave, one of the attractions at Silver Dollar City. The cave, which has been designated a National Landmark by the U.S. Department of the Interior, is important not only because of the subterranean features it contains, but also because the origins of Silver Dollar City are tied to its development.

The first record of Marvel Cave has been passed down orally and deals with a hunting party of Osage Indians who, as tradition has it, cornered a bear in a crevice above the entrance to the cave. When one of the braves, in a show of courage, attempted to dislodge the bear from a rock ledge by attacking it with a knife, both bear and Indian disappeared. Other members of the party, searching in disbelief for the vanished warrior and bear, discovered the entrance to the cave, a sinkhole, located directly above a mammoth cavity in the earth. They notched the trees in the area, a sign of danger to the Indians. The notches remained visible for years and helped early settlers locate the entrance, which they called Devil's Den.

The first recorded exploration occurred in 1869 when Henry T. Blow of St. Louis, a lead mining magnate, led a party of six miners into the cave. The party, hoping to find lead ore, lowered themselves by rope from the sinkhole entrance down through 200 feet into the darkness of the cave.

These first explorers spent a day crawling in the mud and muck, poking their heads into the dark eerie tunnels, and glimpsing thousands of bats clinging to the ceilings. They found no lead before returning to St. Louis, but convinced that the flat wall of one room was composed of marble, they named the cave Marble Cave.

The cave remained undisturbed until 1882 when another group of entrepreneurs, led by Mr. T. Hodges Jones and Truman S. Powell of Barton County, entered the cave in hopes of finding lead. Jones and Powell found huge amounts of bat manure, or guano as it was called, and the flat wall, which they, too, believed to be marble. Two years later T. Hodges Jones bought the property and, with several of his friends, formed the Marble Cave Mining and Manufacturing Company to mine the cave. The company planned a town, Marble City, on the rough hilltop near the cave and in 1884 recorded a plat map at the courthouse in Galena. Although a few lots in the new town were sold, little development seems to have taken place.

By 1889 much of the guano had been mined from the cave, the marble wall proved to be limestone, and no lead ore was found. The mining company, which had developed so quickly, ceased operations.

The history of the cave took another turn in 1889 when William Henry Lynch, a Canadian miner and dairyman, purchased the cave and a square mile around it for $10,000. Mr. Lynch had two daughters, Miriam, an opera singer and instructor, and Genevieve, a registered nurse and poet. This unlikely trio proposed to open the cave for sightseers. The Lynches began operation of their commercial venture in 1894 with a grand celebration and a few visitors. But William Lynch could not make the cave immediately profitable. He went back to Canada for several years to raise additional capital before returning, sometime after 1900, with his daughters to again reopen the cave. The cave has remained open since then, making it one of the oldest continuously running tourist attractions in the Ozarks.

The Lynches operated the cave for nearly fifty years. At first tourists arrived on horseback or in animal-drawn carriages by traveling the old trail which ran from Springfield through Reeds Spring to Marble Cave. Then, when a railroad was built through Roark Valley between Reeds Spring and Branson, visitors could request that the engineer stop the train at a small switch station below the cave. From that point, they made their way up the hill. When motorized vehicles arrived in the Ozarks, the trail from Springfield was the first motor route to Marble Cave. Finally, in the 1930's, when the road to Branson was constructed over Dewey Bald Mountain, tourists could also arrive by vehicle from the east.

Expeditions into the cave were strenuous. Visitors were issued candles and tough, leather-seated coveralls. They climbed down a rickety ladder which dropped two hundred feet through darkness to the floor of the cave. Visitors could spend a full day exploring the passageways, crevices, and tunnels with a guide. They exited up the same ladder they had climbed down. Few other improvements marked the cave although a piano was lowered into the cave so that on special occasions Miss Miriam could give opera recitals.

When William Lynch died on September 13, 1927 at the age of 80, ownership of the cave passed to his two daughters, Miss Miriam and Miss Genevieve. The two daughters, who managed the cave for more than twenty years, changed the name of the cave to Marvel Cave. They lived in a small lodge and frequently rented rooms to their guests. Although they personally cooked many of the guest meals and often served them outside on a long lawn table, they hired guides to lead tours through the cave.

Several people who later became important to Silver Dollar City as guides, builders, and craftsmen were originally employed by the sisters as cave guides. Fannabelle Nickel, an animal lover, became one of the first guides. Ott Teague, a newlywed living on Roark Creek, carted visitors from the railroad switch in Roark Valley up the hill to the Lynch Lodge. And a skinny young boy named Lester Vining would, when he saw tourists arriving, catch the Lynch sisters' goats and tie them up so they would not disturb the visitors to the cave.

A Decade Underground

During the late 1940's, a family of visitors from the Chicago area, Hugo and Mary Herschend and their two sons, Jack and Peter, began visiting the cave. Hugo, who had enjoyed a successful career as a vacuum cleaner salesman, was looking for a retirement project. In 1949, Hugo Herschend signed a 99 year lease with the Lynch sisters for Marvel Cave—an act which would eventually lead to the establishment of Silver Dollar City.

Hugo had many ideas for improving the interior of the cave and expanding promotional activities. He even envisioned a train which would carry visitors out of the cave. But the implementation of the ideas did not come easily. For one thing, Hugo remained in Chicago and tended to his Chicago business to raise needed capital while Mary and the two boys traveled to the Ozarks each summer to conduct tours of the cave and expand the operation.

First things had to come first. Mary Herschend insisted that she have indoor plumbing in her new home before making it her permanent residence. Her house became one of the first rural homes in the county with such conveniences.

In their first summer at the cave the new operators welcomed 8,000 visitors, an average of 100 per day. For the next three years the Herschends hosted summer tourists and made modest improvements in the cave.

The year 1954 was a year of family transition. A marriage came first when Jack Herschend and Sherry Nickel, daughter of cave guide Fannabelle Nickel, exchanged vows in a ceremony which took place in the cave. Later in the year, to the consternation of the family, Hugo Herschend suffered a heart attack. He recuperated and joined the family in the Ozarks to participate in the new enterprise.

Hugo hoped to continue the improvements in the cave. A year later he made an appointment to visit a Branson Bank to request a loan, but was unable to keep that appointment because on that day, November 14, Hugo Herschend suffered a second heart attack and died.

The period of time after Hugo's death was not easy for the mother and two young sons. At the time both boys were away from home: Jack in the military and Peter at college. But Mary Herschend made a firm decision to continue the development of the cave. She sold the remaining family property in Wilmette, Illinois

The early explorers and miners entered Marble Cave in huge buckets tied to ropes and lowered by a windlass. Later visitors descended a rickety ladder until this modern steel stairway was constructed.
(Photo courtesy of Silver Dollar City)

and invested the proceeds to further develop the business. The decision severed her last major contact with her former home; now her only residence was the Ozarks, her only business the cave.

Mary Herschend was equal to the task of providing capable leadership to the new family business. She was a person of strength and integrity. One of seven children born on an Illinois farm, she attended Eureka College in Illinois and Ohio State University. Her first employment was as a librarian in Chicago, where she met and married Hugo Herschend. She enjoyed the challenge of running a business and especially loved the Ozarks. Her inspiration to continue with the new venture came from the tenacious character of the two Lynch sisters she had succeeded at Marvel Cave.

One of Mary's first decisions was to complete the improvements of Marvel Cave which Hugo had envisioned: the footpaths inside the cave and a railway from the depths of the cave to the parking lot above. Cave guides performed much of the work on the walkways. On days when visitation was slow, they would shoulder heavy sacks of cement and carry them down into the cave. Jack and Peter joined in the construction when they returned to the area.

By 1957 the Herschends were ready to build the railroad. Jack served as the chief engineer of the project. He began by mapping the cave to find the most advantageous place to drill a tunnel to the outside. After weeks of exploration, he and the cave guides determined that the nearest place to the surface was in Blondie's Throne, a 97 foot dome pit. The distance to the surface would be 218 feet through solid rock.

Before the building of the railroad could begin, an indoor passageway was cleared so tourists could walk upright to Blondie's Throne. Then the rock was blasted away outside and the tracks were placed in position. Local materials were used for most of the project. The only mishap was almost a catastrophic one; a train cable broke during final construction and the train rammed backward down the tracks, badly injuring Jack's leg. But even this injury, from which Jack recovered, did not appreciably slow progress on the railroad. The railroad was completed within ten years of the Herschends taking control of Marvel Cave.

On May 11, 1958, the Herschends formally dedicated the train. Proving that they already had an eye for publicity, they enlisted Casey Jones, Jr., son of the subject of the ballad, to help initiate the maiden trip up the steep hillside. With the railroad in operation, the development of the cave was complete.

The Herschends immediately began to search for ways to expand their growing attraction. Anticipating an influx of additional tourists to the Ozarks, they wanted to create an attraction which would entice even more visitors to the cave. Although they realized that any new attraction would have to be added above ground, they were uncertain what to provide.

The Beginning of Silver Dollar City

In 1960 the future for tourism in Stone and Taney Counties looked bright. Table Rock Lake had filled with sparkling pure water from the White River. Highway 65 from Springfield to Branson was being rebuilt. American families were responding to their new affluence by vacationing in scenic areas like the Ozarks. And the Herschends, although they could not foresee the magnitude of the tourist boom, had the experience, determination, and good fortune to be at the top of a creative explosion.

The Herschends give Russell Pearson the credit for starting the chain of events that led to Silver Dollar City. Pearson was a carnival man who lived his life dreaming of ways to entertain people. He had already helped build one "old west" town, Frontier City, in Oklahoma City. Pearson arrived at Marvel Cave, unknown and uninvited, in the fall of 1959. He proposed to the Herschends that they build an old Ozark Village where the past could be relived.

The Herschends connected Pearson's idea with the almost forgotten town of Marble. The perfectly timed proposal ignited the creative explosion—but not without an astounding amount of accompanying effort.

Russell Pearson sketched an old Ozark village that could be built on the stone-laden hilltop near the entrance to Marvel Cave. The sketch included five facade-fronted stores, at seven-eighths scale, facing a wide main street where old time Ozark music, contests, and mock family feuds could be held.

Mary Herschend modified and then approved the plan. She liked the concept but considered the facades to be shortcuts. Every inch of her buildings, not just the front, she decreed, would resemble 1890 Ozark buildings. In a kind of environmental impact statement years ahead of its time, she insisted that, during construction, the landscape be altered as little as possible. She demanded that no trees, other than those that absolutely interfered with a construction site, would be removed. When she borrowed $16,000 for the construction of the buildings, everyone knew the project would meet her standards.

Jack, when he returned from service in the spring of 1960, served as foreman for the new town. Meanwhile Peter, who could see little personal future for himself in the new town, arrived in the late spring after he had completed college. He pledged only to help during the busy summer months. Neither has ever left the employment of the family business.

The first addition to the town was an old log cabin in Taney County, the McHaffie homestead, which was being threatened by the backwaters of the new Bull Shoals Lake. And so, when workmen reassembled the logs near Marvel Cave, a part of the past was literally preserved.

The church, originally the Wilson Creek schoolhouse—located near the Sack-and-All store and grist mill northwest of Reeds Spring, Missouri—was moved to Silver Dollar City. The cupola was fashioned from an abandoned log cabin in Roark Valley. Lester Vining personally made the pulpit from a huge oak tree log which had been cut to clear the way for a street. The first services in the church were held June 15, 1960.

The stores and the blacksmith shop were built from local materials by the cave guides who, by now, had come to call themselves "the mole hole gang." They were called on to use even more extensive skills than in the upgrading of the cave. Without the inventive abilities and "make-do" skills of the guides, the buildings would have never been completed. Those buildings remain in everyday use, a testament to the builders' skills and Mary Herschend's insistence on quality.

But the creation of a town required more than just buildings. Other help was needed.

Don Richardson, a publicist for country music stars in Springfield during the Ozark Jubilee era of the 1950's, promoted the new town. He had already helped the Herschends promote extravaganzas in the cave. No advertising budget existed. Except for a few small ads in the local newspaper, no budget would exist for another six years. Richardson, hoping that word of mouth advertising would promote the venture, suggested that the town be named Silver Dollar City and that

visitors be given actual silver dollars as change. Otherwise, he relied on free promotions in newspaper articles and radio and TV coverage to promote the new theme park.

To provide entertainment, Jack and Peter, with the help of Russ Pearson and the "mole hole gang," created their own version of the Hatfield-McCoy feud.

The "old" paint was barely dry on the new buildings when Silver Dollar City opened for the first time on May 1, 1960. Clerks in the old-time stores waited on customers. Guests rode sure-footed burros or in a real stagecoach drawn by handsome horses. From the beginning, the Hatfields and McCoys appeared from the hillsides to raise a hullabaloo in front of guests.

The response from visitors the first year exceeded expectations. And the silver dollars, when spent at other area shops, helped advertise the new tourist town, although they were used for only a short period of time. The Herschends rushed to employ additional help. The new Ozark town was an immediate success.

For the next few years, the fledgling town experienced the excitement of creative growth. The Frisco-Silver Dollar City Line began carrying passengers from the edge of the city, through the woods, and back to the station. Because the original engine could not make the entire run without rebuilding a head of steam, some of the staff at Silver Dollar City created a mock raid to entertain the passengers while the engine regained steam. The ruffians, the Alf Bolin Gang, named for an early band of local outlaws, have become a permanent part of train trips at Silver Dollar City and continue their silly, but entertaining, attempts to rob the train. Other attractions—a new restaurant, pottery shop, and general store—followed in quick succession as the town expanded down the hill. Finally, a flour mill and bakery, named Sullivan's Mill for a man who gave an old miller's stone to the Herschends, was completed. Visitors could watch the slow turning of belts, shafts, and gears transform grain into flour—and smell the aroma of fresh-baked bread.

Meanwhile, new personalities, some who stayed for years, took up residence at the city.

Shad (Lloyd) Heller, who had worked at the Shepherd of the Hills, came to Silver Dollar City to produce plays. Shad was a gentle person. He sported a bushy, white beard. He worked a year, left for a season, returned, and stayed until his death in 1991. He became extremely popular with his fellow workers, and was noted for the pranks he pulled on other employees and guests alike. Although not the city's first blacksmith, he has long been remembered as the blacksmith and first mayor of Silver Dollar City. He and his wife Mollie (whose name off-stage is Ruth) produced and performed many skits at Silver Dollar City.

Peter Engler first began woodcarving at Silver Dollar City in 1963. Until Peter Engler arrived, crafts had been tangential to Silver Dollar City. But when fascinated guests purchased all of the prodigious carver's works, the potential for other handiwork became obvious. The woodcarver opened the door for the multitude of crafts that eventually flourished at Silver Dollar City.

But Peter and Shad were more than just craftsmen performing a trade; they were showmen, too. In private the two were good friends who enjoyed conjuring up antics to spring before unsuspecting guests. Most of their bantering centered around Shad's tenure as mayor—and to the public they became outspoken political opponents. To the amusement of visitors in the park, Shad's terms as mayor were marred by heated public disputes with woodcarver Engler. Peter demanded that the potholes in the street be fixed. They were hard on his wagon wheels. And he demanded that more watering troughs for mules be placed throughout the park. He asked aloud what the mayor and city council would do. The mayor belligerently retorted that the roads were good, taxes would have to be raised, and that Peter was a crabby fellow. Peter would respond by threatening to run for mayor. The pair often polled the guests unexpectedly to see who they thought would make the best mayor.

During this early period everyone helped put on the plays. When the Hatfields and McCoys had a ten minute altercation "every hour on the hour" on the town's main street, shop clerks would close their stores, don the costumes of their particular parts, and rush to Main Street to participate in the play. They would shout and yell and accuse each other of the most horrendous atrocities before firing their shotguns. But, since no one was ever hurt, shopkeepers returned to their shops until the clock had passed another hour and they could resume the feud.

The feuds had a specific purpose. Until 1967 Silver Dollar City had no admission fee; the only charge was for a tour of the cave. Thus, it was not by chance that the Hatfield and McCoy feud was perpetrated near the cave entrance. Immediately after the final shotgun blast, guests were urged to tour the cave. Cave tour receipts meant that the payroll could be met—and the park expanded.

John Corbin and Andy Miller both added their talents during this time. John, who loved to quote Shakespeare as he worked, was employed as a plumber and quickly became familiar with every pipe in the park. But his diverse talents included writing, directing, and acting in skits. One of the early "medicine shows" was his creation. John retired after a few years at Silver Dollar City. Andy Miller, originally employed as a part-time painter and designer, eventually became the conscience of Silver Dollar City, assuring that all buildings, billboards, and promotional material adhered to the city's 1890 theme.

By 1963 Don Richardson was working full-time at Silver Dollar City as a one-man chamber of commerce. He wrote articles for newspapers and travel brochures, and booked appearances for Silver Dollar City craftsmen at radio and television stations and mall shows throughout the midwest.

And Peter Herschend's creative talents quickly blossomed in public relations. Peter always had time to laugh and weave a good story. He accompanied craftsmen on the promotional tours around the midwest. He often stayed an extra day and extended interviews to producers, executives, writers, and travel agents. The increasing gate receipts attest to his promotional genius.

In order to accommodate the abundance of visitors, the park was always in need of expansion, and work crews were constantly hurrying to complete one project so that another could be started. The haste to complete projects provided some startling moments. In 1964 when the decision was made to build Slantin Sam's and Leanin Lil's (now Grandfather's Mansion) and The Tree House, two teams, one under the leadership of Jack and the other led by Peter, raced to complete the two buildings before the Fourth of July when visitors,

paying a quarter each, would tour the attractions. The workmen, who constructed a slide in Slantin Sam's and Leanin Lil's for children to exit, gave the surface a good waxing upon completion. Jack Herschend, insisting on being the first to try, hurled himself down the new slide with a powerful pull at the rails. He ricocheted in a circular motion, and landed sprawling on the rough, rocky hillside approximately twenty paces beyond his predicted stopping spot—on his "tush." Astonished workers rushed to make certain he had survived, and guffawed when they discovered that only his pride was hurt. But it was Peter's team that was declared the winner and dined on steak that night.

The building of the tourist town was a bold and ambitious undertaking. Since the town was growing so quickly and beyond original expectations, no extended plan for the town was possible. With so many determined, hardworking, and creative people contributing to the 1890 recreation, the potential for conflict was great. Could such a project flourish without a serious

Shad and Aunt Mollie Heller became well-known employees of Silver Dollar City. For many years he was the blacksmith and mayor of SDC; their skits and plays were performed throughout the park.
(Left photo courtesy of Silver Dollar City; above photo by Kathleen Van Buskirk)

clash of ideas and personalities? Of course none developed, for Mary Herschend did not allow it. Mary Herschend supplied the decisive leadership and inspiration that ensured the success of the theme park. She was energetic and paid attention to every detail. She made the final decisions on the location of the buildings, the color of paint, the quality of construction, and the content of plays.

Not only did Mary work hard, but she insisted that all employees do their part. If, on days when crowd attendance was low, she ever noticed her employees loitering on the job, she would turn to one of her sons and say "can't you find something for these boys to do?" And, almost immediately, a work crew would be on its way to the newest building under construction. The

The first employees of Silver Dollar City were required to perform in a variety of roles.
Here Shad Heller, Ray Mullenix, Peter Herschend, and John Corbin entertain early park visitors.
(Photo courtesy of Silver Dollar City)

company books were also a focus for her keen mind. For many years Mary personally wrote every check issued by Silver Dollar City.

Not only did Mary Herschend command respect and affection from her employees, but others recognized her talents, too. In 1968 the Federal Small Business Administration honored her as Missouri Small Businessman of the year. Four years later, in 1972, she received the first Missouri Tourism Award for her contributions to tourism.

A significant decision which was less noticeable to the public but certainly important to the continued success of the operation was made in 1967. Peter and Jack Herschend donned still another role when they traded their 1890 garb for suits and ties and participated in a seminar sponsored by the American Management Association. The two young executives from the fledgling theme park sat in on sessions with chief executive officers from major corporations. From this experience they decided to incorporate Silver Dollar

City and establish a professional board of directors. Although the company remained a family owned business, the brothers voluntarily decided to place themselves under the direction of outside control. Jack became the president and Peter the executive vice president, positions which utilize their complementary talents. Both men praise this decision which has controlled Silver Dollar City since 1968.

A period of growth 1969 - 1978

In 1969 a popular television show, the Beverly Hillbillies, was beamed into millions of American homes. The show was a cornball spoof about a family of lovable hill people who had struck it rich and moved to Hollywood. The characters in the show—Granny, Jed, Jethro, and Ellie Mae—pursued their simple needs with an energetic lifestyle that contrasted sharply with the materialism of Hollywood—and the plot for the weekly series was hatched. Because Don Richardson, publicity director for Silver Dollar City, and Paul Henning, producer of the television show, were good friends, Silver Dollar City became the backdrop for five shows. When the Beverly Hillbilly family needed to find a boyfriend for Ellie Mae, the family moved to Silver Dollar City to find an acceptable suitor.

Area newspapers were full of the news. Autographed pictures of the stars were displayed prominently in local restaurants, and Silver Dollar City employees lined up to be extras in the shows. Crowds gathered to watch the filming, and Shad Heller became an instant favorite in homes across America. Even Ellie Mae, although she did not find a permanent boyfriend, told visitors at the set about her enjoyable visit to Silver Dollar City. To express appreciation, at the completion of the filming, the stars feted the workers at Silver Dollar City with an evening dinner.

The national exposure ushered in an era of near miraculous growth for the small, family owned theme park. Gate receipts spiraled upward. The park grew down the hill and into the holler. The huge glass blowing furnace was installed, followed in successive years by the Ozark Marketplace, saloon, courthouse, diving bell, and Tom Sawyer's Landing. Additional restaurants were added and the music festivals begun. In just a few short years, the park doubled in size.

By the end of the 1970's, Silver Dollar City had grown to such a size that no one, not even the management, could keep up with all the activities. Even the employees noticed the change, for no longer was a single employee required to do a multitude of jobs. Carpenters were required only to be carpenters, electricians practiced only their own trade, and craftsmen could spend all of their time handcrafting items while the mole hole gang retreated, permanently, back to the cave. By the end of the decade, Silver Dollar City had a peak summertime payroll of 500 employees.

A company of this size could no longer be bound together solely by the enthusiasm and perseverance of the founders and employees. Yet the company continued to provide quality entertainment. The staff remained courteous and caring to guests. Many customers returned year after year. To ensure that the excellence of Silver Dollar City would continue, the Herschends developed a Mission Statement and a Creed which have been the guiding principles for Silver Dollar City. The statements declare that Silver Dollar City expects to exceed customer expectations, will empower each other as employees, and strives to provide a consistently high quality of family entertainment in an historical setting. They explicitly state that Christian values and ethics will guide the conduct of the park. The statements reflect in words the force of character and example that Mary Herschend epitomized. Her influence on the park continues, even though she passed away in 1983.

The growth of Silver Dollar City proved to be vulnerable when, in 1973, the shortage of gasoline curtailed driving and vacations all across the United States. Fewer guests passed through the turnstiles. The Herschends responded to the immediate crisis by purchasing gasoline on the open market and reselling it to service stations in the area, ensuring that it would be available to tourists when they arrived or for their return home.

The energy crisis also prompted them to look

In 1969 the nationally popular Beverly Hillbillies television show filmed five segments of the series at Silver Dollar City. The filming brought exposure and surging growth to Silver Dollar City. Here Mary Herschend and the cast, including Ellie Mae, Jed, Grandma, and Jethro, pose for a picture.
(Photo courtesy of Silver Dollar City)

beyond the confines of Silver Dollar City and put their financial eggs in more than one basket. In 1975 they purchased another theme park at Pigeon Forge, Tennessee and renamed it Silver Dollar City. Although this decision eventually turned into another highly successful enterprise, the Herschends discovered the new park still left them vulnerable to an erratic oil market because the oil shortage hurt that park's revenues too. The Herschends vowed that their next developments would be in urban areas so that tourists would not have to travel great distances.

By the end of the decade, Peter Herschend relinquished his position as general manager of Silver Dollar City. John Baltes, who is still the general manager at Silver Dollar City, was lured away from another theme park to guide everyday activities.

Diversification

The 1980's ushered in a period of corporate growth. But even this growth, like much of the original city, originated in the inquisitive nature and inventiveness of the Herschends. In the mid-1980's the Herschends installed a water slide at their campground near Silver Dollar City. Because of the enjoyment youngsters derived from the slide, they decided to build a complete park based on water. They knew that other water parks were beginning to spring up across America.

Within five years they opened five water parks: one each in Branson, Oklahoma City, Atlanta, and two in Texas. In 1986 the company joined with country music singer Dolly Parton and changed the name of Silver Dollar City at Pigeon Forge to Dollywood. Attendance there doubled in one year. All the while, additions were being made to the original family theme park, Silver Dollar City. Not surprisingly two of the additions were large water rides, the American Plunge and Lost River.

In 1983 Echo Hollow, a hillside arena seating nearly 4,000 people, was built for the production of country music shows. The addition allowed Silver Dollar City to extend the park day with an evening show. It also brought Silver Dollar City directly into the world of country music.

At first the production crew at Silver Dollar City experimented with a variety of entertainers, always keeping the family orientation. In the fall of 1985 Pat Boone used the arena to film segments of his television shows. In 1989 the energetic and harmonious quartet, the Branson Brothers, opened the season at Silver Dollar City. The immensely talented and popular group became the first Branson music group to sign a contract with a major recording studio, Warner Brothers. The introduction of this large-scale music show also became a portent of things to come.

During this decade, a conscious effort was made to expand the length of the season at Silver Dollar City. The Fall National Craft Festival, which began as a three day event in 1967, was extended to a six week festival with scores of craftsmen coming from across the nation to demonstrate their wares. The new Flower and Garden Festival now inaugurates the season in April, while during June the American Folk Music Festival delights visitors.

But the most successful addition was reserved for Christmas. Now 100 miles of white lights are strung from trees to rooftops and across rail fences, until the whole city twinkles with the joy of the season. The Christmas theme is now being promoted in all of Ozark Mountain Country.

Simultaneously with their own business developments in the decade, the Herschends also joined with others to promote the Stone and Taney County area. In 1981 the Herschend brothers helped form the Ozark Marketing Council, a cooperative group of area businesses. Peter became the president of the group. This council initially coined the name Ozark Mountain Country as a public relations effort to identify the Stone-Taney County area. The name immediately became popular with both media and local residents.

What's ahead for Silver Dollar City?

The interests of the Herschends have branched out in several different directions. They have now built or purchased theme parks throughout the south and southwest. The parks in Texas and Oklahoma have been sold; those in Tennessee and Georgia remain under their control. The organization continues to expand.

What will be the future of Silver Dollar City in a corporation which has several parks under its control? Plans for the park indicate that it will become one of four companion entertainment centers in the Branson area. Joining Silver Dollar City and White Water in Branson in 1992 is the Grand Palace, a 4,000 seat theater dedicated to country music. And plans are being made, in partnership with entertainer Kenny Rogers, for a huge showboat on Table Rock Lake in 1995. Future advertisements will invite guests to attend all four attractions.

Of the many business interests which the Herschends now enjoy, Silver Dollar City is not only their first project but unquestionably their sentimental favorite. Pictures and memorabilia of the early days at the cave and in the park line their modern office walls. They frequently walk the park's streets, talking to employees and guests.

But Silver Dollar City is thirty years old and the challenge of exceeding customer expectations is ever-present. Many of the original employees, who were passionately loyal to the park, are no longer there. Lester Vining, for example, who served in many capacities including cave guide, electrician, actor, train engineer, and jack-of-all trades has retired. Some of the others have died. The year 1991 was particularly sad since several of the original company, including Don Richardson, Andy Miller, Bert Lewallen, and Shad Heller passed away.

Nothing epitomizes the bonds which hold the city together more than the reactions to Shad's passing. Shad had many friends who grieved at his death. Lester Vining, keeping a promise he made to Shad many years ago, dug a hole in frozen soil on a cold January day and placed the urn of Shad Heller's ashes into the ground.

Many of those who helped the Herschends originate the park are now gone. To ensure that the high standards of the park are maintained, Peter and Jack Herschend constantly stress that customer service and quality entertainment are foremost to the park. The creed and statement of mission, which were hammered out years ago, still hang on office walls and are placed in employee handbooks. Administrative staff and park personnel expect everyone associated with the park to abide by the rules of excellent service.

But it is the employees who interact directly with guests who ensure that the theme park remains true to its purpose. Some current employees are still related to that past. Walker Powell, who operates the old lathe and sells baseball bats, is a descendant of one of the early explorers of the cave, and Oma Holt, who stirs the lye soap kettle, actually made the product for home use when she was growing up in the Ozarks.

But new faces, too, have appeared at Silver Dollar City and may be as dedicated and become as influential as the early employees. There is a tendency

Walker Powell, grandson of one of the investors in the Marble Cave mining company before the turn of the century, today works for Silver Dollar City.
(Photo courtesy of SDC)

now for management to employ older, semiretired employees when possible. Others are there because of their outstanding accomplishments with their crafts. Energetic Rita Williams, who spins wool, is an encyclopedia of knowledge about the history of spinning and weaving. And Donna Gilbert, who can pull a white oak splint with all the ability of the master craftswoman that she is, left her career as a school teacher to make baskets. Don Ogilvie, who retired after a successful career with a major corporation, enjoys his hobby of calligraphy. Today he mischievously drips water on children while he shows them how to make paper in the Deep Woods Section of Silver Dollar City. Using his own 19th Century presses, he also prints—on the paper he makes—the verses he writes.

These employees enjoy passing the heritage of the past on to others. They possess the entertaining ability to do so. More than anything else, these people will continue to uphold the commitment to high quality and keep Silver Dollar City the Ozark treasure it has become.

Robert McGill

Shepherd of the Hills Country

Signs all over Southwest Missouri proclaim it; businesses, motels, tourist attractions, and billboards affirm it: the region is Shepherd of the Hills Country. From every direction roads lead vacationers to the Shepherd of the Hills Homestead perched high on a ridge just west of Dewey Bald. From early spring until the end of October, the Homestead introduces visitors to the old J.K. Ross cabin and farm and, via an outdoor drama, to the people and events Harold Bell Wright immortalized in his 1907 novel *The Shepherd of the Hills*.

During the day, guests tour the very log house where Wright first experienced Ozarks hospitality. Old-fashioned jitneys pulled by giant Clydesdale horses offer rides around the upper part of the Homestead. Motorized trams ply the steep wooded hillsides, dropping folks off to watch Ozarks artisans at work and to explore the rustic village which, after dark, becomes a giant stage where Wright's book is brought to life.

Visitors stroll about the Homestead, walk or ride to Inspiration Point, and ascend the 230 foot enclosed tower to enjoy views of the hills and valleys for miles in every direction. Near the base of the tower are stone sculptures of characters from *The Shepherd of the Hills* and the reconstructed ninety year old church similar to those in which Wright preached during the years he lived in the Ozarks.

Wright Visits the Ozarks

When Harold Bell Wright, then a pastor in Pittsburg, Kansas, first visited the log house at the homestead at the turn of the century, the property belonged to J.K. Ross and his wife Anna. Wright was summoned to the area by a call for help from his father and younger brother, George, who were hunting and trapping in northern Arkansas. When Harold and his guide were unable to cross the rain swollen White River, they climbed the steep ridge to the cabin, where they were welcomed warmly and stayed the night.

Drawn by the peaceful beauty of the area and the hospitality of his hosts, Wright returned in 1901 with his family and camped near the Ross home. During

Dewey Bald, much as Harold Bell Wright found it shortly after the turn of the century.
(Photo courtesy of Chloe LaRue)

his stay, he tramped the hills, painted, and worked on the manuscript which would become *That Printer of Udell's*, his first novel.

The story was set in Pittsburg, Kansas, then a mining town with many saloons and brothels. Eager to encourage his growing congregation to become involved in eradicating Pittsburg's evils, Wright authored a lengthy story.

Back in Pittsburg, he read segments of *That Printer of Udell's* at special meetings of his congregation. Friends encouraged him to publish the book to reach a wider audience.

In the summer of 1902, the Ross family received a package containing "a lot of choice magazines and a large family Bible," and most welcome of all, a copy of Wright's recently published novel, *That Printer of Udell's*. A few months after these gifts arrived, Wright came back to hunt the hills and fish the nearby White River.

Recreational pleasures were not on the author's mind in July, 1903 when he returned to the Ross homestead. J.K. and his son Charley were getting ready for a day's work in their sawmill when a horse-drawn dray, loaded with a large tent, carpets, chairs, a desk, and household items needed to set up a summer home, pulled up the dusty mountain trail to the cabin. The tent was erected on what is today called Inspiration Point, in the midst of the farm's recently harvested cornfield.

(Continued on page 25)

Harold Bell Wright *was born on May 4, 1872, in Rome, New York, the second of William and Alma Wright's four sons. Harold's father, an alcoholic, was a carpenter who, in seeking employment, moved his family many times in Harold's early years. To compensate for the boy's disrupted school attendance, his mother read to him from the Bible, Shakespeare, Pilgrim's Progress, and Hiawatha, and taught him to paint and sketch.*

When Harold was ten, however, his mother died. For the next several years, the boy alternately lived with relatives or followed his father from job to job, sometimes living in close proximity to saloons and brothels. No matter where he stayed, the young Harold worked—as grocery boy, quarry or factory hand, or farm laborer.

In his middle teens, traumatized by his father's dissolute behavior, young Wright declared his independence. He rode a freight train to Grafton, Ohio where he developed a sign and house painting business. He also began attending the Disciples of Christ church. At the age of twenty, motivated to study for the ministry, he gained admission to the Preparatory Department of Hiram College in Grafton despite the gaps in his education.

The young college student also continued his painting business. So pressed was he by his responsibilities that he developed a severe case of pneumonia which, in addition to cutting short his college career, damaged his lungs and badly impaired his eyesight. A year later, still unable to resume his studies, he challenged his frail body by building a canoe and traveling down the Mahoning and Ohio Rivers and across the Mississippi.

Harold Bell Wright, author of The Shepherd of the Hills.
(Photo courtesy of Norman Wright)

From there he went by train to the "White Oak District" of the Ozarks west of Springfield, where he was warmly welcomed at his Uncle Ben's farm and reunited with his father. As his strength returned and his eyesight improved, he helped with farm work and painted pictures. He also attended worship services in the one-room log schoolhouse in the valley. On Thanksgiving, when a traveling minister failed to arrive to deliver a sermon, Harold was called on to preach, the first of several invitations he would receive. Shortly thereafter, he moved to Mt. Vernon to take up house painting again.

His reputation as a preacher was to follow him, however. Rural congregations around Mt. Vernon eagerly recruited the tall, good-looking preacher for their worship services. When he was hired as regular pastor at Pierce City, about 25 miles away, Wright rode to his church and home again on horseback every Sunday.

Then in 1898, the much traveled preacher was called to serve the Christian Church at Pittsburg, Kansas. A year later, he took a short leave from his church work and journeyed back to Buffalo, New York, to marry Frances E. Long, a young woman he met at Hiram College. The couple would eventually have three sons. Harold Bell Wright stayed in Pittsburg until 1906, then moved to a church in Lebanon, Missouri, northeast of Springfield.

Along with his preaching, Wright was working hard on The Shepherd of the Hills *well into 1907. During the years he wrote the text, he visited Taney and Stone Counties on a number of occasions. At first he stayed with the Rosses, the family which served as a model for his characters, but later he stayed at the Branson Hotel or a resort in Hollister. These visits obviously had a profound and lasting influence on Wright, for several of his later books also had Ozark settings. By late 1907, however, when the reviews of* The Shepherd of the Hills *first appeared in city newspapers, Wright had moved his family to Redlands, California where he became pastor of the First Christian Church.*

The Shepherd of the Hills, *at first slow to produce income for Wright, was by 1912 making him wealthy. Realizing that he could spread his pastoral message more readily through entertaining stories featuring strong moral themes, he left the ministry to concentrate on his writing.*

Though book sales soon made Wright a millionaire, he never lost sight of his "call to ministry," nor forgot his poverty-stricken childhood. Laurence V. Tagg, in his 1986 biography, Harold Bell Wright, Storyteller to America, *points out that Wright donated his time, writing skills, and large amounts of money to medical and other charitable causes involving children, especially after he suffered from an extended case of tuberculosis which caused him to move to Arizona in 1915.*

Sadly, his tuberculosis, coupled with differences over religion, dealt a mortal blow to Wright's marriage. To the consternation of many of his readers and friends in Shepherd of the Hills country, he and Frances were separated in 1917 and divorced in 1920. Wright's three sons—Gilbert, Paul, and Norman Hall—lived with their mother but maintained contact with their father.

Even in the midst of Wright's illness, he continued to write. His novels, eighteen in all, appeared every year or two into the 1930's. An additional book, To My Sons, *a record of his childhood and an explanation of the forces which governed his life, came out in 1934. His last novel was published in 1942, just two years before his death. Most of Wright's books were available by mail order through the Sears Roebuck catalog and enjoyed tremendous popularity. Twelve were nationwide best sellers and have been reprinted many times. From 1912 through the early 1930's, Wright's books were surpassed in sales only by the Bible. By far the most enduring has been* The Shepherd of the Hills, *reissued more than a dozen times with countless reprintings. Sales of that book have been in the millions, and an additional 50,000 copies continue to be sold each year, mostly in Shepherd of the Hills country.*

Ross sawed lumber to lay out a floor for the tent, and helped arrange the furniture.

For the next three months, Wright, guided by Charley Ross, hiked the countryside, studied the local plants and animals, and came to understand and admire the local people.

The story the author was preparing to write, *The Shepherd of the Hills*, is fiction, an imagined tale woven around the hilltop cabin and the people Wright found living there. He models Old Matt, Aunt Mollie, and Young Matt on the Rosses, adding a daughter to the fictional Matthews family. Into the Matthews' lives comes a gentle, religious stranger from the city, who tends sheep and soon becomes "shepherd" to his neighbors as well. No one knows that the shepherd's son and the Matthews' daughter have, in past years, been secret lovers. The girl dies giving birth to a son, the strange child known as "Little Pete," after her lover has left the area. Grief-stricken Old Matt bitterly hates the man he believes caused his daughter's death.

(continued on page 27)

Old Matt—John Keever Ross

John Keever Ross, whose personality and life were immortalized in The Shepherd of the Hills *as "Uncle Matt," was born in 1853 in the Pennsylvania mountains, the son of John and Asseneth Keever Ross. Raised to be a self-reliant farmer, he had lived in Indiana, Illinois, Kansas, and Iowa before moving to Springfield, Missouri around 1887 with Anna, his second wife, and Charles, the eleven year old son of his deceased first wife. After trying his hand at several ventures in the Springfield area, he claimed 160 acres of government ridgetop land in the White River Hills. By homesteading it for five years, Ross earned title to the land free and clear.*

J. K. and Anna Ross, models for the fictional characters Old Matt and Aunt Mollie.
(Photos courtesy of Jessie May Hackett)

When the family first came to Low Gap, between Dewey Bald and Inspiration Point in the Ozark hills, the area lacked a mill to provide them with lumber. Short of money anyway, father and son felled and hewed logs to build their cabin while the family lived in a rented room in nearby Mutton Hollow. Land was plowed for kitchen and flower gardens for Anna. By the time Harold Bell Wright came their way, a kitchen had been added across the back of the house. From the front of the house one could gaze south across the hills and valleys to the Boston Mountains in Arkansas.

In 1905, as Wright began weaving the daily activities of the Rosses into The Shepherd of the Hills, *his Ozark hosts were facing hard times. Several years of drought had plagued the region, and the family's mountaintop water well was always the first to go dry. A decade of struggling had convinced them that, despite the beauty of the spot, their free government land held little economic promise for the family.*

John, hoping to provide his son with a start in business that would keep him in the Ozarks, mortgaged the farm and invested in a store beside the railroad tracks in a new village called Garber, deep in the valley of Roark Creek just north of Low Gap. He applied for a post office permit, anticipating that his son Charley would be postmaster and assist him in running the store. But one day Charley moved to California to marry a girl he had once dated.

At the end of 1906, with a store and post office to run, J.K. and Anna moved down the steep hill to Garber. J.K. began writing a column for the Branson Echo, *reporting on his new neighbors, the orchards, and the big lumber mill being developed in Roark Valley. He also took on the responsibilities of station master at Garber's box car depot beside the railroad tracks. The couple lived at Garber until their deaths, three months apart, in 1923.*

Wright wove into his story the cultural and geographic isolation of the region, the effects of extended drought, and problems with the Bald Knobbers, a vigilante group organized in 1885 to bring law and order to the countryside but which brought instead years of misery, sorrow, and fear to many local families.

Most of Wright's characters were composites of people who lived in Mutton Hollow, on Compton's Ridge, or at the post office village of Notch. To depict Sammy Lane, young Matt's sweetheart, Wright mixed the looks and charms of Charley Ross's fiancee with those of the daughter of Levi Morrill, the postmaster at Notch. In characterizing the Old Shepherd, he combined the work of a young sheep herder in Mutton Hollow with the personality of a distinguished landowner on Compton Ridge who served in the state legislature. It was plain to all who knew him that Uncle Ike, the postmaster at Notch in the book, was Levi Morrill.

When Notch postmaster Levi Morrill brought his wife and two young children to a 160 acre homestead in eastern Stone County in 1883, he was a 46-year-old "dropout," a transplanted easterner, college graduate, and former newspaperman who had apprenticed with Horace Greeley. In 1895 he set up a post office on his place and named it Notch. After Wright's book came out, Morrill slipped into the identity of the irascible Uncle Ike quite naturally, and ever after answered to that name as if it had been his from birth.

The Ross family, having moved in 1906 from the hilltop farm to Garber near Roark Creek and the newly completed White River Railroad, did not find the notoriety so comfortable. In 1913 Ross wrote *Old Matt's View of It*, a booklet relating his own life history, his friendship with Harold Bell Wright, and the impact *The Shepherd of the Hills* had on his family and friends. He noted that "someone has unconsciously been made a victim to give certain details to the story." One can only guess at the details which bothered the Rosses, but coping with questions from tourists, perhaps even from neighbors, about an imaginary daughter and a disturbed illegitimate grandson must have been very hard for J.K. and Anna.

Nonetheless, J.K. was proud of his continuing association with Wright and the novel. In his booklet, and for the rest of his life, Ross referred to himself, his wife, and his son, even his neighbors, more by their "book names" than by their birth names.

Today the Rosses are most often referred to in the region as Uncle Matt, Aunt Mollie, and Young Matt. As the book increased in popularity, bringing thousands of tourists to Stone and Taney Counties, local folk seemed to lose track of the fact that the story and its characters were fictional.

Early Tourists

For Taney and Stone Counties the book served as a magnet, drawing many curious visitors to the Roark Creek and the upper White River. In 1909, roads leading to Low Gap were dirt and rock, fording every creek, sometimes several times. They were rough but passable for high-set wagons and buggies with iron tires. For automobiles they were disastrous. Therefore, people anxious to visit the mountainous country and to meet the people Wright told of in his novel often selected the picturesque train ride to Reeds Spring or Branson. Many made the strenuous hike across the hills to visit the farm at Low Gap. Some shortened the distance, if not the difficulty, by asking to be let off the train at Garber and then climbing the steep path to "Old Matt's Cabin."

The copyright on *The Shepherd of the Hills* was issued in late 1907 but the people whose lives, appearance, and personalities provided models for Wright's characters did not meet any curious tourists before November, 1908 when the first supplies of the book arrived at the Branson depot.

When the first *Shepherd of the Hills* books arrived in the area, the Ross house at Low Gap had stood empty for more than two years, disturbed only by the weather. In the spring of 1909, excited souvenir hunters began pulling its log walls apart bit by bit. To protect the cabin and keep his taxes paid, Ross found renters who were interested in serving meals to hungry hikers. By 1913, the silent saw and grist mill, with no such protection, was stripped of its wood and all but the heaviest of its machinery. By that time, Ross had sold the farm and paid off the mortgage.

Old Matt's Cabin
still stands on the same spot
where it was originally built.
This photo is from the 1930's.
(Photo courtesy of Jessie
May Hackett)

Visitors hoping to meet Wright's characters had little trouble getting directions. For the rest of their lives, J.K. and Anna Ross at Garber, and Uncle Ike at Notch were essentially "on stage." Almost any nearby pretty girl was likely to be pointed out as Sammy Lane.

Tourist oriented businesses in the area were quick to take advantage of interest in the book and its characters. Almost immediately a boat on Branson's river front became the "Sammy Lane." In the summer of 1913, after the dam impounding Lake Taneycomo was completed across the White River, the Sammy Lane Boat Line began carrying passengers and mail up and down the new lake, and the Sammy Lane Resort was built on the Branson lake front.

That same year, plans were announced for building a fancy hotel in Mutton Hollow. Before it could be started, the log house which was identified locally as "Jim Lane's Cabin" would have to be torn down. Jim Lane was Sammy Lane's father in Wright's book, a fictional character. However, the Branson newspaper noted that identifying the cabin with that character had caused it to be "visited by thousands who have registered their names on the walls until they (the walls) resemble a puzzle from China."

The Jim Lane cabin was moved, not torn down. The hotel was never built. A predictable problem stood in the way of operating such a business in Mutton Hollow. All the railroad depots in the area lay beyond rugged mountain ridges, and few car owners were willing to endanger their machines by taking them over the stump-filled wagon tracks which still provided the only access to Mutton Hollow.

The possibility of such a hotel, however, fostered road improvements. In 1914, residents of Branson, Reeds Spring, and the area between were very anxious to be connected to Springfield by an "automobile road." With a prospect that the state might soon underwrite such a highway, a group of citizens gathered at Notch to plan the work of clearing the right of way and smoothing a road over Dewey Bald. Those who lived along the proposed route gladly offered the needed land. No one was more cooperative than the man who had bought the Ross's cabin at Low Gap and was serving dinner to sightseers there. He even offered to donate $100 toward the project.

The road around Dewey Bald was cleared and leveled and drainage established. Unfortunately, it took only a few gully-washing rains to scour that road into rocky stairstep layers.

By 1919, few visitors found much of interest at the Ross's old cabin anyway. Though still visited by individuals sturdy enough to hike the trail from Garber, the place stood empty most of the time, dilapidated from lack of care, and tattered by careless squatters. Nothing was left of the beautiful flower gardens Anna Ross had planted there.

A Tourist Attraction is Born

Harold Bell Wright assisted in making *The Shepherd of the Hills* into a silent motion picture in 1919, stimulating renewed interest in the novel. About the same time, a colorful "taxi driver," Pearl "Sparky" Spurlock, came to Branson and used the new interest to turn the fate of the old cabin around.

Sparky found a challenge in the rocky Ozark roads, and a cause in the cabin at Low Gap. Through the next twenty-five years, wearing a long calico dress and sunbonnet and puffing on a corncob pipe, she took thousands of gasping tourists on an unforgettable, nerve-jangling car ride through the Shepherd of the Hills country. To keep her passengers from concentrating on the jerks and bumps, she talked incessantly, telling about Old Matt, Aunt Mollie, and Uncle Ike, and repeating Wright's story, with embellishments.

When Anna Ross died in 1923, to her family and friends and especially to Sparky, it was Aunt Mollie who passed away. Three months later Charles Ross came to take his seventy year old father to live with him in California.

The old man told a neighbor that he didn't think he would ever leave the Ozarks. Though Garber was little more than a railroad depot in the upper Roark valley, it was home.

J.K. and Charley began the journey, stopping in Springfield to spend the night with a cousin. But J.K. Ross—Uncle Matt—died there the following day. Charley asked Sparky Spurlock to make arrangements for the funeral to be held in the Evergreen Cemetery near Notch where Anna had been buried a few months earlier.

The two graves went unmarked until 1924 when Mrs. Spurlock launched a campaign among her former passengers to raise the $250 needed for the stone. Poet John G. Neihardt, of Branson, and Robert M. Good, the director of the School of the Ozarks, helped with the dedication ceremonies.

Before Levi Morrill (Uncle Ike) died in 1926, he asked to be buried beside Uncle Matt and Aunt Mollie. His grave also went unmarked until Sparky Spurlock raised another $250 to pay for his monument. Donations came from all over the United States and several foreign countries. In 1929, Congressman Dewey Short assisted Mr. Good with unveiling the stone in the little cemetery between Low Gap and Notch.

Rescuing Old Matt's Cabin

Despite Sparky's continuing interest, the cabin at Low Gap was in serious disrepair when Lizzie McDaniel, daughter of a Springfield banking family,

The statues on Inspiration Point at the Shepherd of the Hills Park.
(Photos by Denise McGill)

became fascinated with Wright's novel and the ramshackle cabin. She rode fifty miles on horseback from her home to visit the site. Finding the place "over-run with pigs and squatters," an indignant Miss Lizzie bought the property and refurbished the house. She also searched the countryside to collect household furnishings, clothing, guns, and memorabilia which had been associated with the Rosses and Harold Bell Wright.

In 1926, with the place presentable again, Miss Lizzie produced an outdoor drama based on *The Shepherd of the Hills*, using the cabin and its surroundings for the stage. Several hundred playgoers stood or walked about while Uncle Matt, the old Shepherd, the young lovers, Little Pete, some Bald Knobbers, and a number of farm animals moved among them, enacting the old story.

For several years Miss Lizzie resided in the refurbished cabin and opened her front room to the public as a living museum. Interest in the museum increased in 1928 when another movie was released based on *The Shepherd of the Hills* book.

At the beginning of 1936, for a dollar a year, Miss McDaniel allowed the State of Missouri to lease Inspiration Point for fifty years as an historical park.

Federal economic recovery programs were, by that time, employing local men to build hard surface roads in the Ozarks. That winter, thanks in good part to publicity generated by Sparky Spurlock, work was in progress on a modern highway between Branson and Reeds Spring, generally following the rocky trail which had been cleared twenty-two years before.

With Easter approaching, Branson's businessmen and church folk began planning an Easter sunrise pageant to be held on Inspiration Point. A big crowd was anticipated.

The WPA hurried work on the highway and rushed to clear and landscape the new park. Telephone lines were installed by the Missouri Standard (Bell) Telephone Company, so the services could be carried on Springfield radio station KWTO.

A temporary stage was built of native timbers while local school children constructed cardboard figures for the park. Thirty Branson citizens rehearsed

the pageant, directed by Karl Klein, who would also be reading the script on the loudspeaker and the radio.

Before dawn that Easter morning, April 12, 1936, some 2,000 people stood on the hillside just below Inspiration Point. The weather was calm and quiet as the sun rose, pulling mists from the nearby river and creeks. The voices of the choristers rang across the hillside, the final note of each hymn echoing through the early morning air.

The players moved silently through the pageant as Klein's solemn voice read the ancient words. Then, as the players rearranged themselves for the final events of the first Easter morning, the sun's rays broke over the ridge tops and caught, on the hill to the north across a steep, rocky creek, the bright form of a giant cross.

For more than an hour, 87 children had waited in the pre-dawn gloom, the dark side of their costumes turned toward Inspiration Point. Their cue came at sunrise, and all turned at once so the white half of their costumes would gleam in the Easter dawn.

The newly paved road which enabled that sunrise service to be held also made it possible for Miss Lizzie to have her house moved from Springfield and reestablished on the ridgetop at Low Gap. She then opened all of Old Matt's Cabin to tourists. Anticipating more visitors now that motoring vacations were possible, she also opened "Miss Lizzie's Tearoom."

National interest in the Shepherd of the Hills Farm received another boost in 1941 when the novel was again made into a motion picture, this time starring John Wayne. As the picture was released, a new edition of the book was distributed, featuring pictures from that movie.

The Shepherd of the Hills had been out of print for some time. In Branson the Taneyhills Library Club, seeing the possibility of a good project for raising funds to support their volunteer "public library," made arrangements to distribute that new edition to local resorts and shops for sale to tourists. The women sold 5,000 copies before that printing was cut off, following the death of Harold Bell Wright in 1944.

When Miss Lizzie died in 1945, the Shepherd of the Hills farm was sold to settle her estate. She had voiced her intention to leave the property to the Branson Civic League, a group of local business women and civic leaders of which she was a member. Those plans had not been completed, but the League, determined to carry out her wish to protect Old Matt's cabin, borrowed the necessary down payment to buy the property and buildings. A year later the Civic League sold all but Inspiration Point and the cabin and barn to Dr. Bruce Trimble and his wife Mary. The Trimbles leased, and in the 1970's purchased, the cabin and barn from the Civic League.

The Trimbles Take Over

At the time of the 1946 transaction, Dr. Trimble was a law professor at the University of Kansas City. For the Trimbles, their retirement project quickly became a full time career. They converted Miss Lizzie's home into a second museum where Mary Trimble's growing collection of Rose O'Neill's Kewpie dolls vied for space with the former owner's antiques and art objects. They opened a gift shop in the old barn and constructed a new building which housed Mollie's Tearoom.

Visitors to the farm continually asked where copies of *The Shepherd of the Hills* could be bought. The book would have been on sale in the gift shop had it been available. Mary Trimble searched the region for used copies to meet the demand. When she traveled to distant cities, she poked through every available bookstore. Each find was a prize. To compensate for the shortage, Dr. Trimble wrote several pamphlets about Harold Bell Wright, the Shepherd of the Hills story, and the farm. Finally, after considerable prodding from both the Trimbles and Branson library supporters, and the release of yet another movie based on the book, a new edition was made available in 1951.

Developing the Shepherd of the Hills farm into a paying enterprise became the basis of everything Bruce and Mary Trimble did through the first half of the 1950's. Their efforts intensified when construction began on Table Rock Dam. The giant lake, which the dam would impound before the decade ended, was certain to bring many more visitors to the area. Dr. Trimble involved the whole community in a project to put

Dr. Bruce and Mrs. Mary Trimble
(Photos courtesy of the Shepherd of the Hills)

sculpted figures of the Shepherd of the Hills characters in the tree-shaded park on Inspiration Point where they first had come to life in Wright's imagination. With the backing and support of businessmen, resort owners, writers, and civic groups all over the region and beyond, Trimble held an art contest to obtain a painted representation of the first figure to be made, The Shepherd.

The contest, judged by Missouri muralist Thomas Hart Benton, was won by 15-year-old Wally Nickel, a high school student at the School of the Ozarks. Springfield art teacher Roberta Stoneman Baker sculpted the seven-foot figure, which was placed on the Point in August, 1954. Statues of Mollie and of Little Pete playing with his dog Brave were set in place a year later.

Dr. Bruce's plan called for four more figures, but it would be many years before those plans were carried out. Trimble also looked forward to developing an outdoor amphitheater just below the top of the ridge so Wright's story could be brought to life for visitors to the farm. He did not live to see his dream carried out.

Mark, the Trimbles' son, later said that when he came to the farm after his father died in 1957, he thought he was coming to help his mother sell the farm. Instead, Mary Trimble continued to develop it, with Mark's help.

In 1959 Table Rock Dam was completed, and crowds flocked to see the lake spreading over the White River bottomlands a few miles south of the Shepherd of the Hills farm. The presence of all the curiosity seekers encouraged the Trimbles, and work finally began on Dr. Bruce's outdoor amphitheater. The Shepherd of the Hills story had been presented in the area, in public readings and as a stage play, many times since Miss Lizzie's "pageant in the round" back in 1926. In the late 1950's it was performed on an open air stage on Branson's waterfront by students from various colleges in the region, and was also produced at the School of the Ozarks.

Meanwhile, on the north side of the ridge at Low Gap, land was cleared and remolded so that theater-goers could sit on the hillside looking down at a part of an old trail, the road which Wright called in his book, "the trail that is nobody knows how old." The flat area was widened to a village street, where J.K.'s old mill was brought to life again, and a "shepherd's cabin" was built nearby. Over five miles of electrical wires were put in place, and dressing facilities were constructed. Mark Trimble enlisted the help of Lloyd (Shad) Heller and a Coffeyville, Kansas stage play director, James Colley, to develop a script and assemble a cast of thirty-three players.

On Saturday night, August 6, 1959, The Shepherd of the Hills play was first presented in the Old Mill Theater at the Shepherd of the Hills farm. Colley directed that production, Shad Heller played the Shepherd, and Mark Trimble was "the Stranger," who introduced the story and provided a running commentary on the action. The actors who performed that night and through the early years of the play were drawn from nearby communities. In the years since, many of them and their children and grandchildren have continued to be involved with the play, and have become leaders

Today Norman Wright, son of the author Harold Bell Wright, maintains a museum of family memorabilia in Mutton Hollow.
(Photo courtesy of Kathleen Van Buskirk)

in the development of many of Branson's current businesses and musical and recreational attractions.

People with memories of those early performances can still be found in the area. Hal Meadows, who performed Young Matt in the early 1960's, recalls that sometimes, in the early years of the play, there were more actors on the stage than paying customers in the audience.

Meadows' first connection with Wright's book was as a youngster when he assisted his father, Chris Meadows, in running the Sammy Lane Boat Line and resort. He also played the part of Young Matt in a 1963 technicolor movie of *The Shepherd of the Hills* which starred Richard Arlen. Some scenes in that movie were filmed at the cabin and on Inspiration Point.

Soon after the opening of the Old Mill Theater, the Trimbles leased the amphitheater to Lloyd and

Ruth Heller, who managed the play for the next five seasons. Lloyd did the directing and acted in the part of the Shepherd. Aunt Mollie was played by Ruth Heller, who soon became so identified with the part that her real name was virtually forgotten in the community.

The Shepherd of the Hills play was not a big operation in those years. Some of the actors handled more than one part. Ruth remembers that, "We would sell tickets, then close the ticket office and run down the hill to go on stage. At first if we had fifty in the audience, we were doing good."

In 1965, with the play being performed nightly except Sunday, from June 21 through Labor Day, the Trimbles began providing free guided tours of Old Matt's Cabin. At the mill, old timers split rails and cut shakes; meals were served in Aunt Molly's Cupboard.

The following year brought more visitors to the farm, and attendance at the play increased. The Trimbles doubled the seating capacity of the outdoor theater, took over management of the play, and hired Hal Meadows as director.

More and more, the amphitheater was filled to capacity. Seating was increased to 1,100, then to 1,700, then to 2,786. The season was gradually lengthened, beginning earlier in the spring, and extending through September, then through October. As the size of the seating section grew, so did the size of the stage, and more horses and wagons were added to the action of the play.

By the mid-1970's both the stage area and the hillside seating had expanded so much that a sound system had to be installed. To allow for movement and action—an important part of the pageant—personal microphones were attached to the clothing of actors who had speaking parts.

Despite the expansions, the theater was often sold out, and many people had to be turned away. In 1978, folding chairs gave way to molded chairs, and a large rain shelter was built so that audiences could reach protection during sudden downpours. Today's audiences enjoy the comfort of theater seats.

Of course it is the impact and presentation of the story which has drawn visitors to the pageant for so many years. The Trimbles looked constantly for innovative ways to provide their audiences with the feel of life in the Ozarks at the turn of the century and to increase understanding of the forces which molded the lives of Harold Bell Wright's Ozarks acquaintances—the forces which continue, in many ways, to mold the lives of those who make visitors feel at home here today.

The entertainment generated by the Trimbles' efforts has been a driving force in the development of Shepherd of the Hills Country as a popular vacation destination. From the time the playgoers are seated on the hillside, they are involved in rustic activities on the stage. They wait with local farmers for the miller to grind a bag of corn; they breathe the dust kicked up by horseshoes being pitched by overall-clad neighbors; and they enjoy the excitement of small children encouraging their frogs in a racing match.

An elderly man trails his flock of sheep across the scene and the play has begun. When Old Matt and Aunt Mollie host a party, teams of high-spirited horses bring wagon and buggy loads of hillfolk to enjoy the lively fiddler's tunes; a "hot-rodding" young buck squeals his buggy and steed to a halt center-stage. Throughout the action, horses tied to surrounding trees browse in their feedbags.

The intermission falls during the square dance, and the audience is invited to come on down and join the festivities. As the story reaches its climax, the Old Shepherd's cabin is set ablaze by Bald Knobbers, and the hillfolks' constant fear of losing their possessions to fire becomes a reality for the audience. Before the evening ends, frontier law and order takes on new meaning as the night is engulfed in a blazing gun battle.

When Mary Trimble died in 1982, her son Mark continued to manage the Old Mill Theater and the Shepherd of the Hills farm, and also began experimenting with new ideas for entertaining visitors to the area.

In the early 1980's, he built a large showroom east of Mutton Hollow where for several years his Ozarks Auto Show offered a fascinating look back at rare and unusual automobiles. Central to the museum were the vehicles he had purchased, beginning with a

1936 Packard Roadster he bought in the mid-1950's. He also spruced up or totally rebuilt many old automobiles. His collection formed the centerpiece of the museum, and one of his turn of the century automobiles became a permanent "player" on the stage of the Old Mill Theater. After several years, Trimble held a big automobile auction and closed the museum.

Mark Trimble also provided active encouragement for the installation of the Harold Bell Wright Museum in Mutton Hollow in 1984, though he had no part in its development. The continuing popularity of the Shepherd of the Hills play brought many questions from visitors for which there were no ready answers. In the 1980's, forty years after Wright's death, few people working at the farm had first hand memories of him. The autobiography he had written in the 1930's had been printed in a very limited edition because neither Wright nor his publisher thought it would be of interest to many readers. Copies are virtually unobtainable.

In Shepherd of the Hills country, answers to tourists' questions were, of necessity, often drawn from local legend and popular rumor rather than from established fact.

Wright Museum Established

A solution to that dearth of well-grounded facts came in the summer of 1984 when Norman Wright, Harold's youngest son, opened a theater-sized museum in Mutton Hollow and displayed books and memorabilia selected from his father's estate.

As a youngster, Norman Wright had spent his summers at his father's ranch in Arizona. After 1922, the times at the ranch were also shared with his father's new wife, Winifred Mary Potter Duncan Wright. For Norman, as for his older brothers, the choice of a career grew out of experiences with his father, who developed movie scripts from several of his novels and assisted on the set as each was translated into popular motion pictures.

Norman's oldest brother, Gilbert, made a career of writing screenplays, short stories, and television scripts. His second brother, Paul, became interested in live theater, and was a rising young actor playing opposite Claudette Colbert on Broadway when he died at the age of twenty-five. Norman started out doing art work for the Disney studio and later developed his own motion picture company, producing many very popular children's movies during his 37 year film-making career.

When Norman Wright retired in 1975, Gilbert had been dead for ten years. As the only surviving son, he found himself responsible for his father's household and literary property, which had been stored in a large warehouse since 1944.

On a visit to the Branson area in the early 1980's, he discussed with his long time friend, Mark Trimble, his search for a useful role for at least some of his father's possessions. Plans for the museum in Mutton Hollow took firm shape in 1983 after Norman and his wife Jean met with Gerald and Amanda Cushman. The Cushmans own the replica village in Mutton Hollow, including the land where the museum with the theater facade now stands.

On display in the museum are Harold Bell Wright's hand-written manuscripts, many of his paintings, and memorabilia from the many motion pictures made from his books. Also on display are furnishings from his home, including all the furniture and equipment from his study, arranged as they were when he worked there.

To provide answers to many of the questions tourists ask about *The Shepherd of the Hills* and its author, Norman wrote and produced a half-hour motion picture which is shown regularly in a small theater in the museum. The film is based on Harold Bell Wright's autobiography, *To My Sons*. Members of his family form the cast; a grandson portrays the writer. The museum, open throughout the spring, summer, and fall seasons, provides a comprehensive and compelling view of the man who was one of the most popular writers of the first third of the twentieth century.

For six years, Norman and Jean Wright spent their summers operating the museum and getting acquainted with people in the area. Poor health and advancing age now dictate that they supervise the museum from their home in San Clemente, California.

Homestead Gets New Owner

The museum had completed its second season when, in 1985, Gary Snadon announced that he had bought the Shepherd of the Hills farm from Mark Trimble. Snadon, a local resident, performed one of the lead roles in the Shepherd of the Hills drama for several seasons in the 1960's. He chose as his business manager Jerry Coffelt, who had been involved with the farm and play for many years.

Soon after Snadon took over the farm, the name of the attraction was changed to The Shepherd of the Hills Homestead and Outdoor Theater. His stated objectives were to keep the play and the farm faithful to *The Shepherd of the Hills* book, and to entertain the customers. His ownership has brought a full schedule of daytime entertainment and activities to the Homestead.

Ozarks artisans and craftsmen now display their skills and products in Miss Lizzie's house. (The furnishings and all the Kewpie dolls and memorabilia were sold at auction by Mark Trimble in 1987.) In September and October a Fall Harvest Craft Village is added to the regular daytime activities.

There have been many other changes. Within two months after the sale of the farm, the 50-year lease on Inspiration Point expired. The little park on the hilltop was closed for a time; then in 1988, a 243 foot tower was built there. From a window-walled elevator, visitors can enjoy the view on the way to the enclosed observation deck at the top. They then walk or ride down to the lower observation level, which is open but protected by an overhang. Guides note that many visitors choose to climb the stairs. The structure, towering above the wooded hilltop, became an instant landmark and a new reference point to travelers in the hills.

The little church, now situated at the tower's base, was originally built in 1901 by the Lutheran congregation at Morgan, Missouri. Snadon purchased it in 1989, when he learned that the surviving members of the congregation might tear it down because it was deteriorating badly. Because of its decaying walls, the building was not moved intact. Instead, its intricately ornamented windows, doors, woodwork, bell tower, pews, and pulpit were salvaged, but the walls, floor and roof were rebuilt with new materials.

The little church is kept open to visitors who often sit and meditate there. Almost daily, a gospel singing group performs in the church, drawing crowds which quickly overflow the limited seating. It has also become a popular place for weddings.

Today Bruce Trimble's sculptured figures, which for thirty years peacefully awaited visitors to the shady park, are found on the east side of the tower. Since 1957, statues of Old Matt, Uncle Ike, Sammy, and Young Matt have been added, bringing Dr. Bruce Trimble's original plan to completion. The sculptor was Michael Lee, an art instructor who now lives in Arizona, but who grew up near Inspiration Point and spent many youthful hours at the farm, helping his grandfather, Homer Coffelt, take visitors on trail rides.

Conscious of Anna Ross's love of flowers, Snadon installed, on the hillside just east of the statuary group, a scaled replica of the chiming floral clock at the 1904 St. Louis World's Fair. The clock's face changes with the seasonal change of flowers.

A whole new season was added to the Homestead's tourist year in 1988 when the region initiated Ozark Mountain Christmas. The Homestead no longer closes when fall colors fade. Now the whole area which used to be known as Low Gap is decorated for Christmas; thousands of lights turn the tower into a gigantic tree. Carols are shared in the little church. Rides are offered in a giant sled pulled, with or without snow, by the Clydesdale horses. Special entertainment and holiday crafts entertain visitors.

Each night, on the broad stage of the amphitheater, a nativity pageant, *The Newborn King*, is narrated to Little Pete by the Old Shepherd. Roman soldiers, donkeys, sheep, even live camels move about the stage, restructured to depict the Holy Land.

Though the locale of the first Christmas story is far removed from the Ozarks that Harold Bell Wright depicted in his book about life around Low Gap so many years ago, the mission which is the subject of the play is at the heart of every story he wrote.

The moral views Wright wove into his tale have shaped the character and social attitudes of many of the people who worked to keep it alive. Inspired by the faith which began with the nativity scene, Harold Bell Wright's book continues to contribute to much that is positive in Shepherd of the Hills country today. There's probably more truth to all those billboards than most people realize.

Kathleen Van Buskirk

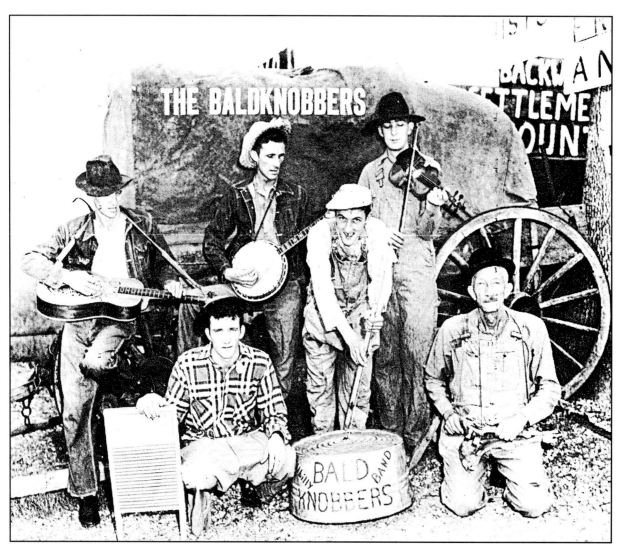

THE BALDKNOBBERS

*An early photograph of
the Baldknobbers,
(l to r) Bill, Jim, Bob, and Lyle
Mabe, Delbert Howard
and Chick Allen.*
(Photo courtesy of the Baldknobbers)

*In 1959 the Baldknobbers rented
the 50 seat basement room of the
Branson Community Center (right)
two nights a week. When
audiences grew, they moved to a
larger auditorium upstairs. Their
performances sparked Branson's
emergence as the country music
capital of the world.*
(Photo by Kathleen Van Buskirk)

Branson:
A Country Music Phenomenon

In 1958, Branson was a small southern Missouri community with no particular distinction which would draw national attention—and with not a single country music show. As of 1991, the music industry in Branson—situated largely along a stretch of Highway 76 known as "the strip"—had 24 theaters with 34 different shows and seats for 42,000 patrons. At the beginning of the 1992 season, with an influx of national headlining singers and musicians and the addition of 12,000 more seats, Branson is being heralded as the "music show capital of the world."

How did Branson, a community which still has a population of less than 4,000 year-round residents, experience such explosive growth in the music industry? The answer is gradually. First one, then several family country music shows established themselves in Branson, thereby laying the foundation for the subsequent growth. In time, nationally known entertainers began performing in Branson, usually for short stints. Meanwhile as the tourist industry grew and brought more visitors who looked for wholesome evening entertainment, the number of shows multiplied, and more and more national celebrities decided to call Branson home.

Origins: Family Country Music Shows 1959-1976

The distinction of being the first country music show in Branson belongs to the Baldknobbers. In 1959, the Mabe brothers—Bill, Jim, Lyle, and Bob—began twice-a-week performances above the old city hall downtown. The four brothers, from a family of eleven children, were natives of Christian County, just north of Taney County. As children, they all enjoyed music and purchased their first guitars out of Sears Roebuck catalogs. By the time they were in high school, the four boys were playing for local pie suppers and fox hunts. Their talents were recognized enough that in 1957 and 1958 the brothers, with their sister Margie, played live music three mornings

a week on radio station KWTO in Springfield.

In 1959, the radio station decided to go to an all record format, a decision which may have been very fortunate for Branson, for the Mabe brothers then opened the first music show in town. Calling themselves the Baldknobbers, the group presented their material on Friday and Saturday nights in a fifty-seat auditorium in the city hall. The season lasted from May through October, with most of the audience composed of fisherman visiting the area and looking for nighttime entertainment.

To present the music they loved, the Mabes developed a show format which combined popular country music with Ozark corn comedy. Songs like "The Doggie in the Window" and "She'll be Coming Around the Mountain" were popular. Two of the Mabe brothers, Jim and Lyle, created comic characters which became an integral part of the show. Jim became Droopy Drawers while Lyle created George Aggernite. "You had to entertain," Lyle says of the early days, "not just sing. People had to have fun." Lyle would appear on stage between musical numbers, dressed in coveralls, a sweatshirt, and a baseball cap set sideways on his head, and tell an outlandish story about an adventure in the Ozarks. He always wrote his own action-filled material. Over the years, in his exuberance, he cracked his ribs by falling off the stage, broke two toes, and once even had a lung collapse while performing. Yet he poured corn on the audience, and they kept coming back. Although he would change material yearly, the audience commonly requested favorite old routines.

For his most popular routine, Lyle, dressed in the outlandish garb of George Aggernite, would rush on stage, huffing and puffing and explain that he was building a new outhouse. "Yes, I had to cut a half moon in the front, a half moon in the back, and two full moons in the middle."

When the master of ceremonies asked him why

he had to build a new outhouse, an excited George Aggernite would stomp his feet, wave his arms, and blurt out, "Oh, one of my brothers got back from the army and brought a hand grenade with him. I didn't know it was live until I pulled the pin," he explained, "so I just threw it over my shoulder and ran. That grenade rolled right up to the outhouse and exploded. Totally destroyed the outhouse," he went on, "and Granny was inside."

"Goodness, was Granny hurt?" the excited announcer would ask.

"No, but she came stomping away from there, mad but relieved," George would respond. "She yelled, 'I'm sure glad I didn't do that in the house!'"

The early years were difficult. At first, the members of the Baldknobbers had to maintain other full-time jobs to support themselves. It was not until one of the brothers made $50.00 a week from his music that he quit his steady job. Jim Mabe, the last to leave his job, did not do so until the late 1960's. The brothers would perform their show on the weekends, sometimes adding a Sunday night engagement in another town—then rush back to their homes to get some sleep before going to their regular jobs on Monday.

Getting an audience was always a concern. The Baldknobbers rigged up a car with a loudspeaker system and drove around Branson announcing the show—before hurrying to the theater to see how many guests had arrived. On nights they were not playing, the Baldknobbers were a part of the Shepherd of the Hills cast, acting and playing live music for the square dance. In return, they were allowed to advertise their show to the audience.

Eventually, the hard work paid off. From the auditorium at the city hall, the show moved to the 200 seat Sammy Lane Pavilion near the waterfront, and then to the old skating rink which seated 500 people. Finally in 1968, nine years after they began in Branson, the Baldknobbers purchased a 14 acre plot on Highway 76 and built an 865 seat theater, a theater which has been expanded twice and now seats 1,700 people.

Even after they moved to the new building,

they continued to work hard. Audiences were still difficult to recruit and the Baldknobbers kept up a grueling schedule. When the Beverly Hillbillies filmed segments of their TV show at Silver Dollar City in 1969, the Baldknobbers, as a way to advertise their own show, were spending their daytime hours at Silver Dollar City, alternating playing thirty minute shows with another band, then performing in their own theater for their regular evening performance. They also devised an effective way to obtain winter work by taking bookings from guests in their audiences during their summer performances.

Today Jim and Bill Mabe still perform nightly in the show. And the Baldknobbers remain not only the first but the longest continuously running show in Branson. The 1992 year will mark their 34th season.

The second show in Branson was the Presley family show. They were the first to build on Highway 76, having done so a year before the Baldknobbers built their building. The Presleys, Lloyd and his son Gary, built this first theater, Presleys' Mountain Music Jubilee, in 1967.

Before they came to Branson, the Presleys had been entertaining in the early 1960's in a cave owned by Herman Mead on County Road DD in Stone county near Kimberling City. Appropriately enough, they called their place Herman Mead's Underground Theater.

During their years performing in the cave, the Presleys not only played their own music but occasionally invited guest stars from the Ozark Jubilee in Springfield to perform. Guests included Slim Wilson, Speedy Haworth, and even the great Red Foley.

The Presleys performed at the cave for several years before they purchased a small farm west of Branson on Highway 76 and decided to see if they could draw an audience on Saturday nights in Branson. This first theater only seated 363 people. But the Presleys remember they would not put up that many straight-back folding chairs if they did not believe the audience would be that large. Sometimes, in fact, they were excited just to see a few cars turn in to see their show. And the Presleys, like the Mabes before them, had to

The first building for a music show was built on 76 Country Boulevard by the Presleys in 1967, making them the first music show to perform on the strip in Branson.
(Photo courtesy of the Presleys)

support themselves with full-time jobs.

The Presleys developed a family oriented music show with country music, lots of friendliness, and an Ozark flavor. Their trademark for the show, the Hillbilly character Herkimer, was developed by Gary Presley in 1962. Gary, who also played guitar in the show, dressed in outlandish garb, blackened his front teeth, told country jokes, and square danced with imaginary partners. Herkimer has remained a favorite with audiences ever since.

The Presleys performed every night of the week during the summer months. Eventually they quit their daytime jobs for show business, and today they normally perform to capacity crowds in their expanded theater which seats 2,000.

The third group on the Branson scene was the Foggy River Boys. The group organized in the Joplin, Missouri area in 1967. All the group's members came from a background of quartet music. Bob Hubbard, who became the lead singer and president of the Foggies, sang with a group called the Fisher's Quartet, which was disbanding. Denzel Koontz, Bob Moskop, and Dale Sullens sang with the Gospelairs, another group which broke up. One evening Moskop, who is now retired, asked Hubbard if he would be interested

in forming a musical partnership. Hubbard agreed to provide leadership but felt that the group should perform variety numbers in addition to gospel material. John Shepherd joined the other members, and rehearsals started.

The group decided to call themselves the Foggy River Boys, taking their name from the popular term for the Cumberland River which flows through Nashville, Tennessee. For several years the Foggies sang mostly for the fun of it in the Joplin area and, in the process, became well known. Then in 1971, the group opened their first theater in Kimberling City, performing both gospel and popular songs like "King of the Road" in the show. Slowly, more and more country music was added to the repertoire. After three years in Kimberling City, the Foggies moved their show to its present location on the strip.

Like the other groups in Branson, all of the Foggies had other jobs when they began and never dreamed they would be performing full time. At first they traveled by car to road shows in their private vehicles. After they moved to Kimberling City, they purchased a van and finally, after opening the theater in Branson, a bus.

The fourth show to move to the Branson area

came from southeast Missouri, the Plummer Family. Darrell and Rosie Plummer and their two children, Melody and Randy, joined the Branson music show scene in 1973. For five years before moving to Branson, the Plummers had considered purchasing property and establishing a theater at the Lake of the Ozarks. Then when they learned about the possibilities in Branson, they visited, fell in love with the town, and established their theater. They would be the first in a long line of entertainers who were drawn into the area because of its beauty and the audience potential.

The Plummer Show performed in Branson until November, 1990 when the family sold the theater to national entertainer Moe Bandy. Randy Plummer still performs in the Roy Clark Celebrity Theater's Celebrity Sound Show.

In 1977, the fifth country music show arrived on the scene. Bob Mabe, a founder of the Baldknobbers, left that show and purchased property further west on the strip. He built an 1,800 seat theater and called it Bob-O-Links Country Hoe Down. Following the traditions of the already established shows, the Bob-O-Links performers played country music, presented comedy, and flavored the entertainment with local humor. The Bob-O-Links were the first show to have full time dancers on stage; the Burdette family, Mom and Dad and their four children, performed with the show from the beginning until the late 1980's.

Growth and a Few Big Names: 1977-1984

Between 1977 and 1980, the Tri-Lakes area was home to only these five shows. During this time, the groups worked together so that people in Missouri and surrounding states would know that Branson was a good place to come for lively, family-oriented country music entertainment. They became active in community affairs and joined the Branson Chamber of Commerce to promote their shows.

The owners learned the necessity of changing the formats of their shows yearly, even the highly successful programs. This became one of the major tasks— replacing dated songs and jokes with new material and new routines. Meanwhile, they also began inviting the

first nationally known entertainers to perform for special occasions. Mel Tillis, Porter Wagoner, Dolly Parton, and Ernest Tubb all performed in Branson during these years.

Major change began in 1981. That was the year the movie *Urban Cowboy* was released by Hollywood moguls, and millions of Americans were enthralled by the film. Young Americans, caught in a country craze, began wearing cowboy hats and boots, listening to country music, and going to country music shows. The effect spilled over to Branson. Ten theaters opened in the Branson area in the next five years, yet none of the original shows left the scene.

As fortune would have it, space for many of the new buildings became available when the School of the Ozarks opened an airport on its campus and the old Branson airstrip, located west of town on Highway 76, ceased operations. Currently Roy Clark, Mickey Gilley, and White Water are located on the old airport property. Other shows were built directly across the highway from the old airport.

One of the first new shows on the strip in 1981 was the Wilkinson Brothers (Larry, Gary, and Charles), who built their own theater. The show featured a band composed of Larry and Gary Wilkinson and other area musicians singing and playing popular country music. Late in the first half, Charley would make an entrance on stage in a white suit to perform his songs. In 1986 the Wilkinsons sold their theater to Boxcar Willie.

In 1981 the Hee Haw Theater opened with a house band and several stars from the Hee Haw television show. Archie Campbell, Buck Trent, and Lulu Roman were guests on the show and lived in Branson parts of each year. Perhaps the show, featuring well-known entertainers on a daily basis, was ahead of its time. At any rate, the show did not take hold and closed in 1983.

The Campbell Ozarks Country Jubilee also opened in Branson in 1981. When Clifford and Maggie Sue Campbell bought a vacant theater on Highway 76, they purchased not only the building, but the right to use the well-known name—Ozark Country Jubilee. That name was made famous by Red Foley who hosted a nationally televised show from Springfield in the 1950's, which featured stars like Brenda Lee, Hank Williams, Sr., and Patsy Cline. Although the Ozark Country Jubilee in Branson did not feature nationally famous stars, it received numerous local awards for its entertainment, featuring the singing dentist, Dr. David Struble, Carlotta Gail, and emcee Bob Leftridge.

In 1982, Chisai Childs produced a new, more varied style of show which dominated the strip for four years. Chisai, who hailed from Grapevine, Texas, purchased the year old Starlite Theater from George Shipman and added the words Grapevine Opry to the name of the theater.

Not only did she develop an entertaining show, but she emceed, sang, and performed comedy while dazzling audiences with an array of costumes. Chisai also excelled in finding and booking talent new to the area. Some of that talent still performs at area music shows, and a few of her performers have reached stardom. She first booked Shoji Tabuchi in Branson. Identical twins John and Paul Cody, Buddy Green, and The Masters Four (now the Texans), performed at her theater before developing their own shows. Other performers, including Jeanie Dee, the Branson Brothers, Johnnie Long, Shawna Smith, Doug Gabriel, and Cliff Wagner, are still familiar to Branson audiences. One of Chisai's other innovations was performing beyond the regular summer season by inaugurating special Christmas and New Year's shows.

In 1983, the Lowe Family built a theater on Highway 76 and opened in June. The group, managed by Ken and Nevon Lowe, featured their four talented daughters who had a background in gospel music. The Lowe Family Theater is the only theater from this period that is still in the hands of the original owners. The sisters—Teresa, Sheila, Sandy, and Kathy—were one of the first groups in Branson to appear on the Grand Ole Opry and on TNN. Currently, Loretta Lynn performs 100 dates yearly with the Lowe Sisters.

The Lowe family had discovered the Ozarks while vacationing in the 1970's and, in 1980, built a theater on Indian Point near Silver Dollar City. When they moved to their newly built theater in Branson in 1983, they leased the old theater to the Braschler Quartet for a year. Shortly after being abandoned, the building was hit by lightning and destroyed.

In 1983, Branson gained its first national attention when Roy Clark became the first nationally known star to allow his name to be used on the marquee of a local theater. Clark, a host of the "Hee Haw" television show, has won numerous awards in the country music business. When Jim Thomas and others invested in the theater along with Clark, the performer personally committed to playing one hundred dates in the theater each year. On weekends, other big name guests including Lee Greenwood, Conway Twitty, Roger Miller, Mel Tillis, Ray Stevens, and Louise Mandrell began coming to Clark's theater—guests who are now becoming a regular part of the Branson scene.

1983 also saw the opening of the Swiss Villa Amphitheater near Lampe in Stone County. This 7,500 seat amphitheater was the first outdoor music show in the area and allowed guests to enjoy concerts underneath the stars while listening to such country music names as George Strait, Reba McEntire, Earl Thomas Conley, Willie Nelson, and George Jones, in addition to rock stars like the Beach Boys, Kentucky Headhunters, and Warrant and Extreme.

Silver Dollar City also plunged into country music in 1983 when it opened Echo Hollow Amphitheater with nearly 4,000 seats. Rodney Dillard, a former regular on the Andy Griffith television show, headlined with his Time Machine Band for several years beginning in 1984. Pat Boone taped several segments of his show at Silver Dollar City in the mid-1980's, and other well-known individuals and groups provided variety to the show. In 1989, the Branson Brothers joined the format and have headlined since that time. They recently signed with Warner Brothers, becoming the first Branson-based group to ink a contract with a major recording studio.

In the spring of 1985, the gospel group, the

Braschler Quartet, located in the former Lowe's Theater on Indian Point, moved into the Musicland U.S.A. theater on Gretna Road in Branson, which had been occupied the previous year by the Lester Family. The Braschler's Show features the quartet as well as comedian Terry Sanders who has appeared on Hee Haw.

Romance novelist Janet Dailey and her husband Bill opened Country Music World in the former Hee Haw theater in 1985. They booked a variety of acts, including a quartet new to the area at that time, "Branson." This quartet performed at several shows for the next few years, changed its name to the Branson Brothers, and eventually signed with Silver Dollar City in 1989. The Daileys also signed Shoji Tabuchi, and John and Paul Cody for one year. In 1989, the Daileys brought Danny Davis and the Nashville Brass to the theater where the band performed until the Daileys sold the theater to Mickey Gilley. Danny Davis moved his group to a theater near Harbortown Mall in Branson.

Country Music Explosion 1985-1991

The Sons of the Pioneers, who had their beginnings in the 1930's and have made over 3,000 recordings, were the first big name entertainers to appear in Branson on a regular basis. The group also appeared in nearly 100 movies and made many western songs famous, including "Tumbling Tumbleweed" and "Cool Waters." During performances, the band still reminds audiences that one of their originating members was Roy Rogers. When the Pioneers came to Branson in 1985, they performed as the second half of the show with the Lowe sisters. In 1986, they moved to the Foggy River Boys Theater where they now provide daily matinees and a Monday evening show. Since arriving in Branson, the Sons of the Pioneers have been inducted into the Grammy Hall of Fame.

The show that, more than any other, signaled the coming of a new era, was the one developed by the lovable old country music hobo, Boxcar Willie. During his music career, Boxcar Willie has sold over 10 million records, especially overseas in England, New Zealand, and other countries. Some of his hits include "Luther," "We Made Memories," and numerous train songs which are associated with the hobo image he portrays on stage.

Boxcar Willie fused music and his hobo image because, as a young child growing up in Texas, his dad played fiddle and the family lived near the railroad tracks. "My whole family was poor and we barely had enough money to buy a battery to listen to the Grand Ole Opry on the radio on a Saturday night," Boxcar Willie tells people at his show. "We made our own music and our entertainment. Dad worked for the railroad, and I had the real thing—a full train set in my front yard."

Boxcar talks of his musical style as if he were offering a recipe for a cake. "What you do is take a little bit of George Jones, a little bit of Roy Acuff, a little bit of Hank Williams Sr., Ernest Tubb, and Jimmie Rogers, and then mix in some Boxcar Willie songs. If you have a good band behind you and present it well on stage, then you have my style."

Boxcar, whose career gained momentum when he was declared a national Gong Show winner, appeared at various music theaters in Branson before he announced that he would be moving here for the 1987 season. At the time, he said, "I wanted to get off the road and spend more time with my family. Having a theater here is something my wife and my family can do together." To make the decision though, Boxcar agonized about borrowing the more than one million dollars necessary to purchase and renovate the former Wilkinson Brothers Theater. But he and his family made the plunge in 1986. To advertise his show, Boxcar, who is a member of the Grand Ole Opry, would appear on the Nashville Network and invite fans to "pass through Branson and come and see me while you're on your way to Nashville." The campaign worked. Boxcar Willie filled his theater night after night, and other stars from Nashville, hoping to get off the road, were taking notice.

Other changes were also taking place on the Branson music scene. Existing shows extended the range of their music and offered a wider variety of hours, including morning and after-dinner shows. One of the most innovative new formats was begun by Glenn and Venus Robinson who opened the 76 Music Mall Complex in August, 1987. Located on Highway 76, the complex featured the Sounds of Time Show with music and comedy from the 1930's to the 1980's. A comedy matinee was added the following year. By 1991, four different shows were offered on a daily basis, along with the Max Bacon Family Gospel Sunday Matinee Show. Other shows included the Texas Gold Minors, the Down Home Country Music Show, and the Al Brumley, Jr. Show. Al Brumley's show was one of the first morning shows and featured a tribute to his father, Missouri gospel composer Al Brumley Sr., who wrote hundreds of gospel songs, including the classics, "I'll Fly Away," and "Turn Your Radio On."

But by the late 1980's, the new theaters and big-name entertainers were grabbing the headlines. Trivia buffs and Branson watchers began having a heyday keeping up with who was coming and leaving Branson, a heyday that continues to the present—except that many more are coming and staying than leaving.

In 1989, locally based entertainer Shoji Tabuchi and his investors renovated the former Ozark Auto Show Museum building, and Shoji opened his own variety show. He moved to a new 2,000 seat theater on Shepherd of the Hills Expressway in 1990. The versatile entertainer, his wife Dorothy and daughter Christina, perform in the show which uses props, costuming, and extensive dance numbers.

Many big name stars from outside the area began arriving in Branson in 1989, too. For example, in 1988 Chisai Childs leased her Starlite Theater to Ray Price for the season. Then, in late 1989, Cristy Lane purchased the theater. Lane, billed as an international star, is known for her hit recordings of "One Day at a Time" and "Amazing Grace." She has received awards from foreign countries, including Nigeria and India, for her million-selling records.

Also in 1989, Freddy Fender, known for such hits as "Wasted Days and Wasted Nights" and "Before the Next Teardrop Falls," established Freddy Fender's Tex-Mex Theater. After the 1989 season, Fender left to become part of the Tex-Mex group, the Texas Tornadoes.

In 1990, Danny Davis and the Nashville Brass left the County Music World Theater due to its sale. Davis took over the former Show Palace and renamed it the Danny Davis Theater. His band played there until the end of the 1991 season. Davis and the Nashville Brass are known for the country brass and big band sound. He performs at the Christy Lane Theater in 1992.

In December of 1989, the 1976 Country Music Association Entertainer of the Year, Mel Tillis, called a press conference and announced that he would be coming to Branson. He took over the former Tabuchi location in the old Auto Show building and renamed the theater the Mel Tillis Ozark Theater, opening in the spring of 1990. Tillis has appeared in numerous motion pictures and written many hit records. Two of his most popular compositions are "Detroit City" and "Ruby, Don't Take Your Love to Town."

In the spring of 1990, "Urban Cowboy" Mickey Gilley, known for his hits "Roomful of Roses," "Stand by Me," and "Talk to Me," purchased the Country Music World Theater which had featured Danny Davis. The influx of stars continued when Jim Stafford—comedian, songwriter, and entertainer—first appeared on a regular basis at a dinner theater, the Wildwood Flower. In the fall of 1990, he moved to the Stars of Ozarks Theater, which he purchased in November of 1991 and renamed the Jim Stafford Theater. Stafford, who is known for co-hosting TV's "Those Amazing Animals" and for hits such as "Spiders and Snakes" and "Cow Patty," also wrote for the Smothers Brothers television show.

Meanwhile, Silver Dollar City also stepped squarely into the middle of the Branson music scene in 1990 with the startling announcement that it would build two major projects in the Branson area. The first would be the Grand Palace on Highway 76, a theater designed to seat 4,000. The ornate building with the ante-bellum look of a southern mansion, complete with a circular lobby, opened in the spring of 1992. Two nationally known entertainers, Louise Mandrell and

*Branson stars, including artists long familiar to Branson audiences and those new to the area.
The mixture is creating a music explosion—and draws crowds from across the United States.*
(Photo courtesy of the Branson Daily News)

Glen Campbell, named to host the shows, will appear on a rotating schedule along with performing guest artists. Some of those scheduled to visit are Vince Gill, Randy Travis, the Statler Brothers, Roger Miller, the Oak Ridge Boys, and Ricky Skaggs.

Silver Dollar City also announced a White River Landing project with a showboat on Table Rock Lake. Scheduled to begin operations in the mid-1990's, with Kenny Rogers as a partner, the show boat will seat 1,000 people.

Hard on the heels of Silver Dollar City's news came the announcement that Darrel and Rosie Plummer were retiring. Their theater was sold to entertainer Moe Bandy and his business partner, Mac Stringfellow, of Texas. Bandy got his start in country music by learning to play the banjo and fiddle from his father, Marion Bandy, who played in various bands. In the 1960's Moe Bandy started recording in Nashville, but he did not have his first big hit, "I Just Started Hating Cheatin'

Songs Today," until 1972. Since then he has had 50 chart records, of which 30 were in the top ten. Bandy, who is known for the hits "Bandy the Rodeo Clown," and "Til I'm Too Old to Die Young," also sang President George Bush's unofficial 1988 campaign theme song "Americana." Bandy opened his completely refurbished theater in April, 1991.

Other surprises during the year included Bob Nichols developing an Ozark Morning Show and performing at the Wildwood Flower. That show moved in late summer to Campbell's Ozark Country Jubilee and added entertainer Buck Trent. The Baldknobbers revealed their newly renovated theater front and lobby. In August, 1991, the Norris Twins of the Baldknobber's cast announced that they were leaving the show to become regular cast members on the Hee Haw television show.

Comedian Ray Stevens (with his musicians, the French Fried Far-Out Legion Band) opened his 2,011 seat theater at Highway 76 and Shepherd of the Hills Expressway in June, 1991. The theater cost $4 million and features an Arab motif, complete with a "Clyde the Camel" logo. For six years in a row, Stevens has won the Comedian of the Year Award from "Music City News" and Nashville Network. His hit songs include "Ahab the Arab," "The Streak," "Mississippi Squirrel Revival," and "Everything is Beautiful."

1991—The Year of Announcements

From March through the end of 1991, the Branson music story grew and grew. In press conference after press conference, announcement after announcement, and story after story, one music project after another unfolded. Between press conferences, music lovers spent their time speculating about whether stars who were visiting Branson might be here for the purpose of establishing themselves locally. Throughout the entire 1991 season—as the bands played—the building of an even larger music industry was being announced for 1992. It took a score card to keep up with the announcements.

First, Mel Tillis announced in March that he would leave the Ozark Theater at the end of the 1991 season and build a new 2,100 seat theater on Highway 65 north of Branson, the first show to be built that far off the "strip." He also announced that he would feature Barbara Fairchild, who is known for her country and gospel music, and a dance group.

In April, developer David Green of California announced a $30 million theme park centered around country music veterans, Johnny and June Carter Cash. To be called "Cash Country," the new theater would have 2,500 seats. The complex would also have a museum and retail shops with room for later expansion of a theme park. That project was delayed, but Johnny vowed to perform at least 75 days in Branson during the 1992 season. Cash is known for such hits as "I Walk the Line" and "Ring of Fire."

Shortly thereafter came the announcement of the opening of a 2,000-plus seat gospel theater called Celebration Theater, featuring contemporary gospel artists like Bill Gaither. Gaither is known for such compositions as "The King Is Coming," as well as for his modern religious cantatas. The show performs in the old Bob-O-Links Theater and features entertainers Marilyn McCoo, Paul Overstreet, the Nelons, and the Cathedrals.

In August, after months of speculation and rumor in Branson, Andy Williams announced that he would build the Andy Williams Moon River Theater. At his press conference, Andy promised a show filled with his soft music, a distinct break from the country music on the strip. In addition to the 2,000 seat theater, his complex will feature a restaurant and motel.

Music was not the only item on the music industry's agenda in 1991. Ever increasing crowds of people could mean snarling lines of automobiles and impatient waits at restaurants. To prepare for the expected incoming traffic, Branson residents passed a half-cent sales tax in August, with the revenues intended for transportation. The proceeds are expected to bring in approximately one and a half million dollars a year for the next seven years to ease the traffic burden and finance new road construction. Almost immediately after passage of the tax, bulldozers were running up and down Branson hillsides cutting and slashing new roads where, not too many years ago, Ozark farmers raised strawberries and tomatoes.

But roads are only infrastructure and, for music people, a necessary diversion from the real task of making music. A new $25 million twin complex of 3,300 seat and 1,000 seat theaters, a hotel, and a restaurant was announced in late August by Global Productions of Dallas, Texas. The theaters are scheduled to open in 1993. The Gatlin Brothers, who have had such hits as "Houston" and "All the Gold in California," will perform at one of the theaters.

Meanwhile, L. Dino Kartsonakis, "America's Premier Pianist and Showman," announced that his show would open in April, 1992 at the former Legends Theater location.

Another deal was struck in mid-September with Willie Nelson taking over the Mel Tillis Ozark Theater, which now is called the Willie Nelson Ozark Theater. A

Willie Nelson Museum is also planned for the building. At his press conference, Willie, known for such hits as "On the Road Again," "Blue Eyes Crying in the Rain," and "You Were Always on My Mind," echoed a common sentiment among country music performers when asked why he came to Branson. "A lot of my friends are here in Branson already, and a lot of music fans come to Branson."

In late January, 1992, Merle Haggard, known for such hits as "Okie from Muskogee" and "Cherokee Maiden," announced that he would be performing 70 dates at the Willie Nelson Ozark Theater in 1992.

Because of all the announcements about new music shows, national news coverage sources began to converge on Branson. A steady stream of stories appeared in major newspapers and national magazines. *Entertainment Today, The Atlanta Constitution, U.S.A. Today, The Los Angeles Times, Time Magazine,* and *The Chicago Tribune,* as well as numerous television networks and stations, did stories on Branson's challenge to Nashville, calling Branson the "New Nashville" and the "New Entertainment Mecca."

In December, 1991, Morley Safer of the television show "60 Minutes" presented a 13-minute segment on Branson. The show, more akin to a Chamber of Commerce commercial than the kind of hard-hitting journalistic piece for which the show is known, was aired into 40 million homes across the country. Local officials estimated that the tab for an equal amount of commercial advertising would have exceeded seven million dollars. Many residents who remember the influx of new visitors following the filming of the Beverly Hillbillies at Silver Dollar City in 1969 believe the "60 Minutes" airing will result in a similar explosion of tourists for Branson.

While most entertainment ventures have been successful in the Branson area, a few have come and gone, especially in the 1980's and early 1990's. Most closings have been due to retirements, it is true, but a few, after having left their mark, went out of business.

The 1992 season opened an exciting year for Branson. The year also marked the thirty-fourth season since the Mabes were apprehensive about filling a fifty-seat theater on Friday and Saturday nights. But apprehension was again evident—about the challenge of filling 50,000 seats.

James D. Lancaster Jr.
Robert McGill

It Ain't Easy to Become a Star

The Shoji Tabuchi Story

All music performers in Branson have their own hopes, dreams, and desires. A few become stars, but only after many ups and downs and years of hard work. Stardom depends upon a small measure of luck and timing, and a great deal of talent and tenacity. Stars "pay their dues." Mel Tillis talks freely about his struggle to overcome stuttering. Moe Bandy played in near obscurity for years before finally having a hit song, while Willie Nelson's career has resembled a roller coaster ride. But, perhaps no other career has been as unusual as that of Shoji Tabuchi.

Born in war ravaged Daishoji, Japan in 1949, Shoji Tabuchi began his musical career as do many musicians—under his parents' tutelage. Shoji's mother enrolled her seven year old son and his sister in a music school which featured the Suzuki technique of playing the violin.

While Shoji did well with the violin, he was not inspired to a musical career until he heard a performance by an American musician, Roy Acuff, who was touring Japan. During the performance a member of Acuff's band, Howard Forrester, or "Big Howdy" as he was called, played the melodious "Listen to the Mockingbird." The song gave Shoji a focus for his life. From that moment on, he wanted to become a country music performer.

While he completed his high school and college education in the stringent Japanese school system, Shoji found time to continue to play the violin which, by now, he was playing as a fiddle. At his college in Osaka he formed a band, the "Bluegrass Ramblers," which played on campus and at parties around the city. In one contest, featuring all of the school's bands, Shoji's group was voted "best band on campus."

In 1967, after he had completed his college course work but before the graduation ceremonies, he boarded the luxury liner, *U.S. Cleveland*, with a dormi-tory class ticket. When he left Japan, Shoji took with him the $500 allowed by Japanese law, and an additional $100, hidden so authorities could not find it. He asked his mother to pick up his graduation diploma.

When he left Japan for the United States, Shoji's dream was to appear before three American audiences: the Grand Ole Opry in Nashville, the Louisiana Hayride, and the Dominion Barn Dance at Wheeling, West Virginia. But Shoji's resources were meager. When he arrived in San Francisco, he had little more than a few personal belongings, the $600 in his pocket, and one fiddle. He did not know anyone in San Francisco and could not speak English. Furthermore, he found that he could not join the musician's union because of the type of visa which had been granted to him. Therefore, the customary work of professional musicians was off-limits. But he did find employment: washing, detailing, and waxing cars.

Eventually he found musical work. In his one year in San Francisco, Shoji was befriended by an officer in the United States Coast Guard who helped him book parties and, for a brief period, he even played at the "Hungri i," opening for the Rodney Dillard band. Rodney became the first of a long string of musicians Shoji would meet and then come across again later in Branson. Buck Owens, the second, met Shoji and had him open for his show at the Corral Club in San Jose, California.

In 1968, Shoji received his first steady job, as a member of a band at the Starlight Club in Riverside, Missouri, just outside of Kansas City. The job, which lasted six months, served as an excellent apprenticeship, for it allowed Shoji to learn how to back up main performers. Occasionally, he was allowed to play solo on his fiddle.

When Roy Acuff gave a performance in Kansas City in 1968, Shoji was able to meet the man who had inspired his career. Roy listened to Shoji play and, recognizing his talent, immediately invited him to come to Nashville to appear on the Grand Old Opry.

Shoji jumped at the chance. The following Friday and Saturday night, Shoji fulfilled his dream of playing at the Grand Ole Opry and received a standing ovation for both his performances.

On this brief visit to Nashville, Shoji also met—on a street corner—another country music musician from Japan, Mike Ito. The chance meeting began a close friendship which has influenced both performers. Mike preceded Shoji to Branson where he now plays for the Baldknobbers.

Shoji quickly learned, as many other performers had before him, that a triumphant appearance on the Grand Ole Opry did not necessarily lead to a successful career in country music. His next job was in the X-ray department at St. Francis hospital in Wichita, Kansas where he worked during the daytime while playing nights at the Western Swinger Club on 47th Street. But Shoji's talent was gaining recognition. He often soloed at the club, and disk jockeys on Wichita radio station KFDI gave him considerable air time.

Within a year, Tillman Franks, who had helped several country music stars, hired him to tour with and open for country music star, David Houston. Shoji flew to Louisiana in late 1969 and, for the next eleven years, made Louisiana his home while he traveled across the country performing.

For five years, Shoji traveled with Houston, opening the show, learning about life on the road in country music, and meeting many of the Nashville stars who would later come to Branson, including Mel Tillis, who remains his good friend. In 1975 Shoji was ready for a change and, for one month, he played back-up in a band formed by retired Pittsburgh Steeler quarterback, Terry Bradshaw. Mercifully for all, Terry realized that his future career was in sports rather than country music, and he retreated back to the broadcasting industry. Shoji, after the brief stint, chose to become a solo performer of country music.

Working as a solo artist in country music is never easy. But working solo, Shoji gained the experience he would later need to manage his own show. Solo performers, even when they have agents, must make many business decisions. Shoji, because he had already established many contacts, was able, either personally or through his agent, to gain bookings across the midwest and south. He made many contacts and learned to follow through on bookings, setting up additional shows as he traveled. Working solo conditioned him to find opportunities and to help create them where they seemed not to exist. To make the difficult life of travel more pleasurable, Shoji—tired of sleeping in hotels and motels and eating restaurant cooking—purchased a motor home, which he drove himself, and began preparing some of his own meals.

Working as a solo performer also helped him become more versatile as an entertainer. Since Shoji did not have a band of his own, he used house or pick-up bands to support his role as the major performer. These bands varied in ability; on rare occasions they were excellent; sometimes they were good, but most often they were mediocre. At every stop, Shoji had to adjust to a different band even though he was the major attraction. He learned to improvise and, above all, to improve his entertainment abilities.

During the time that Shoji was a soloist, conditions for moving to Branson materialized. In the late 1970's, Shoji booked dates with the Grapevine Opry in Grapevine, Texas where he played with Chisai Childs and other country music performers. When Chisai opened her own show in 1981 at the Starlite Theater in Branson, she asked Shoji to become a part of the show. At first, Shoji refused. But in early 1981, he was traveling from Springfield, Illinois to Grapevine, Texas when he decided to stop in Branson to visit his old friend, Mike Ito, and survey the local music scene. Although Mike was not at home, the Branson country music world impressed Shoji. Within a few short months, he signed with Chisai and began to make his reputation in Branson.

Recognition and opportunity came quickly when Branson audiences responded enthusiastically to his talents. Within a few short years, he would play for Chisai at the Starlite Theater, and for Bill and Janet Dailey at Country Music World. Following those venues, he teamed up with his energetic and talented wife, Dorothy, whom he met in Branson, to develop and perform in his own music show. In 1990, he built his own theater, one of the most luxurious in Branson, where he, Dorothy, and daughter Christina headline a robust and versatile program twice daily throughout the season.

Robert McGill

An Ear for Music

She had an ear for music,
The neighbors used to say
As they gathered in our happy home
To hear her sing and play.
She caught and held the rhythm
Of winging birds and bees,
She lightly snatched the raptures
Of the singing, sighing breeze.
Now her little children's voices
With her sweet music blend.
For that quaint old cottage organ
Is still her faithful friend,
For that mystic gift, God given,
Brings from distant, dreamy spheres
Rich melody and glory
Through all these later years.

Mary Elizabeth Mahnkey

Peter Engler and Ron Conn
A Woodcarving Resurgence

Historically, woodcarving has been an important American industry. Shipbuilders placed huge carvings on the bows of their ships; owners of fashionable houses commissioned carved mantles and decorative entranceways; families used wooden utensils; and hobbyists produced "Sunday toys" for children—small dolls, birds, and animals.

But by the mid-twentieth century, woodcarving in the United States had virtually disappeared. Metal ships had no need for carvings; home architects had turned to straight, fashionable—although often veneered—designs rather than the ornate detail of woodcarving. Stainless steel replaced most wooden utensils; those still being made were more quickly shaped by machines. Only the carvers of decoys in prime waterfowl hunting areas and the carvers of Sunday toys, primarily in the Ozarks and the Appalachians, still practiced their craft.

Now, however, because of an artistic revival which started right here in the Ozarks, the craft of woodcarving is again thriving as an American industry. And one person, Peter Engler, is largely responsible for the comeback of woodcarving in the Branson area.

In the late 1940's as a boy in northern Arkansas, Peter learned from older family members about wood, carving tools, and the crafting of Sunday toys. His interest lasted only a few short years before other pursuits—school and athletics—dominated his time. In 1958 after serving in the Marines in the Korean War, Peter returned to Lakeview, Arkansas where his mother owned a small tourist-oriented gift shop. At first, Engler intended only to learn how to operate the business. However, developing the talents which he had used as a youngster, he soon began to carve objects which could be sold at the gift shop. The carving, which he enjoyed, served as a diversion from his work. By combining his carving talents with his newly

Woodcarver Peter Engler, who is largely responsible for the resurgence of woodcarving in the Ozarks.
(Photo by Denise McGill)

acquired marketing know-how, Peter would soon energize a languishing industry.

When the young woodcarver heard about the new village of Silver Dollar City in 1962, he visited Mary Herschend to discuss the possibility of carving a cigar store Indian. The two talked—not only about the project, but about merchandising. Peter would soon move into the area with his family and open a woodcarving shop at Silver Dollar City, a shop which foreshadowed the growth of the craft industry at the expanding family theme park.

As his own business grew, Engler opened, in 1968, what he hoped would be a production shop in a small building north of Reeds Springs, a location he called the Wilderness Clockworks. Engler intended to use the building only as a workshop to produce carvings which would be sold elsewhere, but he very quickly found that potential customers wanted to see his works at his new location. He added a retail store to the building and invited "would be" carvers to participate in carving sessions in his back room. Other carvers from the area responded to his invitation, notably Robert Robertson who made archery equipment; Dave and Wendy Rauch, the former owners of the shop; and Junior Cobb and Ivan Denton, talented and well-known carvers from Arkansas.

A woodcarved hillbilly caricature.
(Photo by Denise McGill)

The carvers compared works, traded tips, and critiqued each other's productions. The attention to detail and the demanding self-direction indispensable to being an excellent carver were always evident. Because of the mixture of personalities and carving styles, the carvers began to call their group a "soup." Their mutual support eventually led to a resurgence of the craft of woodcarving in the Ozarks. Although they did not realize it at the time, the "soup" at Engler's Wilderness Clockworks would catapult several of the members into national prominence as woodcarvers.

Peter Engler sold both his Wilderness Clockworks and Silver Dollar City shops in 1975 in order to move his base of operations to Branson. Ron Conn, an executive at Silver Dollar City, purchased the shop there and continued to promote woodcarving.

Conn, though not a carver himself, enthusiastically supported the craft and quickly began to market exquisite carvings. His strategy was to encourage the best available carvers by guaranteeing purchase of all their work. Their responsibilities would be to provide an adequate and steady supply and to develop their skills in order to produce successively better and more valuable carvings. Conn, in return, would advertise and market every piece.

Conn's timing was perfect. The finest carvings in the United States were soon being carved in the Branson area, and the interest exceeded even Conn's expectations. A national market of eager purchasers quickly developed. Within five years, Conn had five retail galleries, and he employed seventy-two carvers, including many of the best in the area. The carvings of some artists were purchased well in advance of their completion. On several occasions, Conn held drawings of the names of people willing to pay the asking price of completed pieces. Purchasers included movie stars Burl Ives, Jane Fonda, and Burt Reynolds, two former Presidents of the United States, and major corporations across the United States. Prices for the museum quality pieces ranged to $30,000.

Conn tells of several unusual experiences. On one occasion a browser in one of his shops purchased two carvings valued in excess of $23,000, paying for them on the spot with ten and twenty dollar bills. Conn and his associates joyfully piled the loose bills on a silver platter and photographed the proceeds of the unexpected sale. Several months later Conn received a telephone call from an inquisitive employee of the Internal Revenue Service who explained that the buyer was a drug dealer who had been laundering money by investing in crafts. Conn eventually sold the same carvings again, this time on behalf of the Internal Revenue Service.

Conn's insistence on the highest standards produced another memorable incident. Once, when one of his carvers failed to live up to his potential, Conn refused to purchase one of his pieces and even threatened to burn all of the man's carvings stored in inventory. The carver, who had always found excuses for his lack of improvement, soon produced significantly better material.

Both Conn and Engler continue their woodcarving activities today. Conn still operates the woodcarving shop at Silver Dollar City and makes carvings available to retail shops and commercial accounts throughout the United States. Engler's activities include, but now extend beyond, woodcarving. In 1986, Engler opened a small woodcarving shop on Highway 76 in Branson. In addition to selling carvings, the shop, patterned after the Wilderness Clockworks, features working carvers, and offers tools, supplies, and instructions to those who would like to learn the craft. The following year, in 1987, a huge building attached to Engler's small carving shop became available and Engler suddenly found himself renting a building many times larger than his original establishment. He remodeled the building, patterning the frontal architecture after a similar building his grandfather had owned a century before

in Minnesota, and called it The Engler Block. Then he encouraged friends and business associates to market a variety of crafts through his building. Today many craft shops, including a fine arts gallery, are located in The Engler Block.

Peter Engler, incidentally, was the first area merchant to emphasize the Christmas season as a marketing period. He decorated his store with a particularly brilliant array of lights and Christmas ornaments two years before other businesses in the area began advertising an Ozark Mountain Christmas.

Currently, a thriving woodcarving industry exists in Ozark Mountain Country, and the two-county area remains the national center for woodcarving. Many of the finest carvers in the nation reside in the area. Expert carvers who live elsewhere often look to the Branson area for creative support and markets. Although the demand for artistic carvings is not as high as it was during its peak in the late 1970's, carvings from the area are still sent to collectors and museums all across the country. A variety of carvings, including expressive faces, hillbilly caricatures, cowboys, horses and animals, and even hobby horses are available. A resurgence of architectural carvings, highlighted by mantles and doorways, is currently underway.

The modern day pioneers in woodcarving and marketing, Peter Engler and Ron Conn, continue to make woodcarvings available in their retail shops and through the wholesale and corporate accounts they hold. A few other craft shops in the area also have woodcarvings available so that visitors to the area can readily find fine carvings. But it is the carvers—those artisans both past and present—who fascinate us with their skills. Their works bring joy and happiness—and inspire awe.

Robert McGill

Woodcarving

Child: Mister, how did you carve that Blue Jay?
Woodcarver: I just chipped away everything
that wasn't a bird.

Woodcarving, like the execution of so many crafts, looks deceptively simple in the hands of a master craftsman. The carver studies a piece of wood; soon the chips are falling. As the artist maintains a slow, steady pace of work, a shapeless piece of wood begins to take on character. The viewer looks on in amazement as the woodcarver shapes the final product, be it an animal or human form.

Opportunities for viewing woodcarvers at work are limited because many of the carvers in Ozark Mountain Country work in small home shops. Currently, only The Engler Block in Branson and Silver Dollar City have galleries where the public can observe a practicing carver. But these opportunities make the Ozarks one of the best places to see the craft practiced. Indeed, Ozark Mountain Country is one of the few centers of woodcarving in the nation. As many as thirty-five area carvers make a full time living from their craft. Many others—retirees and business professionals—supplement their income with carving.

Woodcarvers develop their skills through classes, apprenticeships, experimentation, and most of all, daily work. A beginner must first master the use of tools, which come in various shapes and sizes: flat chisels, rounded gouges, and square cornered V-tools. Carvers use massive tools, which they pound with a mallet, to tear away wood in the carving of a large piece, such as a cigar store Indian. Extremely small tools serve to cut away minute pieces of wood for fine detail. Veteran woodcarvers eventually collect hundreds of different tools. The sharpening and maintenance of these tools is an art in itself. Carvers utilize a variety of sharpening stones, grinding compounds, and honing straps for keeping edges sharp.

The selection of wood is a very important part of the trade because each type of wood has different properties. Basswood, or linden, is the favorite wood used by carvers because it rarely splinters, is easily cut,

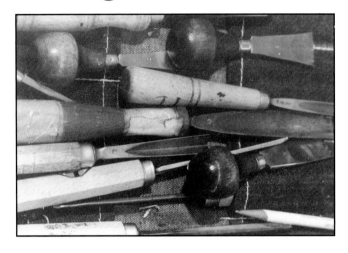

A few of Peter Engler's woodcarving tools.
(Photo by Denise McGill)

and can be painted or readily finished. It is commonly used in mantles, hillbilly caricatures, and animals. Sassafras limbs when cut in the wintertime hold their bark for several years, and so are favored for the carving of expressive faces. Red cedar, which has a rich two-tone grain, is also used for the same purpose. Walnut, a hard, dark, and beautifully grained wood, is preferred when a natural finish is desired. The premier wood for carvers is butternut, a wood which is lighter in color than walnut but with an equally distinctive grain. Museum quality carvings, especially animals and characters with a western motif, are usually carved from butternut.

Most carvers experiment with different items before settling in on their "specialty." Animal carvers spend time in the field and in zoos studying the animals they produce; carvers of the human figure pore over books on human anatomy. Many of the excellent carvers first design their carvings in modeling clay which allows them to experiment with poses, expressions, and designs before actually setting the subject in wood. But no matter what the carver may tell you, the art takes time and practice to master. If you try it, you will soon learn that there is more to the craft than "chipping away everything that isn't a bird."

Robert McGill

If I Lived Down on White River

If I lived down on White River
I know just what I would do.
I would fish and swim and hunt for pearls
And build me a big canoe.

I would go floating down White River
And maybe I would see
Some of the many lovely things
God made for boys like me.

A mother duck and her little ones
Might come gently floating near
And far across an open ridge
I might see a big brown deer.

At night I would not be afraid
For I'd stop at a gravel bar
And go to sleep in my blankets
Watching the evening star.

Mary Elizabeth Mahnkey

Section II
The White River Tamed

    If the entertainment industry has brought national attention to Ozark Mountain Country, it was the taming of the White River which changed the character of the region from a largely rural area of subsistence farms to a tourist center. In 1959, in fact, two important local events coincided: the Bald Knobbers opened their first music show and Table Rock Lake filled with waters backing up behind the newly built dam.

    This section of the book focuses on the history of the development of the White River Valley and area roads and includes an article on Congressman Dewey Short who played a major role in seeing the Table Rock dam project completed. Because fishing and the outdoors have always been a part of the attraction of Ozark Mountain Country, we also offer articles on fishing, wildlife, birdwatching, the Mark Twain National Forest, flora, and geology.

The Wild White River

Before the White River in southwest Missouri disappeared beneath Bull Shoals and Table Rock Lakes in the 1950's, it had a reputation as the wildest river in the midwest. Though the people of the Ozarks hated to see the free-flowing river with its deep-cut valleys and towering bluffs disappear, they have come to appreciate the freedom from disastrous flooding that the great dams have brought to the White River Valley—as well as the electric power and water sports.

The river begins as a clear spring in Arkansas' Boston Mountains, near the village of St. Paul, fifty miles south of Eureka Springs, Arkansas. It enters the Mississippi River 250 air miles away, just north of the mouth of the Arkansas River.

For centuries, the river rushed northwest, collided with the plateau at Fayetteville, Arkansas, and shifted northeastward, chewing a several hundred foot deep chasm between two high bluffs just south of the Missouri border, now mostly inundated by Beaver Lake. The free-flowing river then circled through the southeast corner of Barry County, wound a serpentine path across southern Stone and Taney Counties, then plunged southeast toward the swampy Arkansas lowlands, a journey of 700 miles or more. All along the river's upper course, picturesque high bluffs lined the fertile bottomlands.

To the pioneering immigrants who began settling Taney and Stone Counties 175 years ago, and to the native Americans who preceded them, the river was a life sustaining force—a highway into the region, a provider of fish, and a vital source of water.

When six-inch rains deluged the 12,000 square miles of hills and valleys which make up its upper watershed, the White River went on towering rampages; surging waters up to fifty feet deep tore trees and stone from beaches and limestone bluffs. Such debris became a part of the river's destructive force downstream. As the floodwater slowed, its load of silt and debris was dumped on the bottomlands, or created new snags and sandbars in the riverbed.

When Taney County was established in 1837, its boundaries extended to much of present day Stone County and parts of several other modern counties. In the 1840 census covering that very large county, there were 3,265 people living in 385 households.

Those pioneering settlers immediately began adapting the upper White River Valley to meet their survival needs. They cleared and plowed the bottomlands; fished, hunted, and trapped the region's wildlife; and prepared animal pelts to trade for other necessities. Though the pioneers feared the river's destructive ways, they were quick to make use of the water's power. Some sought out spring-fed streams which could be dammed to power mills for grinding grain, ginning cotton, and sawing logs into lumber.

Before the Civil War, most newcomers came to Taney County by way of the White River, usually in long, narrow, high-sided flatboats, which could carry large cargoes yet draw only a foot or two of water when fully loaded. Sails, oars, or long poles were used to propel the craft upstream and over the sandy shallows and rocky shoals.

Essential supplies also arrived by flatboat. Cargoes to be sent downriver to market depended on sufficient water to float flatboats or log rafts. The journey was always dangerous. Dumped cargo could be buried almost instantly by the river's heavy load of silt; shipments of fat cattle, tied to a flatboat's deck, had no chance of swimming to safety if the craft foundered.

Steamboats tried to reach the tiny village of Forsyth, the Taney County seat, as early as 1842. A leader in the effort to make the upper White River a reliable highway into the Ozarks was Springfieldian John P. Campbell. He hoped to open navigation to the mouth of the James and thus bring the world's markets to Springfield's doors.

By 1844, Campbell had a channel cleared through the numerous shoals below the Buffalo River in Arkansas. Eight years later, the first steamboat, the *Yohogony*, reached Forsyth, but only after its cargo of salt was off-loaded to wagons so the vessel could get through the treacherous Elbow Shoals south of that town. At least two shallow draft steamers managed to reach the mouth of the James in the 1850's, but the financial rewards were not worth the struggle.

Steamboat traffic upriver to Forsyth, and sometimes a few miles further, was revived after the Civil War and continued into the 20th century. However the upper White River remained a half-tamed bronco, and derelict boats littered its rocky shallows, testimony to the dangers of the voyage.

Those hazards were compounded after the Civil War by a constant traffic of logs being floated to market. As railroad tracks were extended into the Ozarks, farmers cut down white oak and sold it for railroad ties, then later cut other tree species—maple, black walnut, pine, and cedar—and sold them for fence posts, wagon parts, lumber, furniture, and cedar pencils. The logs were floated downstream to collecting yards—at the mouth of the James River and at almost every creek. Formed into huge rafts and fastened together into long trains of rafts, the logs were piloted downriver to the nearest factory or railroad center.

After the completion of the White River Railroad Line through Roark and Turkey Creek valleys in 1906, the new towns of Branson and Hollister became hubs for log shipping. Loggers downstream from Branson floated their rafts south to Cotter, Arkansas. Pleasure fishermen also used the busy river at the turn of the century, enjoying the hillmen's fishing methods—spearing, grabbing, trapping, seining, noodling, and most pleasurable of all, floatfishing. Float fishermen could drift in boats around several switchbacks of the James River with a pole and line, and have only a short portage back to their starting point. With the coming of the railroad, floatfishing enthusiasts, beginning at Galena, could enjoy a 125-mile float trip down the James and the White to Branson, where a fifty minute train ride would return boat and boaters to their starting point. At the end of a 250-mile float to Cotter, the train trip back to Galena took two hours.

Another potential for economic gain from the river was developed in 1897 when a mussel shell yielded a large, lustrous pearl. Fortune hunters flocked to every stream, looking for mussels with pearls.

Word went out, around 1900, that the shells themselves could be sold to button factories, and piles of mussel shells were collected to be loaded on boats and sent downstream to market. Later the pearl seekers found that they could saw tube-like "button blanks" from the shells' pearly lining instead of paying to ship the whole shells. The industry continued until the 1940's. Uncounted piles of riddled shells disappeared from view when Bull Shoals and Table Rock Lakes were impounded.

The White River was at its busiest in 1906 when the railroad was completed, but suddenly its navigability seemed unimportant. Now that rapid travel by land was assured, business interests began urging Congress to declare the upper river "unnavigable" so it could be

The Moark, a sidewheeler built in 1906, carried passengers and goods between Forsyth and Branson when the water was deep enough to handle the boat.
(Photo courtesy of Chloe LaRue)

harnessed to produce electricity.

In 1907, plans were formulated for a dam called "Table Rock," upstream from Branson. However, four years later, when a group of private investors organized the Ozark Power and Water Company and began construction of the first White River hydroelectric dam, the site was a dozen miles down the river, near Forsyth. The resulting impoundment, Lake Taneycomo, filled the floor of the 22-mile-long canyon to its western gate at the high bluff topped by a large table of white stone which today provides a magnificent view of its namesake, Table Rock Dam.

The first damming of the White River caused considerable furor. In addition to conservation concerns, many objected to the idea of licensing a private company to build on and profit by a public waterway.

Powersite Dam includes a 210-foot-long powerhouse on the south, a 546-foot-long spillway, and a 440-foot core wall on the north side of the river. The dam is seventy-five feet high on its face, the depth of the water it impounds at the dam is 50 feet.

To build the dam, more than a thousand workers, many of them local men, were hired and paid a livable wage, a new concept in the area. Most of the construction materials came to Branson by train and were brought down river on barges built on that town's waterfront. Much of the 2.3 million dollar construction cost went directly into the local economy.

Workers were housed in barracks-type buildings on the hillside overlooking the damsite. The company provided a commissary, school, post office, and other civic amenities, creating the town of Camp Ozark, rivaling Branson as the largest community in Stone or Taney County at that time. When the dam was completed, the company town disappeared as quickly as it had been built.

On May 9, 1913, the day Powersite Dam's gates were closed, heavy rains were falling. Less than two days later water was spilling over the crest of the dam. Within the week, an excursion boat pulling a barge, both loaded with local citizens, made the round-trip from Branson to celebrate the completion of the dam.

Lake Taneycomo, the first sizable impounded lake in Missouri, drowned the mouths of creeks, buried many roads, and altered operations at several ferry crossings. A wagon bridge across the river was completed that summer at Branson, where the traffic in floating logs was diminishing due to depletion of the hardwood forests. Fishing camps and vacation cottages were built along the lake, and a sizable resort community, Rockaway Beach, began developing near Bull Creek.

The power plant brought electric lights to some nearby communities, though most of the electricity from the dam went to Springfield and the mining towns in western Missouri. For the most part, the White River remained free-flowing. Taneycomo's spillway dam was an impediment only to the passage of fish and watercraft.

Repeatedly, through the next twenty-three years, the Empire District Electric Company, a regional power company which took over Powersite Dam, sought to construct a second, much higher dam at various sites in the vicinity of Table Rock. Due to public opposition, lack of financing, and uncertainty about where such a dam should be located, work was never begun.

In 1935, Congress finally terminated Empire's permit to build, and pressure began for federal funding of a series of hydroelectric dams on the White River and its tributaries.

Repeated flood damage, made worse by farming practices, finally forced the taming of the White River. The floods that roared through Taneycomo's canyons became higher and more intense. Downriver, floodwater no longer spread out through miles of swamps. The wetlands had been stripped, and drained by a system of canals. When the White went on a rampage, 600,000 acres of cotton, corn, and beans were threatened with inundation. One year out of three in the 1930's, damaging White River floods of epic proportions devastated homes, businesses, and crops.

In late 1941, Congress approved a four dam, $134,000,000 flood control and hydroelectric power project on the upper White River. The initial dams were built in Arkansas, though the lakes they impound stretch into Missouri. Work had already begun on the first dam, Norfork, at the mouth of the North Fork of the White River near Mountain Home, Arkansas. As work was completed there, the construction equipment was moved up the White River to Bull Shoals where the second dam was started in 1947.

When 256-foot-high Bull Shoals Dam was completed in 1951, it backed the river up 75 miles, to the base of Powersite Dam. While Bull Shoals was being built, bottomlands were purchased, roads and bridges relocated, and cemeteries moved to high ground. Most of the town of Forsyth was relocated from beside the

White River—where it had stood for more than 100 years—to the top of a nearby bluff.

People who lived at Protem, in the southeast corner of Taney County, were offered options: they could trade for nearby land above any danger of flooding, move several miles up the road, or sell out and go elsewhere. The bottomlands, which supported the local economy, would be flooded. Although the lake never actually threatened Protem, the town shrank to a small village.

Bull Shoals Lake filled rapidly. People below the dam expected immediate protection from flooding, but when heavy rains fell, a single dam could not retain the run-off from 12,000 square miles. Disastrous floods continued both below and above the new dam. In 1951 work still had not begun on Table Rock Dam. Strong objections to that dam were being heard. If Table Rock Dam were built, much valuable farmland and attendant tax revenues would be lost. The cost in wildlife habitat was unacceptable. Fluctuating water levels would discourage recreation and tourism.

Congress also was dragging its heels. The cost of the first two dams had greatly exceeded expectations; only $17,000,000 remained of the money earmarked for the entire hydroelectric dam project, and the projected costs of Table Rock had risen to $76,000,000.

Despite the complaints and its own fiscal problems, Congress knew the project must be completed. In addition to the continuing problems with flooding, almost every county in southwest Missouri was losing population, and more cheap power was needed to foster growth and prosperity in the region.

Nonetheless, the delays multiplied. The damsite was changed in late 1951 when rock borings revealed a problem at the original site. Money to begin construction was appropriated in January, 1952, but work was delayed for two more years while the Corps of Engineers restudied the entire plan. Building finally commenced in October, 1954. Throughout the project, at each of its sessions, the Congress was forced to consider anew whether funds would be made available to continue construction.

Construction on the dam which impounded Table Rock Lake began in 1954. By 1955 concrete work had begun. Many visitors came to the area to view the progress on the dam. Table Rock Dam was completed in 1958.
(Photos courtesy of the Corps of Engineers, Branson)

1959, the year after the completion of Table Rock Dam, was significant for Branson and Stone and Taney Counties. During 1959 Silver Dollar City opened its gates for the first time, the Shepherd of the Hills pageant began, and the Baldknobbers presented the first music show in Branson.

(Photo courtesy of the Corps of Engineers, Branson)

The building was complicated by the length of the earthen embankment required to tailor the dam to its finally selected site. The 2,256-foot-long Bull Shoals Dam is built almost entirely of concrete, but Table Rock's 1,602 foot concrete section is extended to 6,423 feet by a long earthen and rock-filled embankment. The cost of Table Rock Dam was held to $65,420,000 by chopping rock and gravel from the top of nearby Baird Mountain and delivering it to the damsite via an aerial conveyor system.

The completion of Table Rock Dam in 1958, and the impoundment of Beaver Lake upstream in Arkansas in 1964, finally provided relief from repeated severe flooding all along the White River. Though many people were displaced, and though an incalculable loss of natural beauty resulted from the impoundments, the lakes provide a new kind of beauty, and the financial and recreational gains have been substantial.

Tourism, which increased with the completion of each dam, has developed into the region's major industry. Though savings from prevented flood damage are hard to assess, there is little doubt that the power generated and all the other benefits have much more than paid for the construction.

Water drawn from deep in Table Rock Lake permanently changed Lake Taneycomo's year-round temperature to a bone-chilling fifty-five degrees, but the loss of swimming holes and warm water fish habitats was turned to advantage. In 1958, a hatchery was built at the foot of Table Rock Dam to keep Taneycomo's cold waters supplied with trout.

Today the White River seems to be tamed. The United States Corps of Engineers and the operators of the dams' many generators have, over the past thirty years, developed careful plans to balance electrical generation, recreation, and flood control on what once was the wildest river in the Midwest.

Kathleen Van Buskirk

Floods in the late 1980's necessitated the opening of all flood gates on Table Rock Dam and the removal of the spill-boards from Power-site Dam.

(Left photo by Denise McGill; below by Kathleen Van Buskirk)

The Silver Tongued Orator
Dewey Short

I deeply and sincerely regret that this body [Congress] has degenerated into a supine, subservient, soporific, superfluous, supercilious, pusillanimous body of nitwits, the greatest ever gathered beneath the dome of our National Capitol, who cowardly abdicate their powers and, in violation of their oaths to protect and defend the Constitution against all of the Nation's enemies, both foreign and domestic, turn over these constitutional prerogatives, not only granted but imposed upon them, to a group of tax-eating, conceited autocratic bureaucrats—a bunch of theoretical, intellectual, professorial nincompoops out of Columbia University, at the other end of Pennsylvania Avenue—who were never elected by the American people to any office and who are responsible to no constituency. These brain trusters and 'New Dealers' are the ones who wrote this resolution, instead of the Members of this House whose duty it is, and whose sole duty it is, to draft legislation.
Dewey Short, 1935

Born April 7, 1898 in Galena, Missouri to Jackson Grant and Permelia Cordelia Long Short, Dewey Jackson Short would often in years to come remark on his family heritage and allow as to how he was both the "long and the short of it." Endowed with a gregarious personality, superior intelligence, and a remarkable gift for oratory, Dewey Short was destined to become known far and wide as the "Orator of the Ozarks," and to serve his district in the U.S. House of Representatives for twenty-four years.

When Dewey was a youngster, Galena was a marvelous place for a boy to grow up, for it was the floatfishing mecca of the United States. The young lad kept busy, not only with school, but with helping visitors prepare for float trips down the James River. He would meet visitors at the train station, haul luggage and tourists in his jenny-pulled hack, tote supplies, and sell ice. But he also had his sights firmly fixed on obtaining an education; by 1911, he kept his own checking account at the local bank so that he could save money for college.

Young Dewey Short graduated as valedictorian from Galena High School in 1915 then attended Marionville College for two years. He received his degree from Baker University in Baldwin City, Kansas in 1919. Having decided to enter the ministry, Short attended Boston College School of Theology from 1919 to 1922

and graduated with honors. With a fellowship to study abroad, Short and his friend, Earl Marlatt, traveled to Europe to study at Berlin, Heidelberg, and Oxford in 1922-23. Upon his return, Short became Professor of Philosophy and Psychology at Southwestern College in Winfield, Kansas.

With a spell-binding address to the Republican faithful assembled at the Lincoln Day festivities in Springfield on February 12, 1926, Short drew widespread attention to his speaking abilities. Short's speech, "Republicanism and Americanism," created a sensation and placed him in great demand for speaking engagements throughout Missouri.

Intrigued by the prospects of political office, Short ran successfully in 1928 for the congressional seat in the 14th district, a district which extended from Stone County on the west to the Mississippi River on the east. After serving one term, he was defeated in the Democratic landslide of 1930 following the onslaught of the Great Depression.

After traveling again in Europe and visiting the Soviet Union, Short ran unsuccessfully for the U.S. Senate in 1932. In 1934, however, he captured the congressional seat in the newly formed 7th district of southwest Missouri, a position he held until his eventual defeat in 1956.

In 1935, Short's oratorical flair became the

object of national attention when, highly distressed by the New Deal's concentration of power in the federal government, he unleashed a relentless attack against his fellow congressional members on the floor of the House, including the excerpt quoted in the headnote.

The Washington press reported his tirade. *Time* magazine carried his picture and termed the speech "notable," done in "his best revivalistic style." Short had made his mark as a major opponent of New Deal policies, and thereafter his voice was heard often in the halls of Congress and at meetings and rallies throughout the country.

With his keen insight and barbed tongue, Short expounded his political beliefs in terms that caught the attention of political observers everywhere. In 1937, Short stated that people "seem today to be suffering with the 'gimmes.' It is 'gimme this and gimme that.' There is very little difference between Republicans and Democrats when it comes to that sad affliction."

On individual initiative, Short quipped: "I have always been old-fashioned enough to believe it is much better to 'git up and get' than it is to 'sit down and set'. The only animal I know which can sit and still produce dividends is the old hen."

Even Short's political opponents recognized his great talents and ability. After one of Short's oratorical displays in the House of Representatives, one of his Democratic colleagues remarked:

He is, indeed, a gentleman of fine attainments. He came to the House with a sparkling reputation that he has fully justified. I have frequently heard him designated as the sage of the Ozarks. In dealing with any question he is a master, a recognized savant, always having at hand a fund of devastating information that disarms and paralyzes an opponent before the opponent fairly starts. No great question is finally settled before he speaks.

Perhaps Short's most enduring tangible accomplishment is Table Rock Dam and Lake. The proposal to dam the White River and its James River arm was introduced in Congress in 1906 when Short was eight years old. In 1929, during Short's first year in Congress,

the Empire District Electric Company announced its plan to construct a hydroelectric project in Stone County known as "Table Rock." Although the project was approved by the Federal Power Commission, Empire failed to proceed as planned and eventually its license was withdrawn.

During his second year in Congress in 1930, in a speech delivered to the Springfield Rotary club, Short declared that the completion of a Table Rock dam project was only a matter of time, and he envisioned the establishment of a national park in Stone or Taney County. "I am sure that the Table Rock dam will go through, but we must be patient," he said. "The market crash has delayed it, as it has delayed other projects."

As early as 1933, the White River Boosters League in Branson asked Short to jointly sponsor its cooperative effort with the Springfield Chamber of Commerce to make the Table Rock Dam a reality. Short promised his continued cooperation, stating that the proper procedure had never been followed "nor has there been the concerted action in Washington that is necessary to bring our desired end to a consummation." At the time, Short was out of office. But on his return to Congress in 1935, he was in a position to push the project.

Just as the Great Depression had derailed the Table Rock project earlier, World War II postponed its completion. Both the Bull Shoals and Table Rock dam projects were authorized by Congress before the war, but the Table Rock proposal was not funded due to the emphasis on the war effort. When the Allied victory was assured, Short spoke at the hearings of the House Subcommittee of the Committee on Appropriations to urge the allocation of funds for the construction of the dam and reservoir.

Short made his final push for the dam in 1953. Speaking on the floor of the House in support of appropriations for the construction of the dam, Short stated, "For the 20 years that I have been in Congress I have been working for Table Rock Dam." He noted that the appropriation for the construction of Bull Shoals Dam downstream had passed in 1946, and the dam was nearly completed. In 1952, some $3,000,000 was available for the Table Rock project. Short urged that the money be spent and that the project proceed immediately.

In 1954, President Eisenhower signed the bill which provided $76,000,000 for construction of the Table Rock Dam, and bids were let in October of that year. In a letter to Short, Eisenhower praised him for the manner in which he "bulldogged" the project through Congress.

On June 19, 1959, the formal dedication of the Table Rock Dam signaled victory for Short and others who had long labored for Table Rock Lake. Ironically, Short participated in the ceremony not as a Congressman, but as the Under Secretary of the Army, sharing the platform with Charlie Brown, the Democratic Congressman for the Seventh District whose victory over Short in 1956 ended Short's Congressional career.

Short died on November 19, 1979. His body, as he requested, was returned to Galena for burial in the cemetery on top of the hill overlooking the town. Short never lost his affection and pride for his modest upbringing in Stone County. He was fond of saying, "Really, I am just a plain, ordinary country boy, a native hillbilly from the Ozarks in southwest Missouri, where we still cover our houses with bull hides and use their tails for lightning rods."

In 1984 Short received posthumous recognition for his efforts to build Table Rock Lake when the House of Representatives passed a bill designating the visitor's center at Table Rock Dam the "Dewey J. Short Table Rock Lake Visitor's Center." But the most enduring legacy of this statesman is the lifetime of dedicated public service and his advocacy of individual freedom.

Robert S. Wiley

Robert S. Wiley, a lawyer in Crane, Mo., is the author of a biography of Dewey Short, *Dewey Short Orator of the Ozarks.*.

The Challenge of These Hills
Roads

On the road known as West 76 or Mountain Country Boulevard, it often seems as if everyone is trying to get to the same place at the same time. A drive into the hills in almost any direction quickly reveals why the traffic problems are so difficult to solve—because of the hilly terrain, one may be forced to drive for miles to reach a spot just over the next ridge.

Travel has always been a challenge in the area. The earliest settlers solved the problem by following old Indian trails along the James and White Rivers. But as the population grew and commerce increased, wagon roads became a necessity. In the mid-1830's a road was developed between Springfield (then the county seat of most of Southwest Missouri) and the White River at Swan Creek (the eventual townsite of Forsyth), so Springfield residents would have access to the White River.

Before the Civil War disrupted community development in southwest Missouri, such wagon roads connected all the county seats in the area, as evidenced by an 1860's atlas map. The map also shows the Wire Road, which crossed the northwest corner of Stone County and was used by the Butterfield Stage in the 1850's and by Union and Confederate troops during the Civil War.

When commerce began to grow again in the 1870's, north-south roads were cleared and widened for use by large freight wagons. The major freighting route in Stone County followed a well-established Indian trail called the Wilderness Road. From Springfield it more or less followed today's Highways 160 and 13 south through Spokane, past the Linchpin Campground (south of Reeds Spring), and through Blue Eye to Berryville, Arkansas.

In Taney County there were three major freight roads, two connecting Springfield's railhead with communities as far south as Harrison and Lead Hill, Arkansas, and one connecting a railhead at Chadwick, Missouri with Yellville, Arkansas and the busy farming centers on the east side of Taney County.

Ponderous freight wagons traveled to market loaded with cotton, tobacco, animal pelts, farm produce, and railroad ties. They returned loaded with merchandise to be sold in stores along the route. The round trip took as much as two weeks, with nights spent in campgrounds along the way. The roads wound back and forth, climbing steep hills and meandering along the ridge tops. When the dirt paths were thick with ice, heavy cleats had to be strapped to the feet of the straining horses to allow them to climb without slipping.

By the 1880's, a whole network of roads had developed and required constant upkeep. Counties were divided into road districts managed by road overseers who took an annual census of men over 21 and scheduled them for work on the roads. Such labor was called "working off the poll tax." Those who did not work their two to four days each year paid the tax.

One of the tasks assigned to the road overseers in 1887 was to see that every fork or crossroads had direction or "finger" signs on posts, easily visible so people would know they were heading where they wanted to go.

Poll tax work also involved keeping trees and brush out of the roadways, clearing ditches, pulling out and sometimes blasting out rocks, filling mud holes, establishing safe fords across creeks, and building culverts. The jobs were accomplished with axes, shovels, pry bars, hand saws, and a wagon rigged so that when the end panels were removed the floor boards could be tilted sideways to dump loads of dirt.

When mule-drawn graders and scrapers were required, a farmer who volunteered his team for the work got double credit on his taxes. To slice through the roots that clogged ditches and humped roads, a "rooter" was used—a plow with two guide handles and a single vertical cutting blade. To force the blade

Before bridges, the current of the White River powered many ferries. Early roads were few and precarious.
(Photo courtesy of Chloe LaRue)

through the roots so they could be pulled out, four big mules were required.

The men of Stone and Taney Counties became so familiar with road work that, in 1914, citizens of Reeds Spring, Branson, and vicinity formed two cooperative road districts to build a highway between the two towns. The road crossed the slope of Dewey Bald and ran past the Shepherd of the Hills farm and Marble Cave. Though parts of the road soon eroded into steep, rocky stairsteps, for much of its length it was a picturesque country lane, lined with trees and a number of comfortable homes and farm houses. In 1936 that route was reconstructed and paved. Today it is known as Highway 76.

At the time the road across Dewey Bald was first developed, the two dozen or so ferry crossings on the White River and the James, long licensed and controlled as parts of the region's transportation system, had begun to be replaced by bridges. Today only the Peel Ferry, which takes cars across Bull Shoals Lake at Highway 125 south of Protem, is still operating. All the others, whether boats, or well built rafts large enough to carry wagons with teams, were replaced with bridges by the late 1950's.

The first ferries discontinued service in 1914, after four bridges were built across the new Lake Taneycomo. The bridge which crossed the lake at the foot of Branson's Main Street, as well as the nearby bridge which took traffic across the wide mouth of Roark

Creek, were designed to carry wagons with iron-shod wheels. A short time later automobile bridges (designed to carry rubber-tired vehicles) were constructed across Coon and Turkey Creeks on the road connecting Branson with downtown Hollister. Another automobile bridge was built across the James River at Galena.

By the 1920's the early "wagon bridges" were being upgraded to carry automobiles, and other major crossings along the White River were getting steel bridges as part of a highway improvement program in which the roads now known as Highway 13 and 265 in Stone County and Highways 248 (first named Highway 3 and then U.S. 65) and 160 in Taney County came into being. Each was formed from an amalgam of old freight roads, widened and graveled to carry two lanes of traffic in all kinds of weather. Those new highways still wound along the ridge tops and up and down steep hillsides, but many crossed the larger streams on steel bridges.

Through the next forty-five years, tourists motoring into White River country on warm summer days found local basket makers sitting under shade trees along old U.S. 65 north of Branson, displaying their baskets and hoping for buyers.

Arriving motorists voiced many complaints about the unpaved streets and roads in Taney County and southern Stone County, but little was done about the problem until the mid-1920's when local businessmen and residents began buying cars. In 1929, funds for road improvement became available from local property taxes and state and federal sources, and efforts were begun to "pave" all the streets and secondary roads with gravel.

The gravel was a mixed blessing. In town, the larger rocks, dressed with finer gravel called "chat," packed down to a solid surface. In the surrounding hills, speeding cars scoured out the gravel in the center of the roads and piled it up on the sides. A driver who slipped into that deeper gravel at forty-five miles an hour was likely to find his car spinning off in some unintended direction; flying rocks were hazardous to windshields, gas tanks, and nearby pedestrians, and fast stops were guaranteed to strip the tread from tires.

Upgrading U.S. 65 to concrete or asphalt from Springfield to the Arkansas border began in 1929, but the effort slowed during the Depression. The work was completed eight years later as a WPA project to provide jobs for the unemployed. In the process, the highway through Branson and Hollister was rerouted from Commercial, Main, and the steel bridge to what is now Business 65. New concrete bridges were built over Lake Taneycomo, all three creeks, and the railroad tracks in Hollister.

Since World War II all major highways in these two counties have been given modern hard surfaces, secondary roads have "chip and seal" surfaces, old bridges have been replaced, and some frequently used low-water crossings have been bridged. In a continuing series of engineering feats, begun in the mid-1960's, a new U.S. 65 has been cut through the mountains from Springfield to the Arkansas border south of Branson, reducing the driving distance by half and creating a much safer and marvelously scenic drive. Eventually the highway will be four lanes all the way to the state line.

Roads in Stone County have undergone a similar transformation. The picturesque Y Bridge at Galena, which replaced the earlier steel bridge in 1928, recently was cut off from traffic and reduced to an historical curiosity after a modern high bridge was built upstream, part of a new by-pass Highway 13. The new bridge and Highway 13 are now also a part of

Highway 265, a western approach to the Branson area being developed using bits of several existing highways. Highway 265 will become a main artery into the area from Interstate 44 west.

The impoundment of Table Rock Lake in 1959 brought many changes to the roads and highways of Stone and western Taney Counties, as had happened in eastern Taney County with the impounding of Bull Shoals in 1952. Many bridges which dated from the 1920's, including those at Forsyth and at present day Kimberling City, were replaced. The new Kimberling Bridge, much longer and higher than its predecessor, dwarfed the older structure in photographs taken before Table Rock Lake Dam was closed in 1959. The old bridge, left in place, was submerged by the new lake.

Along with that old bridge, miles of serpentine river roads were submerged, necessitating the building of several new highways. Of prime importance to both Stone and Taney Counties is Missouri Highway 86, which once angled across Long Creek into Stone County from south of Branson. Now it begins at U.S. 65 a mile or so north of the Arkansas border, and follows the southern side of Table Rock Lake, crossing the Long Creek Arm over a very photogenic bridge. At Blue Eye, 86 turns north on Highway 13 for a few miles before continuing west.

In the past few years, as vacationers have flocked in ever-increasing numbers to the attractions on West 76, that highway has been widened and improved several times. Most recently a network of interconnected by-pass roads has been engineered through surrounding valleys to help relieve congestion. Even before those roads were completed, new shows and motels were being built along them.

Motorists trying to reach theme parks and music shows have long found driving on West Highway 76, alias Mountain Country Boulevard, exasperating. Often they ask why the congestion problems have not been solved. Given the many attractions in these hills, and the miles of deep valleys and ridges on either side of Highway 76, it may take a gigantic aerial railway to iron out all the problems.

Kathleen Van Buskirk

Fishing the Area Lakes

The White River, which starts as a spring in the Boston Mountains of Arkansas, once was feared as a raging and temperamental river during seasonal flooding. Now the river's course through Stone and Taney Counties has been calmed into three lakes: Bull Shoals, Taneycomo, and Table Rock. In 1911-13, the Ozark Power and Water Company built the overflow dam and hydroelectric plant at Powersite, which holds back the water of Lake Taneycomo in Taney County. On either end of this lake, in the 1950's, the Army Corps of Engineers created Bull Shoals and Table Rock Lakes.

Some say that the heart and soul of the White were ripped out in the name of hydroelectric power and flood control. The impoundments can never really replace the untamed White River in all its natural glory. But, as it turned out, each lake acquired a national reputation for good fishing. Although the lakes share the White's lifestream, each offers different challenges to the fisherman. Let's explore the lakes one at a time.

Lake Taneycomo

Despite current water quality problems, Taneycomo holds the distinction of being one of the most productive, easily accessed trout lakes in the nation. A fisherman of average ability can catch a limit of five fish almost any day of the year, except perhaps in August and September when a lack of oxygen in the water makes trout sluggish and difficult to catch. Frigid water from the depths of Table Rock is flushed through the dam on a regular basis. These cool waters are ideally suited for trout, although warm water species also do well in backwater tributaries and near the Powersite dam.

Large brood rainbow trout from Shepherd of the Hills Hatchery, directly below Table Rock dam on Lake Taneycomo, are released into the lake in October. Fly fishermen and spin casters concentrate their efforts near several hatchery outlet streams running into the lake. Those fishing at night stand the best chance of catching a lunker. Fish from three to eight pounds,

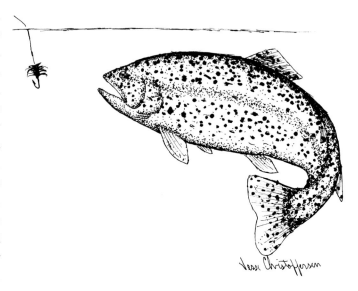

Vessi Christoffersen

caught on flies or nightcrawlers, provide the incentive for staying up all night. Some anglers take intermittent naps throughout the night in their camping vehicles to bolster their staying power. Since water releases from Table Rock into Taneycomo are unpredictable, the fisherman-camper can time his casting to coincide with prime lake levels. Good times to fish include the initial rise of water or when no water is being released. A heavy release of water, however, makes it extremely difficult to keep fly, lure, or bait in the strike zone. A highly effective method for daytime fishing is to boat upstream nearly to the dam and then, during water releases, drift back downstream bouncing weighted baits such as corn, salmon eggs, or power baits off the bottom.

If by some odd chance the fishing is slow at Taneycomo, a visit to the fish hatchery is a welcome break. The visitor can learn about the science of fish culture, observe live fish in the raceways, and view movies about the stocking program at the lake.

Trout in the lake are caught on corn, salmon

eggs, worms, miniature marshmallows, power bait (a scented concoction that comes in a small jar and can be molded on single or treble hook), small spinners, and brown, black, or olive green marabou jigs. Small spoons, like the Little Cleo, also work.

Boat fishermen have an advantage because they can cover more water, but bank anglers and those using chest-high waders can also do well. Feeder streams and their backwaters like Bee and Bull Creeks are excellent in May and June for bluegill and bass. Bluegill baits include worms, crickets, and popping bug lures. Bass, close to shoreline cover, are caught on floating minnows. Jig and pork rind frog, as well as plastic worms, are other good choices.

A $5 Missouri trout stamp and a current fishing license are legal prerequisites. Boats can be rented at the Main Street boat dock in Branson. Those towing their own boats can launch at a public ramp close by. Many resorts on the lake have boat slips and fishing docks. A well-managed public recreational vehicle campground is located on the waterfront near the Main Street dock and tackle store.

Bull Shoals Lake

Taney County lays claim to the headwaters of man-made Bull Shoals Lake. The Bull looks like a wide, flat, meandering river in Missouri; only after it sweeps into Arkansas does it take on the spread out face of an impoundment. Some of the best fishing in the entire lake is found in Taney County. An area immediately below Powersite, called the "potholes," is famous for attracting good numbers and a wide variety of game fish including walleye, white bass, striped bass, crappie, and trout. The fishing is good there throughout the year. The mouths of feeder streams like Swan and Beaver Creeks are also excellent spots.

In linear miles, Bull Shoals' shoreline is about equal to Table Rock. There are few coves and a noticeable absence of visible structure—standing dead timber. For these reasons, some anglers feel the Bull is harder to fish than other Missouri lakes and, in some ways, it is. But for knowledgeable anglers, the fishing can be quite good. The lake receives far less pressure from fishermen than Table Rock and does not have the stringent length limits for bass and walleye that other area impoundments have. The crappie fishing is generally better than on Table Rock. The fishermen who do well on Bull Shoals have learned to rely on electronic "fish finder" graphs or chart recorders to locate humps and depressions in the lake bottom which hold largemouth and smallmouth bass, as well as walleyes.

Once fish are located, the best method is a vertical presentation of lure or live bait—dropping the offering straight down rather than casting. Silver jigging spoons, jig and pork frog, live bait (minnows, nightcrawlers, crawdads), and plastic grubs are used on relatively light lines of from six to eight pound test. Because the water of Bull Shoals is extremely clear most of the year, light line is necessary. Trolling with a deep running plug and small silver spoon rigged on a three-way swivel is another good method for the lake.

Because of the clear water in summer and fall, night fishing is popular. Some anglers use a black light that makes fluorescent monofilament line glow in the dark. They mount the unit on the gunwales of the boat and have good visibility and line control without spooking the fish. Still other fishermen use the light of the moon or gas lanterns with reflectors.

In the spring, during the spawning runs, one of the best places to fish is just below Powersite Dam in the potholes area. Conditions change from day to day, depending on how much water is being released from Taneycomo. Natives of the area will sample the water each day during the spring, making several casts. When water temperature and water levels are right, the fish respond in short order. Veteran fishermen there do not spend a lot of time casting without a bite. The potholes can be terrific one day and a bust the next. But when techniques and luck mesh, the day is long remembered. The area can be fished by boat or, when water levels permit, from the bank. The first two miles below the dam can produce some outstanding white bass fishing in late March and April. That same stretch of river contains a good population of walleye. A jig and minnow combination or plain minnow fished with hook and split shot are good walleye baits. White bass are caught on chartreuse or white jigs, or three-inch floating minnows jerked just under the surface.

Some excellent catfishing with rod/reel, trot lines, limb lines, and jug lines is found in the Taney County portion of the lake.

Unfortunately, in the spring Bull Shoals has a lot of water dumped into it as a result of releases from Table Rock. In some years the lake does not return to normal power pool until mid-summer. The tremendous fluctuation in water levels has hurt fish populations and the area's tourist trade. But for those who want solitude on a lake whose beauty is renowned, the Bull, impounded in 1951, is a sleeper.

Table Rock Lake

Perhaps the biggest drawing card in southwest Missouri is Table Rock Lake. Rimmed by rolling hills covered with hardwood, and blessed with clear, deep water, the lake offers some of the finest year-round spotted bass fishing in the nation, making it a major draw for bass tournaments.

The lake's super clarity is a mixed blessing. Anglers who do not use methods and baits which take full advantage of ultra-clear water often go home frustrated. To enjoy consistent success for legal bass (15-inch minimum length limit) on Table Rock, fishermen must use techniques designed for clear water.

The clear water areas of the lake lie in the arms south of the dam. The clearest arm is Long Creek, followed by Cow Creek and the waters south of Shell Knob. Fisheries biologists from the Missouri Department of Conservation have electro-fished most of the lake and found the greatest percentage of largemouth bass over four pounds to be in those clear waters. They also agree with local fishermen that the clearer water presents a more difficult fishing challenge and that there is less pressure in those areas than in spots at the lower (northern) end of Table Rock Lake.

While the Long Creek arm is sparkling clear, the James River arm, near Cape Fair is commonly murky. A heavy rain turns the James muddy in short order and the mud and silt wind up in the lake. But many bass fish-

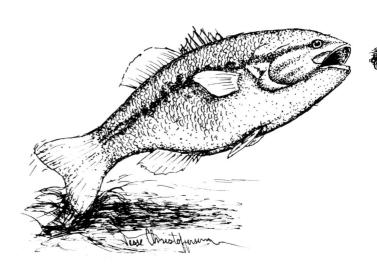

ermen like to fish in areas with stained or colored water because such waters warm up in late winter and early spring faster than the clear water spots.

The fish in stained water are generally easier to catch. The James River arm of the lake receives heavy fishing pressure. Favorite local spots such as Piney Creek, Wooly Creek, and marker 15 (where Flat Creek and the James meet) attract large numbers of boats, especially during April and May.

Generally, fishermen catch more bass in the James arm, but those fish run smaller in size than upper and mid-lake bass. Mid-lake offers attractive options. Aunts Creek, Joe Bald, Mill Creek, and the Highway 13 boatdock area attract a loyal following of anglers who vouch there is no better stretch on the lake to fish. The area abounds in shallow coves and flats as well as deep water drop-offs. The largest concentration of spotted and smallmouth bass is found in the lake's midsection.

Smallmouth also congregate in rocky areas adjacent to the dam. It is estimated by fisheries biologists that spotted bass account for about twenty-five percent of the bass population in the lake's clear sections. Spinning equipment and lines from six to eight pound test are best suited for clear water fishing. Plastic grubs, jig and pork frog, gidzits and four-inch plastic worms work fine. Jigs tipped with live minnow are favorites.

Table Rock is also home to the paddlefish (sometimes called spoonbill) which were introduced into the lake in the mid-1980's when the Osage River/Truman Lake paddlefish fishery was lost to the dam at Warsaw. When rainfall is sufficient in the spring and the river is high, the fish make a spawning run up the James. Snaggers use long, stout rods and large, weighted treble hooks from bank or boat in hopes of latching into a 60-pounder. The paddlefish has done well in Table Rock. Initially interest was high in the snagging opportunities for this prehistoric creature, which can weigh up to 80 pounds. But chlordane contamination in the James River arm of Table Rock prompted the state health department to issue an advisory in June, 1991 against eating paddlefish. Snagging waned thereafter.

Some of the best catfishing in the area is found in the James River arm of the lake. Most cats are taken with trot lines baited with goldfish.

From its creation in the 1950's up until the early 1980's, Table Rock was known primarily as a fishing lake. However, times are changing for Table Rock. More and more recreational boaters are using the lake, operating anything from runabouts to 30 foot cruisers. Water skiers and jet skiers also find the lake to their liking. And shoreline development above the Corps of Engineers' public boundary is progressing at a brisk pace. Despite the increasing bustle, Table Rock still yields good fishing, some of the best of which can be enjoyed from November through April.

For a change of pace, and fishing as good if not better than the lakes, the streams that feed those impoundments are good bets. A fisherman using a canoe, john boat, or wading in tennis shoes and cutoff jeans will find that the clear streams offer solitude and fast action throughout the summer.

Charlie Farmer

The Fisherman

He was a fisherman
And he made his camp
Down where the firefly
Lit her lamp.
Away from bright lights
And traffic roar
On White River's
Friendly sandy shore.
His old tent stood
'Neath a tall black oak
Where from the tip top
A rain crow spoke.
His lures and his snares
and his silken lines
He hung to dry
Mid flowering vines.
He gathered drift wood
To cook his meals
And boiled his coffee
Hunkered on his heels.
He was a fisherman
Following far
Rugged trails
And a beckoning star.

Mary Elizabeth Mahnkey

Life in the Woods, Fields, and Marshes

Call it the "good old days" syndrome. I have often heard an old timer say, "Son, back in the old days there were so many ducks flying in autumn, the sky turned black," or… "The goggle-eye were so thick in the stream we couldn't keep them off our hooks."

But, let's examine conditions 50 or 60 years ago. Back then, the hardwood forests had been cut down for timber. The early settlers, dependent on wild game for food, had killed off most of the deer and turkey and trapped out the furbearers to augment their family incomes. Wildlife game management was in its infancy. With the exception of bobwhite quail, rabbits, and migratory birds, wildlife in southwest Missouri was scarce.

But a change has taken place. The hunting traditions of the early settlers are alive again today; thousands of hunters take to the woods during hunting season every year in Stone and Taney Counties. There are many more deer and wild turkeys than fifty years ago; and the ruffed grouse, which was extirpated from the two counties, has been reintroduced. Conservation department game managers affirm that there are more smaller animals too: squirrels, bobcats, raccoons, otters, and opossums. This turnabout is the result of the efforts of local residents and state and federal officials. Citizens are more concerned about wildlife now. Conservation and environmental education has led to a greater appreciation for wildlife habitat needs. And the Missouri Department of Conservation and U.S. Forest Service (Mark Twain National Forest) have purchased thousands of acres which they manage for wildlife and open for public hunting. Contributing to the increased wildlife populations are the state hunting rules and seasons, allowing for a harvest of surplus game to match the carrying capacity of the land.

Armadillo

The armor-encased armadillo, a common resi-

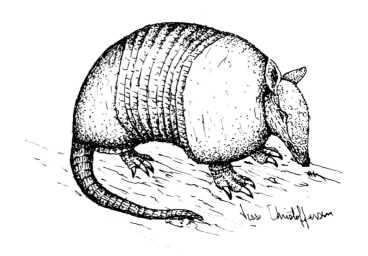

dent of the South, particularly Texas, has been expanding its range northward and is now frequently seen in southern Missouri. My most frequent sightings of live and road-killed animals have been in Stone, Taney, and Barry Counties. For the past five years, during spring and fall turkey seasons near Shell Knob, I have seen the meandering trails of armadillos in the leaf litter. As I waited for deer and turkey, the armored one has waddled within 15 yards of my blind. Look for these chiefly nocturnal animals in forests where they root along, searching for insects in the leaf litter. If you frighten one, it will curl up in a ball.

Beaver

The beaver, once nearly trapped to extinction in the Ozarks, has come back on its own. You may, if you spend enough time near streams or lakes, see one. Sapling beaver chews commonly wash up on the banks of Bull Shoals, Taneycomo, and Table Rock Lakes. The best time for viewing animals is at dawn and dusk. Look for beaver dams and lodges near tributary or backwater sloughs. And if you startle the animal swimming on the surface, listen for the shot-like crack of the broad, leathery tail as it slaps the water.

Black Bear

There are documented sightings of wild black bears in recent years in Taney and Stone Counties. But do not expect to take a hike in the Mark Twain Forest and bump into one of these critters. In spite of the extensive time I have spent in the woods, I have yet to sight a bear in Missouri. Bears are plentiful in northern Arkansas where the state Fish and Game Department has established an open hunting season on them. The few bears in the Missouri Ozarks no doubt wandered into our state from lands south of us. The Missouri Department of Conservation has no plans to manage for bears, nor is a season projected for them in the near future. The chances of seeing a wild bear in the Missouri Ozarks? About the same as winning the lottery.

Bobcat

I was bowhunting for deer in the Mark Twain Forest near Cassville a few years ago when a large cat, followed by six kittens, pranced within 20 yards of my tree stand. Domestic cats deep in the woods, I wondered? It took several seconds before I realized the felines were bobcats—a family of kittens being led by their mother. Sighting bobcats during daylight is quite rare. The animals are nocturnal hunters, elusive and extremely wary. Though seldom seen, bobcats are com-

mon in Taney and Stone Counties. The prime habitat certainly exists. And trappers in the area bag their share each season.

Cottontail Rabbit

One of the animals that the bobcat feeds on is the cottontail, an animal found in fair numbers in both counties. Cottontails, which require scruffy cover and do not fare well on clean farms with pasture grasses, have declined in numbers since the demise of row crop farming in the Ozarks. The increase in the predator population (coyotes, owls, and hawks) also keeps the population in check. Cottontail populations are cyclical. The Missouri Department of Conservation wildlife areas in the two counties harbor some rabbits as do patches on private and public land with sufficient protective cover. Compared to central and northern Missouri, the rabbit hunting is only fair.

Coyote

Coyotes have learned to outsmart man and consequently are holding their own in an age of shrinking natural habitat. I know Stone and Taney Counties have plenty of coyote because, when camping, I am nearly always treated to a howling good serenade, be it spring or fall. The coyote outwits dogs, trappers, poison baiters, and wolf hunters. I occasionally call them in with turkey yelps and kee-kees during spring and fall. The coyote invariably has a hungry look in its eye, fully expecting to run down a hen trying to hook up with a gobbler. For good sport in the winter after the conventional hunting seasons, use a predator call from a camouflaged stand or a blind deep in the forest. You can call normally shy coyotes to within 20 yards.

Deer

In 1990, hunters killed 161,141 deer in Missouri. Those are good numbers considering the short, nine-day firearm season. The fact is, that even with a significant harvest, deer populations are stable or increasing.

Taney and Stone Counties offer good hunting opportunities, with a suitable mix of public forest and private land hunting. The most challenging hunting is available during the three-month bowhunting season that opens October 1 each year. During firearms season, normally in mid-November, most animals relinquish habitual behavior and turn to escape and survival tactics, like staying in thick cover and not moving during daylight. Before the firearms season, archers can hunt unpressured whitetails with little or no interference from other hunters. The best hunting is generally from portable or handmade tree stands which aid visibility and keep human scent above the keen noses of deer.

Special seasons for muzzleloader and primitive weapons also give Missouri hunters extra hunting opportunities and offer greater challenges than the rifle season.

Dove

Dove populations in Stone and Taney Counties are not as high as in Missouri counties with extensive grain fields. Occasionally a cut field of sorghum, corn, oats, or weeds yields good area dove hunting. For dove hunters, the bootheel area, the west central, and the northern half of the state are best choices.

Ducks

Lake Taneycomo, the backwaters of Bull Shoals, and Table Rock offer fair duck hunting. Some of the feeder streams and backwaters of Taneycomo are the top choices. Generally, a substantial freeze to the north, which ices over lakes like Stockton, Pomme de Terre, and Truman, is necessary for hunting to be good in this area. The ducks then move to Stone and Taney County waters for resting.

Geese

One of the brightest spots on the conservation horizon, nationally and locally, is the dramatic increase in the number of Canada geese. While duck numbers are down drastically across the country, geese are thriving. Local flocks of Canada geese in Stone and Taney Counties provide good viewing for the naturalist and fair to good hunting. Local flocks established through the Missouri Department of Conservation stockings stay year-round rather than migrate. It is becoming quite common to see geese, regardless of the time of year, on nearly every outing to Bull Shoals, Taneycomo, and Table Rock. Some areas on Taneycomo are closed to goose hunting. Ironically, as Canada geese grow in numbers, so do the number of citizen complaints about the birds "messing up" yards and eating flowers and plants. Other species of geese—snow, blue, and white-fronted geese—can be seen in high-flying flocks at various times from November through March. Occasionally they will land on area lakes or use local grain fields.

Grouse

One of the distinctive woodland sounds of early spring is the drumming of the ruffed grouse, a hollow booming which slowly increases in rapidity. Currently the Missouri Department of Conservation is reintroducing wild ruffed grouse (from Ohio in exchange for wild turkeys from Missouri) into suitable habitat, including locations in Stone and Taney Counties. Ruffed grouse require a mix of young and old growth forest with ample ground cover. Hunters can anticipate an open season in the future once the birds become well established.

Mink

Last summer, at a popular public recreation area near the dam on Table Rock, my family and I watched a family of minks in action. Two of the large animals were taking turns diving for crawdads on the rocky bottom. For an hour, without stopping, the adults would dive into the water and bring up a three or four inch crawdad to carry back to the tiny juvenile minks. Every so often the entire family, young and old, would scurry down to water's edge for a quick swim. We watched with swim fins and face masks from ten yards away. Look for mink around rocky banks on Table Rock, Taneycomo, and Bull Shoals. It appears this sleek member of the weasel family is on the increase.

Opossum

Judging by road kills, there is no shortage of 'possum in the Ozarks. They are everywhere, but live sightings are not all that common. The American marsupial is largely nocturnal. If you are looking for some nighttime excitement, use a strong-beamed flashlight and take a hike down the banks of an Ozark stream. Shine the light in the lower branches of trees along your route. Chances are you will come in contact with a live, hanging opossum. Most of my nighttime encounters are during summer frog hunting expeditions. 'Possum stew was once a common Ozark dish—probably in hard times—but I confess, I have never tried it.

Otter

Otters are making a comeback in the Missouri Ozarks thanks to the Missouri Department of Conservation's efforts in trading wild turkeys to Louisiana for river otters. The animal was once native to the state and, if the stocking program is successful, all of us will be sighting more of the acrobatic swimmers in the future.

Owls

It would be a serious error of omission not to mention Ozark owls and in particular the Barred Owl. We have the Screech and Great Horned as well, but they are not as prominent in the counties as the bird whose call sounds like: "Who Cooks for You…Who Cooks for You All." A turkey season without hearing the call of the Barred Owls just would not be a season at all. By imitating an owl call, I have shocked many a gobbler into responding. Barred Owls are highly vocal in the springtime and early summer, and as much a part of the season as whip-poor-wills and spring peepers. You can purchase a commercially made owl hooter at a store that sells hunting gear. Or you can learn to voice hoot. Either way, it is fun calling an owl into camp. But don't shoot them. They are a federally protected species, as are all raptors.

Panther

A friend of mine, Ron Kruger, reports sighting a cougar in the Devil's Backbone Wilderness area. The panther had run right through a hunting camp which I had left temporarily. Kruger is not one to fib. Joe Hollingshad, our guide, said he had seen several panthers in the area since he was a boy. Ron swears by his sighting. The Missouri Conservation Department takes a neutral stance on whether or not panthers (also known as mountain lions, cougar, or puma) exist in the Ozarks. So if you see one, try and get a clear, well-exposed photo. The Missouri Conservation Commission would like to have one.

Quail

The bobwhite is another example of a dwindling species in the Ozarks and more specifically, in Stone and Taney Counties. The habitat just is not there any more. Some birds survive on marginal habitat, but a severe winter cuts them down. While efforts are being made by the Missouri Conservation Department to better the quail situation, dairy operations, clean farming, and the demise of hedgerows and multiflora rose hurts the quail population. Still, hearing the bobwhite call in spring and early summer during nesting season and occasionally seeing birds on the ground or flying across a roadway are pleasures of Ozark living. You can call birds in for photography by using a quail whistle, available from hunting supply shops.

Raccoon

Unfortunately, roadkills are the commonest indicator that the ring-tailed furry bandits still exist in good numbers. Ozark coon hunters, a thriving fraternity of dog and coon fanciers, know firsthand that the animal's numbers are strong because the forest habitat is healthy. The animal in Missouri is important enough that it is part of the identifying logo of the Missouri Department of Conservation. It is just too bad the curious little animals are so nocturnal. The bandits are fascinating creatures.

Several years ago, while frog hunting down on Bull Creek from a canoe, we came across a family of coons hunting snails and mussels on a gravel bar. We caught their faces in the beam of our lanterns and I wish I could have preserved that fleeting picture with a photo. The group melted quickly into the darkness, purring loudly as they scampered onto the bank.

Skunk

At times the skunk and opossum seem to vie for the title of number one road kill. Apparently numbers are significant. I rarely see live skunks, but I smell their presence frequently during fall and winter hunts. At times, I even use a commercially prepared skunk scent to hide my human odor when deer hunting. Deer do not seem to mind skunk, but are terrified of human scent.

In spite of their notorious odor, skunks have an attractive black and white color pattern and are fascinating to observe, especially if one is lucky enough to see a mother tripping along with her young.

Squirrel

Squirrel hunting is the most underrated and underused shooting sport. It is ideal for teaching kids how to hunt. The Ozarks have an abundance of woodlands to hunt squirrels. Squirrel meat is tasty. The

only negative I can come up with is the chore of skinning squirrels. Various methods for shedding the tough hide look good on paper but in practice are difficult—no matter what.

Squirrel hunting in Taney and Stone Counties is excellent, just as it is in most of the Ozarks. The fox squirrel is found primarily along field borders and the gray variety in deep hardwoods. The best time to stalk squirrels is from mid-August to mid-September when the animals are honing their teeth on hickory nuts. Floating an Ozark stream in May and June (the season opens on the Saturday of Memorial Day weekend each year) is also an effective method of slipping up on this elusive, but highly sporting Ozark animal. Hunters commonly take the daily limit of six.

Tarantula

One of the most dramatic displays of wildlife I have ever witnessed in the Ozarks occurred during October in Taney County near the Mincy wildlife area. My family and I came across a mass migration of tarantulas crossing a road, at least 100 spiders on the blacktop at one time—all moving in the same direction. Since then, I have made trips to the area to see if the sighting could be duplicated. And while I have seen two or three at a time on the road or in the woods, nothing matches the magnitude of that sighting eight years ago. You need not fear these creatures; they avoid human contact and their bite is not considered dangerous to man. The hairy creature just looks threatening.

Turkey

There were those, including Ben Franklin, who believed the wild turkey should have been our national symbol. I agree. The wild bird is noble and smart. The turkeys of Taney and Stone Counties, though found in good numbers, are wary. It takes a good hunter, skilled at calling, positioning, and camouflage, to lure one into shotgun range. While spring and fall turkey hunters concentrate most of their efforts from dawn until mid-morning, most of my casual sightings from a vehicle have been from noon until 2 p.m. Drive some of the dirt roads in the forest for a chance to see a lone bird or a flock. Missouri is generally considered to be one of the top three states in the nation for turkey hunting. Whether you hunt spring or fall, there is no finer sport and no better time to be in the Ozark woodlands. Gobbler season opens in late April, the fall season in mid-October, but hunting must cease at noon each day.

Woodcock

Every October, the woodcock or timber doodle migrates into southern Missouri. The plump gamebird, with the long bill and helicopter take-off, seeks out bottomlands, moist woodlands, river banks, and marshes. With its 3-4 inch bill, it probes the soft earth for earthworms or insects. The weather and the availability of food and resting areas determines the length of stay. Birds found in good numbers one day may be gone the next. But other flights may come in to take their place.

Woodcock hunting is certainly not traditional sport in the Ozarks or our counties, but the opportunity is present. The season runs from mid-October to mid-November. I have flushed woodcock along Swan and Beaver Creeks. Hiking along those streams in October could very well turn up this fascinating bird for the gun, or just the dramatic flush.

Charlie Farmer

Bird Watching

Whether you are just a backyard-feeder watcher or a serious birder, southwest Missouri can be an enjoyable and rewarding place to observe birds. A diversity of bird species take advantage of the wide variety of habitats available in Stone and Taney Counties.

What kind of birds might one expect to see in southwest Missouri and where can they be found? Generally speaking, bird species found in Stone and Taney Counties are typical of other east-central U.S. forests. Probably the best place to see birds at any time of the year is the Table Rock Dam and State Park area, including the Shepherd of the Hills Fish Hatchery below the dam. During spring migration, the trees near the water are filled with migrating songbirds: warblers, vireos, thrushes, and buntings (including the Painted Bunting during the early summer months). During the hottest days of summer, observable activity decreases as the birds nest. However, during the fall and winter, the areas around the dam draw various species of diving ducks, grebes, and loons. Not only is the Common Loon quite common, but the waters near the dam have hosted stray winter Pacific, Red-throated, and even Yellow-billed Loons in recent years. The largest wintering Black and Turkey Vulture roost in southwest Missouri can also be found across from the boat launch ramp at the fish hatchery on Lake Taneycomo.

The campus of the College of the Ozarks offers several attractions to visitors and residents of the area. In addition to the Ralph Foster Museum, the college has an old-time grist mill and green houses full of exotic orchid and cactus species. Productive birding is possible on campus, but be sure to obtain permission from campus security if you plan to leave the beaten path. In winter, watch the fields and pond near the entrance for Brewer's and Rusty Blackbirds, Lesser Scaup, and Ring-necked Ducks.

Birding can be fruitful on the rivers in the area, especially the James. Float trips are possible

For beginning birders who are looking for an aide to identifying species, Roger Tory Peterson's *A Field Guide to the Birds of Eastern and Central North America* (4th edition) is an excellent field guide. To help observers distinguish between bird species which might be confused, Peterson pioneered the method of separating important field characteristics and noting them with arrows in his illustrations. If you may be birding in the Rockies or the far west, Peterson has a companion edition for western birds. But if you would like to have a one volume text which covers all the birds encountered north of Mexico, you have two choices in purchasing a field guide: Robbins, Bruun, and Zim, *A Guide to Field Identification: Birds of North America*, or *The National Geographic Society's Field Guide to the Birds of North America*. The first text is somewhat easier to use; the second offers more detailed information.

through local canoe rentals, and the river moves slowly enough during the summer months that even a moderately experienced canoeist does not have to worry about tipping the canoe and soaking a pair of binoculars. A 4 hour float trip from Horse Creek to Galena, or a 7 to 8 hour trip from Hootentown Bridge to Galena may turn up Green-backed and Great Blue Herons, Spotted Sandpipers, and Prothonotary Warblers.

A special treat for winter visitors to the area is the chance to see the magnificent Bald Eagle. Adult eagles can easily be identified by a combination of the bird's massive size and white head and tail. Young eagles do not develop the white coloration until they are approximately four years of age; the young birds generally have a mottled white and black appearance when seen soaring and they can be told from the smaller hawks and the Osprey by their size and slightly different configuration—most notably, a larger head profile. Look for Bald Eagles along lake or river edges or soaring on thermal updrafts.

Glades offer a very special type of birding habitat in southwest Missouri. Interspersed through our hardwood forest, glade habitat is normally found in areas with shallow soils. The Hercules Glade Wilderness in eastern Taney county contains expansive glades although small glades can be found in many other places in the Tri-Lakes area. Birds commonly found in glade habitats during the breeding season include the Yellow-breasted Chat, Prairie Warbler, Field Sparrow, and Blue-gray Gnatcatcher.

Historical censuses of bird species' diversity and abundance are lacking in our area, but during the last decade dedicated birdwatchers have begun to keep records of both numbers and species encountered in the western Ozarks. The drive to collect data has been initiated by Patrick Mahnkey and Jeff Hayes. They now maintain a record file and routinely publish sightings for each season in the *Western Ozarks Birders Newsletter.* Anyone interested may subscribe to the WOBN by writing to Pat Mahnkey, P. O. Box 53, Forsyth, MO 65653. While there is no subscription price, a donation of $5 will cover printing and mailing costs for one year (4

issues). The newsletter also contains articles about conservation issues, bird behavior, and related topics. Interested individuals may also submit articles for the newsletter.

A not-for-profit agency, The Ozark Center for Wildlife Research, has recently been incorporated by Dr. Jane Fitzgerald of Reeds Spring. The goals of the research center are to educate the local public about native wildlife, to monitor bird populations using both census and bird-banding techniques, and to gather data on non-game wildlife species. Such research will enable the center to make recommendations at both the regional and local levels on how to preserve wildlife habitat in developing areas. The center is also involved in studies of vulture roost ecology and bird populations on U.S. Forest Service land.

Birding is a fascinating hobby. What child is not excited by finding a bird nest? Who can fail to thrill to the majesty of our wintering eagles or to the strikingly beautiful color patterns of a spring warbler? The beauty of the Ozarks is enriched by the beauty of its feathered inhabitants. Here in Ozark Mountain Country, we are proud of our rich bird life and we encourage all to enjoy and protect it.

Jane Fitzgerald

A Recovered Forest
Mark Twain National Forest

Could the conditions of any forest be worse? By the 1930's the original magnificent virgin hard-wood forests of the Ozarks had fallen to the ax. Lumbermen and tie hackers had selected the best trees, and farmers had cleared away much of the forest for land on which to grow tomatoes and strawberries. The slash and burn practice of establishing pasture contributed to a loss of topsoil during heavy rains.

The effort to reestablish the forests of Stone and Taney County, as well as much of the rest of the Ozarks, is tied directly to the National Forest Service, established by federal legislation in 1891. National Forests formed at that time were carved from prime virgin western forest land already owned by the federal government—thus preventing the indiscriminate logging which had depleted many eastern forests.

In 1911 Congress passed the Weeks Law which allowed the government to purchase parcels of land from private owners in order to establish National Forests. This law allowed Missouri to have a National Forest. But the establishment of the forest in Missouri also required the passage of state legislation which pledged that Missouri would cooperate with the National Forest Service. Beginning in 1933 and continuing throughout the decade, the Missouri State Legislature passed a series of enabling acts which created the Mark Twain National Forest in thirty-nine counties in the Ozarks. Since the wooded hillsides had been ravaged, the new forest was called a recovering forest.

The purchase of land parcels began immediately and continued throughout the decade of the '30's. Farmers, caught in the nation's worst ever depression, were often anxious to sell. Still, the transactions were often difficult to complete; haggling over land prices and the need for congressional funding all complicated the purchases of parcels. By World War II the mass purchases stopped.

Most of the present National Forest land—15,964 acres in Stone County and 63,901 acres in Taney County—was purchased by 1940. The huge acreage, particularly in eastern Taney County, forced residents to move off the land and caused several businesses—and towns—to close. Since the initial acquisitions, only a few intermittent acres have been added to the forests, and a small number of parcels have been traded for private land.

The purpose of the National Forest is to assure multiple use of the forest, including outdoor recreation, timber harvesting, livestock grazing, the conservation of wildlife, and the protection of watersheds. To fulfill these goals the Forest Service has implemented a variety of practices.

During the early years, thousand of acres throughout the Ozarks were reforested, when possible, by keeping man, livestock, and fire away from the forest so that natural regeneration could take place. Other areas required a massive transplanting of seedlings, an effort accomplished only through backbreaking hand labor. Stone and Barry Counties both required the transplanting of seedlings. To plant the small trees in these counties, a Civilian Conservation Corp camp was established at Shell Knob, west of Stone County, in 1935 and operated until 1942. An average of 120 fifteen and sixteen year old boys from the southern half of Missouri lived in the military-style camp, on six month assignments. Every day they went to the surrounding hillsides to plant oak or pine seedlings, build roads or, when necessary, fight fires.

Over the years the forests matured and other management practices, including ridding the forests of unwanted species, thinning stands to relieve overcrowding, and topping large trees to allow younger, shorter ones to grow, were adopted to speed forest growth.

Before 1930, the native forests of the area were depleted by the cutting and shipping of logs and railroad ties.
(Right photo courtesy of Chloe LaRue; below, courtesy of Alden Hembree)

Eventually, timber harvesting again became important. The Forest Service oversees the selection of trees to be logged, the bidding on and execution of a timber cut, and the clean-up. Today the revenue from the sale of timber nearly equals the cost of forest management.

One-fourth of the revenue of timber sales is returned, proportionally, to the 39 counties to help pay for schools and roads. An additional smaller payment (a payment in lieu of taxes or PILT) is also made to each county. Both Stone and Taney Counties benefit from these payments.

Wildlife, too, has benefited from the forests. By 1930 almost all the large animals, including buffalo, elk, mountain lion, and even deer and turkey, had been severely reduced or eliminated from the Ozarks. But, because of the improvements to the forest and with the

cooperation of the Missouri Conservation Commission and conservation groups, deer and turkey have been reintroduced to the Ozarks.

Taney County was the third county in the National Forest to receive a stocking of deer. In 1937 a herd of deer was taken from the Skaggs Ranch east of Branson (the ranch is now called Drury Refuge) to the Hercules Glades area and released in a deer-tight fenced area. After the deer adjusted, the fences were removed and the deer roamed the open woods, becoming the nucleus of a new herd in the county.

Small game, including opossum, raccoons, squirrels, muskrats, minks, and the reintroduced otter have also benefited from the forest.

The forests remain open to recreational uses. By far the most popular activity of visitors in the forest is to drive the logging trails, viewing the scenery and hoping to catch a glimpse of a turkey in flight or a deer. Hiking and camping are also popular, while in the fall many hunters pursue deer, squirrels, and other game animals in the National Forest. Game must be taken in accordance with the regulations of the Missouri Conservation Commission.

Fishing and canoeing are popular on the many miles of streams in the forest, while the forest edges serve as excellent areas for birdwatchers to view nesting and migratory songbirds.

In 1976 the Hercules Glades Area on the eastern edge of Taney County and the Piney Creek Area, located on the Barry and Stone County boundary line, were designated Wilderness Areas. The designation drastically changed the use of the areas. Timber cutting is prohibited in wilderness areas, and visitors are limited to small groups with non-motorized transportation. Hiking is a prime activity in these areas. But the National Forest Service cautions visitors to secure a map of the area, learn the rules of conduct, and obtain adequate clothing, shelter, food, and water before hiking, especially on the extensive trails of the Hercules Glades area. The Hercules Glades area, a 12,436 acre tract of land with 42 miles of trails, is somewhat larger than its counterpart, the 8,124 acre Piney Creek Area with 13.2

The Taney County portion of the Forest is administered by the Ava District while Stone County is in the Cassville District. The Mark Twain National Forest is part of the National Forest Service, U.S. Department of Agriculture.

miles of trails. These areas contain some of the most beautiful scenery in the two counties.

One major controversy surrounds the Mark Twain National Forest in Stone and Taney Counties. The forest service occasionally exchanges land that it owns for private parcels. The practice is controversial because local environmental groups believe that individuals with political connections have, at times, received choice pieces of National Forest Service land in exchange for land of lesser value. Environmental groups now closely monitor the land exchange program.

In spite of such controversy, the Mark Twain National Forest has been largely responsible for reestablishing the extensive hardwood forests of southern Missouri.

Robert McGill

Ozark Flora

The Ozark plateau, once covered by shallow seas, has been a continuous land area for more than 230 million years, making it one of the earth's oldest geological regions and possibly home to some of the earliest types of land plants. The first documentation we have of the vegetation, however, comes from early white explorers and settlers. In 1819, Henry R. Schoolcraft, an early Ozarks explorer, described the valley at the confluence of Bull Creek and the White River (in Taney County) as a "heavy-wooded forest" with a landscape of "verdant woods and naked peaks" (the latter probably referring to the glades that are found on area hilltops). Along the White River, Schoolcraft noted "the abundance and variety of forest trees and shrubs on banks and valleys," while on bluffs he describes "pines, post-oaks and cedars." Original land survey records from Stone and Taney Counties indicate that oak-hickory forest was present on the uplands while ash, oak, elm, and cane thickets were found along the river bottoms.

In 1819 Schoolcraft could not have anticipated that the mature forests he found in the upper White River region would be harvested within 100 years of his travels through the area. Beginning with the increase in white settlement during the 1830's, more and more land was cleared for farmland and building materials. Forests suffered the most, however, when the demand for railroad ties increased around the turn of the century, making timber from the Ozark forests a marketable commodity. From approximately 1910 to 1925, Reeds Spring in Stone County became the largest supplier of white oak railroad ties in the United States. 500,000 ties were shipped in 1912 alone. Forests were severely depleted during the period, and as a consequence, no remaining tracts of virgin forest survive in either Stone or Taney Counties.

Although all Ozark forest land is now second-growth, stands given time to regenerate often have species compositions similar to those documented in original land survey records. Once again, oaks and

For those interested in learning more about Ozark plants and wildlife, spring tours focusing on the identification and natural history of native birds and wildflowers are offered by the Ozark Center for Wildlife Research. For more information, interested individuals or groups may contact the center at the following address:

Ozark Center for Wildlife Research
P. O. Box 83
Reeds Spring, MO 65737

hickories dominate uplands and slopes, while sycamores, maples, elms, and ashes are more common in the bottomlands. In areas where regrowth is more recent, red cedar, honey locust, hackberry, persimmon, and sassafras—species which colonize disturbed sites—predominate.

In many areas of Stone and Taney Counties, forested landscapes are interrupted by expanses of grasslands dotted with scattered cedars. This particular type of habitat is called a "glade," and occurs on thin, dry limestone soils. Several habitat specific animals and plants such as collared lizards, roadrunners, and ladies' tresses orchids occur in these glades. Both Dewey Bald at Henning forest on Highway 76 near Branson, and Hercules Glade Wilderness area in eastern Taney county have hiking trails through glades for those interested in experiencing this unique habitat.

Just as the Ozark landscape changes on a spatial scale, it also changes with the seasons. Although the flowers of many tree species are inconspicuous, there are a few showy species that beg notice in spring. The bright white flowers of the serviceberry (locally called "sarvis" or "sarvisberry") appear in March, and are the first to signal the end of winter. The lovely pink-lavender colored blooms of the redbud follow the serviceberry and usually reach their peak just as the snow-white blossoms of the dogwood unfold in April.

Many of the area's woodland wildflowers also

bloom in early spring and can be found emerging from the moist soils and leaf litter of the forest floor. Some of the most common varieties found from March to May include rue anemone, false rue anemone, bloodroot, dutchman's breeches, may apple, trillium, dog-tooth violet, liverleaf, and toothwort. By about the middle of May, the forest trees develop their full foliage in myriad shades of green, cutting off light to the forest floor.

As summer progresses, most wildflowers thrive in open or semi-open areas like fields, glades, roadsides, or dry wooded slopes. Several of these plants bear flowers on large rounded heads—butterfly weed, yarrow, and queen-anne's lace; many have daisy-like shapes—purple coneflowers, black-eyed susans, and sunflowers; and by mid-summer some, like blackberries, blueberries, and gooseberries, produce edible fruit. Although the diversity of wildflowers in the Ozarks is great, most of the flowers can be identified with the help of a pictorial field guide such as *Missouri Wildflowers* by Edgar Denison.

September brings yet another change in the Ozark landscape as the forest trees begin to cloak themselves in their fall colors. Maples become orange, hickories bright yellow, and oaks red, scarlet, or brown, depending on species. The trees typically are most vivid around the third week of October although the intensity and duration of color varies from year to year.

An account of the Ozarks' vegetation would not be complete without some mention of the wide variety of plants used by Indians prior to white settlement. Acorns and many varieties of wild berries and seeds provided roughage, vitamins, and variety in a diet based on wild game. Pemmican, a high energy travel food, typically consisted of the dried and pulverized meat of small mammals, mixed with the fruit of the persimmon, paw paw, or serviceberry trees. Wood from osage orange trees (also called bois d'arc or wood of the bow)

was used to construct bows while arrows were fashioned from dogwood, willow, and cedar. River cane was used for atlatl darts (a "throwing tool" developed 10,000 years before the bow and arrow) as well as fashioned into a three prong gig for spearing fish and small birds. Various woods were used for deadfall traps to capture ground dwelling animals. Milkweed, an important fibrous plant, was used as bowstring twine if sinew was not available.

Plants also kept the Indians warm. Wigwam frames were made of willow and osage orange and were covered with the bark of various trees. Stalks of cedar and yucca were used as "bow and drill" or "hand and drill" fire starters.

Acorns, fruits of the pokeweed, and plants such as wild onion and bloodroot were used as dyes. Lichens, a partnership of a blue-green algae and a fungus, were used to set the dyes. Bloodroot was also used medicinally as an expectorant and diuretic, along with many other plant derived substances. Useful plants that were scarce in one region but abundant in another provided currency for barter.

American Indians are respected for their conservation ethic, an extension of their philosophy and religions. Indians are said to have harvested only resources that were necessary for their individual and tribal maintenance, and to have used all parts of what was harvested. It is hard to know what impact American Indians would have had on the land if their populations were as dense as many countries' populations today, but perhaps if modern cultures were to approach the earth's gifts with the same respect as the Indians, we would have fewer environmental problems.

Jane Fitzgerald

Note:

Much of the information concerning the use of plants by Indians was gleaned from an interview with Mr. Bo Brown, a native Ozarkian and professional naturalist who has studied Indian ways and our native flora and fauna for many years. For anyone who may search for wild edibles, Bo cautions that many edible plants have dangerous look-a-likes that may be harmful or even fatal if ingested.

References:

Denison, Edgar. 1989. *Missouri Wildflowers.* Missouri Department of Conservation.

Ingenthron, Elmo. 1978. *Indians of the Ozark Plateau.* The School of the Ozarks Press, Point Lookout, MO.

Krochmal, Arnold and Connie. 1984. *Field Guide to Medicinal Plants.* Times Books, N.Y.

Phillips, Jan. 1989. *Wild Edibles of Missouri.* Missouri Department of Conservation.

Don't Disturb the Wildflowers

Please, don't pick the wildflowers. If you enjoy our native plant life, be fore-warned: most wildflowers do not transplant well. The propagation of native plants should start with seed obtained from reputable growers and nurseries.

Mood

Each stone, each stick, each flower, each leaf
Speaks to me of the old time grief.
Yet when I walk this way in the spring
They laugh and I laugh, they sing and I sing.

Mary Elizabeth Mahnkey

Geology

Moving Water
The Rocks
The Landscape

The term "Ozark Mountains" is somewhat of a misnomer. As an old saying goes: the Ozarks region does not have high mountains, just deep valleys. Though sometimes told as a joke, the statement is highly accurate: the region is a plateau which has been dissected and eroded by countless streams, creating a land of valleys, rolling hills, and winding ridge tops. Springfield, where the terrain is relatively flat, lies atop remaining portions of the plateau; Stone and Taney Counties are in the dissected portions, cut by numerous streams.

The visitor to the Ozarks may be struck by many unusual features in the landscape: matching bluffs on opposite sides of a valley, hillsides bestrewn with rocks, cedar or grass covered glades in the midst of an Oak-Hickory forest, and numerous caves. To understand why the present landscape looks the way it does, we must first understand what shaped the land in the distant past.

Millions of years ago, the Ozark region was covered by a shallow sea. Countless shelled animals died and left their remains on the sea floor. As these accumulated to a great depth, they became compressed into rock, specifically limestone and dolomite. The dolomite, found at lower elevations in the area because it is older, was deposited on the sea floor during the Ordovician period (roughly 435 to 500 million years ago). The limestone, found at the higher elevations because it is younger, was deposited during the Mississippian period (roughly 310 to 350 million years ago). Mixed in with these rocks are a little bit of sandstone, some shale, and a lot of chert. Over great eons of time, the land rose and the sea drained away. Since that time various forces have acted on the original rock to produce the present landscape.

The valleys have been formed by the action of streams cutting downward into the plateau which predated our present topography of hills and hollows. As the water cut its course down through the landscape, it commonly left bluffs on both sides of the water's course. Thus to this day in many places in the Ozarks, you can stand on a ridge and see other ridges in the distance at the same elevation with the same type of rock.

The chert, much of which occurs as nodules or thin beds within the limestone and dolomite, is insoluble. Thus, when limestone and dolomite, which are soluble in slightly acidic water, dissolve away, chert is left behind and accumulates. That is why most of the soils of the region are so rocky, at times causing entire hillsides to be fields of stone.

Most of the glades in the area lie atop the upper portions of what is known as the Cotter Formation. These rock units contain more insoluble material (such as chert) than most other geologic units in the area, and thus soil accumulates more slowly. Because thin soils do not hold much moisture and thus cannot support a hardwood forest, the vegetation of the glades is dominated by plants capable of tolerating the drought susceptible shallow soils: native grasses and Eastern red cedars.

If the Ozark region were to be described geologically with one phrase, it might best be called "The Land of Hollow Hills." Beneath both the hills and the valleys lie extensive cave systems. A number of these are open to the public and are well worth a visit: particularly Marvel Cave at Silver Dollar City and Talking Rocks Cavern.

Like the surface landscape, caves are formed because limestone can be dissolved by water. The openings of caves originally form along fractures (called joints) and along the bedding planes which separate adjacent layers of rock. These initial openings are slowly widened through time as water dissolves away more and more rock. Ultimately, caves form along the joints and bedding planes which were most effective in transporting water to the springs of the region. As the valleys deepen, the caves are drained and the passages become open, allowing cave formations to begin to grow.

New formations in a cave grow from soluble limestone and dolomite carried into the cave by surface water. As rainfall, itself slightly acidic, strikes the land's surface and moves through the leaf litter and into the soil, it takes carbon dioxide into solution; it is this carbonic acid solution which enables the water to dissolve the limestone and dolomite. The dissolving of bedrock is, of course, a very slow process. In Table Rock Lake country it takes 5,000 to 7,500 pounds of water to dissolve a pound of rock. Once the water passes into air filled cave openings, it begins to lose some carbon dioxide to the cave atmosphere, very much the way a can of soda pop loses its fizz when opened and exposed to the air. Because the water cannot retain all of the dissolved rock in solution, small amounts of the dissolved material are redeposited in the caves. Slowly, ever so slowly, the cave formations build—one drip at a time. There is no standard or typical rate of deposition; the speed of a cave formation's growth depends on a number of factors.

Unlike the limestone and dolomite, the cave formations (stalactites, stalagmites, draperies, and flowstone) are crystalline and very beautiful. Caves—when we introduce light to observe them—are unusual and intriguing places. But in addition to being tantalizing, they can serve as barometers of how we treat our natural resources. For cave country has characteristics not found in other landscapes. For example, caves in the Ozarks often have streams flowing through them or waterfalls entering through the ceilings. This tells us that, in cave country, water can move very rapidly from the surface into the groundwater system because of the fractured and soluble nature of the landscape. Therefore, if we contaminate surface water, we may also contaminate wells—commonly used as the primary source of drinking water throughout the Ozarks.

Cave country is characterized not only by caves, but also by springs, sinkholes, and disappearing streams. If you hike through an Ozark forest, you are liable to come upon depressions in the terrain known as sinkholes. These are points where sediment and dissolved rock have been flushed into the groundwater system. You may also notice that most of the small streams crossing the roads of the region are dry and contain sizable gravel channels. During and immediately after storms, they can carry substantial quantities of water although they typically flow for only a few days out of the year—in spite of the region's average annual precipitation of about 40 inches. These are called losing streams because they "lose" water to the groundwater systems which feed caves, springs, and wells. Protecting the quality of water reaching these "losing streams" is an important part of groundwater quality protection.

Caves and springs have long been thought of as features isolated and totally separate from the surface of the land where man normally spends his time. Terms such as "the world of caves" and "the world of darkness" have been applied to the subsurface in cave country. But it is important that we understand that the surface and subsurface are not separate worlds, but instead are part of the same system.

In Cave Country, whatever goes down must come up. Contaminants allowed to sink into the ground may reappear in short order in a cave, well, or a spring. Many of our water quality and water contamination problems in the area are due to the interaction of the surface and the subsurface. Too many people incorrectly believe that we live on an infinite filter which is capable of cleansing any water introduced underground. Here in the Ozarks, we actually live on a sponge where the voids are capable of transporting contaminated water from one point to another.

The key to protecting water quality is to prevent contaminants from entering the groundwater system in the first place—and that takes care and vigilance. The study of ecology emphasizes that everything is tied to everything else. The interrelationship of the surface and subsurface waters of the Ozarks is a good vehicle for demonstrating the interconnectedness of all natural systems. During your time here in the Ozarks, whether you are a resident or visitor, think before depositing anything on the ground that you would not want in a glass of your own drinking water.

Tom Aley

Tom Aley is the Director of The Ozark Underground Laboratory, a research facility near Protem dedicated to the study of groundwater hydrology and methods of protecting water quality.

Section III

The Living Was Hard

To the early settlers of Ozark Mountain Country, life was hard. As the growing population depleted the once abundant game, residents were forced to exact a subsistence living from their small farms. When row crops like corn were planted on the steep hillsides, the region's soils, never rich or deep except on the regularly inundated flood plains, were scoured by gully washing rains. By the last decades of the nineteenth century, the economic history of the region became a story of various attempts of the local population to supplement their meager incomes.

Various industries were tried with little or only mixed success; two examples are lead mining and the collection of mussel shells from area rivers for the button industry. The first sustained boom to the area's economy resulted from the harvesting of local timber when the nation's expanding rail system created demand for a seemingly endless supply of cross ties. After the forests were cleared of their virgin timber, the revenue vacuum was filled by the development of the tomato and strawberry industries. The production of moonshine was sometimes used by the remote hill people for supplementary income.

The story of Ozark Mountain Country is also a story of a people and their culture and values. To a great extent, the area was once defined by its isolation. It comes as no surprise then that the folklore and traditional music of the region has its origins deep in antiquity. The Ozark hills were settled by yeoman farmers who moved into the area from the mountains of the Carolinas, Tennessee, and Kentucky—individuals who were themselves descendants of farmers from Scotland, England, and Ireland. These hill people brought with them stories and tales from their ancient homelands. Vance Randolph, the famous folklorist, collected any number of tales in the Ozarks which find parallels in Chaucer's Canterbury Tales and other medieval literature. The language patterns of the remote hill people also maintain many older expressions, often rich in metaphor.

To give the reader a feel for the values of the area, we have included essays on folklore collector Vance Randolph and on Mary Elizabeth Mahnkey, a local writer who in her widely published columns expressed in elegant terms the simple values of the Ozark people. Her poems, in fact, have been placed throughout the book. Finally we end the section with essays on two famous outsiders who moved into the area and did much of their work while living here: epic poet of the American frontier, John Neihardt, and artist Rose O'Neill, creator of the famous Kewpie Dolls.

Hacking Ties

Tie-hackers wait in line at Reeds Spring to unload their ties at a yard near the railroad. (Photo courtesy of Chloe LaRue)

At the turn of this century, during a period of expansive national growth, railroads were America's engine of progress. The great industrial magnates split their time between their business offices and the wilds of the surging nation, devising ways to interconnect centers of commerce with "iron horses."

The railroads, which crisscrossed maps like spider webs, were built on a foundation of railroad ties, eight feet long and six by eight inches thick. Millions were needed, and they could not be made of just any old piece of timber. The ties had to be shaped from wood which, when laid on a bed of gravel, was very slow to rot or decay. In the Ozarks, two tree species fit the order: white oak and post oak. Since the local area had an abundance of both trees, tie making, called "tie-hacking" in the region, became a local industry— even before railroads came into the area.

The "tie-hackers," as they called themselves, alternated their work days: one in the woods felling and cutting the trees, and one taking their ties to market. Like many of the industries on the old frontier, tie-hacking was hard, demanding work. Only one part of the chore—finding the trees—was not difficult; white oaks were abundant in the area.

Though the towering trees often were situated on public land or on others' property, such details seldom deterred most hackers who often talked of hacking ties on "grandmother's"—meaning on someone else's property. Because of the sheer abundance of trees, few people objected to having some of their trees cut.

The tools of the tie-hackers were a cross-cut saw, a single-bitted cutting axe, wedges, and a broad-axe. Since it took two people working in methodical rhythm to work a two-handled cross-cut saw, hackers worked in pairs. Often the second person on the cross-cut saw was the hacker's wife or child.

Felling trees was difficult and dangerous.

White oak trees were large at the trunk and towering. To fell a tree, the workers had to plan which way the tree would fall, normally by studying its "lean" relative to the surrounding area. Then they would cut a huge notch in the tree in the direction of the fall. Finally, they would finish the job by sawing into the tree from the direction opposite of the notch. Dead limbs were always a concern; from the vibration of the saw, these "widow makers" might fall and cause serious injury or even death. Another danger, especially in a dense forest, would arise if a falling tree got hung up on an adjacent tree and did not drop cleanly.

Even when the tree was safely on the ground, the hacker's job had just begun. The trunk needed to be cut into eight foot lengths suitable for railroad ties. Then the hackers would use wedges to split the thick eight foot sections so that several ties could be made from each length. Finally these timbers would be shaped into ties. With a single-bitted axe, the hacker would notch into the side of a timber, at one foot intervals, to the depth needed to complete the tie. Most ties were cut six by eight inches, but bridge timbers were normally seven by nine. To complete each tie, the hacker used the broadaxe to flatten the sides and ready it for market. The pieces cut off by the broadaxe, the "juggles," were allowed to dry, then hauled off as firewood for local homes. For a tie-hacking team, a good day's effort was ten to twelve ties; twenty would be phenomenal.

Getting a tie from the forest to market was not easy. The deep hollows of the area made the chore agonizing. Some hackers were able to train horses to pull ties up the hillsides without being led. A person at the top of the hill would unhook the tie and send the horse, still unled, back down into the hollow.

The hackers would generally sell their ties to buyers at hillside yards, well above but close to the area's rivers, the James and the White. Buyers graded the ties and marked them with a half-moon or full-moon, depending on the amount of heartwood in the tie—the more heartwood the better. Though the ties were purchased on a year round basis, they were only floated to market during the wet seasons, usually in the spring when the water was high. In the nineteenth century, the destination was Cotter, Arkansas. From there, the ties were shipped to railroad construction sites all over the United States.

Floating ties was a dangerous business. From the tie-yards, the ties were thrown into calm backwater pools where they were made into string rafts, using large hickory poles and huge nails. On the James River, rafts (often called "frogs") ranged from 100 to 350 ties, but the larger White River accommodated rafts easily numbering 1,000 ties, or more.

A steersman at the front and a snubsman on the rear poled the ties, straining to round the bends and bypass the boulders as the rivers swirled with excessive spring runoff. The logs would be wet and slippery, and the churning of the river could make the ride treacherous. Many men were injured and occasionally a life was lost.

When the railroad arrived locally, shortly after the turn of the century, ties were marketed, not on the hillsides, but in the railroad towns along the tracks, especially Reeds Spring and Branson. The hardy breed of men who rode the ties on the ribbon of water had to search for new ways to make a living. Horses and mules, instead of water, now supplied the power to get the ties to the railroad cars which would transport them to the construction sites.

Prices for ties varied, beginning at $.25 each before the turn of the century, shooting up to $1.00 a piece for a while, but then plummeting so far downward in the early 1920's that tie-hacking ceased to be profitable and died out in the area.

Outside of farming, tie-hacking was the first important industry in the local hills, and hundreds of thousands of ties were floated down river or shipped out via railroad. No effort was ever made to keep an accurate account of the numbers, but the forests of the area were depleted of much of their white oak and post oak. The job, however, was the right one for the people at the time—a hardy people working at a challenging and exhausting job.

Robert McGill

Red Gold - Ozark Tomatoes

So this local fellow got plumb aggervated at his ornery hawgs. Took his muzzle-loader and filled it with seeds of the love apple [tomato] and shot at them hawgs. Them seeds took root and growed. When them plump, red 'maters was ripe, they felled off and rolled down the hillside, peeling 'emselves as they gathered speed. Bounced right inta a boiling cauldron, and that's how we knew we cud grow 'maters in these hills.

Ozark Folktale

This oft-told tale expresses two themes commonly found in Ozark tales: good fortune and a desire to obtain wealth without effort. Unfortunately, despite the suggestions of the tale, tomato growing is extremely hard work. While the industry made significant contributions to the local economy from the 1890's until the 1960's, it also produced oceans of laborers' sweat. Life was hard in Ozark Mountain Country, and growing and canning tomatoes was its epitome: tough, exhausting, and insufferably hot labor.

The Ozarks met the basic requirements for a tomato canning industry. Tomatoes would flourish on Stone and Taney County hillsides. Sparkling springs, bubbling out of many hollows, provided abundant water for washing, scalding, and cooking tomatoes. And the farmers' large extended families provided the work force for the tomato fields and canneries.

The tomato canning industry lasted for nearly seventy years. The first cannery in the two county area was built by Waldo Powell in 1895 in the central part of Stone County, near Talking Rocks Cave. Accurate records, if they ever existed, have been lost, but by the 1920's there were probably sixty small canneries in Stone and Taney Counties. In the 1930's, when production peaked, large canneries expanded and drove some of the smaller ones out of business. By that time, too, a large and politically astute organization, the Ozark Canners Association, held a yearly meeting, usually in Springfield, and lobbied for the industry's interests. Although the industry was still large enough during World War II to pride itself on the contributions it made to the war effort, it dwindled and died in the 1960's.

In the 1890's when canning first became an industry, the work started the winter before the first crop was planted. A farmer and his children—the more the better—began an onslaught on virgin timberland with cross-cut saw and chopping axe. Small trees and brush were cut and removed and large trees were girdled to kill them. North or east-facing hillsides were favored because they would be partially shielded from the blazing heat of the afternoon summer sun. When the large trees were dead, small trees removed, and as many stumps as possible uprooted, work began on the soil.

Mules were the preferred draft animal for preparing the soil. Farmers hitched the laboring animals to a bull-tongue plow, then criss-crossed the field at one foot intervals, digging up the roots of the trees and loosening the ground. All available children were put to work in the field dragging the dead roots to a central spot where they were stacked and burned. Man and beast passed over the field another time with a spring harrow to work out the rough spots. Finally, just before planting, a single mule, hitched to a smaller single stock plow, again criss-crossed the field, this time at four foot intervals, to mark the intersections where the tomato plants would be set.

Raising tomato plants was a two-stage operation: first, seeds were planted in a small area to produce seedlings; later, the young plants were transplanted to the hillside fields to mature and produce fruit. Tomato seeds were traditionally planted on the second day of April, which was also school meeting and election day. Tomato producers discovered that a perfect place to plant tomato seeds was in the ground where a brush pile had been burned. The heat from the fire killed out weed seeds, allowing the fragile new tomato

*Operators of the early tomato canneries used horse-drawn wagons to haul empty cans
from railroad sidings to their canneries in horse-drawn wagons.*

plants to emerge without competition. If necessary, farmers would protect the seedlings from frost on a cold night by covering them with paper.

The second stage, transplanting the fragile plants in the fields, began six weeks after planting seeds, during the middle of May when the spring sun had warmed the ground. Tender six inch tomato plants were dug from the ground and bundled, to be planted in the field. Since transplanting on steep, rocky hillsides was time-consuming, the task was best suited to large families. One person would lay plants at the intersections where the seedlings would be set. Several other family members, walking down the rows, poked holes in the ground with a small punch called a dibble, set the plants by placing them into the holes, and covered the roots with soil. Tomato fields averaged

four acres. A fifteen acre field required an extraordinary effort.

Farmers prayed for rain in the early summer while they weeded the tomato plants. A farmer, trailing his mule which was hitched to a cultivator, trod up and down each row, slowly shifting the soil and uprooting the weeds. The first green knobs had set by the first of July, and the pinkish orange tomatoes developed by mid-August. Harvest lasted until the cool weather of autumn. Family members picking the ripe fruit on the rocky hillsides on hot August days were motivated by the anticipation of reward for their summer's effort, for tomatoes were immediately transported to the canning factories where the growers were paid for their fruit.

Tomato production, of course, changed over the years. In the 1920's, fertilizer began to be used and yields increased. When hybrid tomatoes were developed in the 1930's, yields increased even more. Tractors replaced horses and mules in the 1940's, and the work became somewhat easier. But nothing ever replaced the arduous, backbreaking chore of picking tomatoes by hand.

While the canning season was filled with hard work, it was also a festive occasion because families, relatives, and friends would come to the canneries—sometimes from miles around—to work, laugh, and play together. While they worked, hillfolk could catch up on community gossip, and discuss politics, religion, and family matters. Though laborers often lived in crowded bedrooms, abandoned houses, and tents during canning season, the season was always anticipated because of the camaraderie and because, for some, picking and canning were the only sources of cash income.

Before the turn of the century, some of the very first canneries were located outdoors. In preparation for canning, family members would set cookers and cappers under shade trees. Harvested tomatoes were then scalded and skinned. Early tomato cans were manufactured in eastern steel towns, such as Pittsburgh, and shipped by rail to the nearest railhead. The early cans were sealed by the manufacturer, except for a small, one and a half inch diameter hole in the top. At the canneries tomatoes were squeezed through funnels and into the cans. The cans, after being hand-soldered shut, were cooked, cooled, and stacked to ready them for a buyer. Only 500 to 1,000 cans a year were processed by these early canners.

Eventually, canneries were set up inside buildings, insufferably hot buildings since they captured the heat from the hot August sun while the cauldrons of hot water inside raised the temperature even further. And while men and children were busy picking and transporting tomatoes from the fields, women stood on the production lines in the hot, humid buildings, preparing, packing, and canning tomatoes. The process of canning was essentially the same in all canneries. The heavy crates of newly-picked tomatoes were first spread out on tables where poor tomatoes were culled. The remaining tomatoes were washed, poured into a hot vat, scalded, and then dumped into buckets. Buckets, three at a time, were placed on a conveyer belt and passed to each woman. The first bucket contained the scalded tomatoes, while the other two were empty. Each woman then peeled the tomatoes from her own full bucket, placing the peeled tomatoes in one of the empty buckets while letting the core and skins fall into the third bucket. The worker received a token for every bucket of tomatoes she peeled, and then at the end of the week she redeemed the tokens for wages. By using ultra-sharp skinning spoons to core the tomatoes, the women could pop-squeeze the fruit right out of its skin. If the skin stuck to the tomato, the sharp blade of the "tomato spoon" was used to cut the tomato skin off. But let a spoon slip, and a woman would find her hand gushing with blood.

The peeled tomatoes were packed into cans, sealed, and cooked to preserve the contents. Mechanical sealers soon replaced the hand soldering iron, and the number of cans that could be sealed increased to several hundred an hour in the large canneries. The final process in canning was cooling, boxing, and storing the processed tomatoes so they could be shipped to buyers.

Before the railroads were built, canners hauled a few tomatoes to Hollister and shipped them by boats to markets down the White River. But with the coming of the railroads, industry buyers for food wholesale companies began arriving by rail. The buyers, who scoured the countryside in the fall for tomatoes, supplied labels from their parent companies, and shipped box loads of tomatoes to stores across the nation and even to foreign countries.

Ironically, the very conditions which improved the production of the tomato industry also brought about its demise in the Ozarks. The innovations—the use of fertilizer, hybrid seeds, and tractors—were better suited to large fields in California and Florida than to hillside patches in the Ozarks. And inside the canneries, newer, more expensive equipment was always

The first tomato canning factory in the area, above, was owned by Waldo Powell before the turn of the century. The last one, below, was operated by Bob Emerson of Reeds Spring.

(Above photo courtesy of Alden Hembree; below by Kathleen Van Buskirk)

needed to speed the process while federal regulations constantly upgraded sanitary requirements. Ozark canneries simply could not justify the massive expenditures required to continue in the business.

World War II artificially supported the canning industry, but once the war ended, canneries began to shut down. Those canning factories situated along the railroads survived the longest. Crane, Elsey, Galena, Reeds Spring, and Branson all had canneries into the late 1950's, or longer. The last canning factory in the area, which belonged to Bob Emerson of Reeds Spring, closed in 1968.

For years the tomato canning industry was a way of life for many Stone and Taney County farmers. The industry supported the financial needs of families and, in turn, families built much of their social and community life around the industry. Several Stone County canners became prominent in the region-wide Ozark Canners Association; four served as president: Roy Nelson, Porter Lucas, W. C. Cope, and Bob Emerson. Their efforts contributed to uniform quality in the product, greater efficiency in the processing plants, and the establishment of labeling and insecticide regulations. The distinction of being the most colorful individual associated with the industry undoubtedly belonged to Frank Mease of Reeds Spring, who at one time owned seven canneries. This entrepreneur, who became wealthy through his agricultural enterprises, also wrote stories for health food magazines and, to show off his good health, would, when he was past eighty, stand on his head atop a straight-back chair in the bed of a pickup truck—while his son drove him through town.

Some people find it difficult to believe that many of today's heavily wooded hillsides were once tomato fields, but the plow scars and old farm roads, still visible in many of these woods, attest to the legacy of the tomatoes.

In the summertime tomatoes are still available at roadside stands. Often, these tomatoes are raised on the same hillsides, by descendants of the same families who produced them for the canneries. And the fresh, vine-ripened tomatoes remain a testament to the quality of Ozark produce.

Robert McGill

Strawberry Time in the Ozarks

Who can forget the old wood-burning cook stoves used by our mothers and grandmothers? The stove, in addition to its use in preparing meals, canning garden vegetables, or heating water for the Saturday night bath, often warmed small fingers and toes after a snowball fight or a long walk home from the country school.

Each year in mid-May, when Ozark strawberries began to ripen, the sturdy old range assumed a different function, that of holding a large assortment of kettles and pans filled with red, ripe strawberries and sugar—ingredients of delicious strawberry preserves and jam. A never-to-be forgotten aroma filled the room as the thick concoction bubbled merrily on the stove. (In fact, the favorite variety of strawberry in the area was the Aroma, eventually to be replaced by the improved Blakemore.) Soon the finished product was poured into previously sterilized jars and set to cool. The preserves and jams were stored away to be eaten "when the snow flies," as my mother always said.

Growing strawberries instead of the usual row crops was an entirely different concept of farming for the residents of Stone County, Missouri during the Depression years of the 1930's. While profits derived from the sale of the strawberry crop provided growers with an income to be used for paying taxes and making payments on the family farm, harvesting of the crop also put ready cash in the pockets of a large number of area pickers.

Long hours of labor were necessary before the strawberry fields yielded their harvest of plump and juicy, ruby-red berries. New ground—farmland that had not previously been in cultivation—was the ideal location for the strawberry fields. The first step was to clear the plot of brush. A horse, or preferably a mule, was hitched to a double shovel or a turning plow for loosening roots and vegetation. The next step was to harrow the ground several times and lay off the rows. The tender strawberry plants were then set with a sharp-pointed tool known as a dibble.

More, long tedious hours of labor were required as the plants developed. Strawberries develop runners which set new plants, and these long trailing appendages had to be laid by hand and trained to follow the existing row. The strawberry fields were fertilized by a laborer who carried a large bucket and threw a handful of fertilizer around—but never directly on—each plant. The addition not only nourished the strawberry plants but fast growing weeds and grasses as well. The job of eradicating weeds was a never ending chore. All members of the family, from the youngest to the eldest, pitched in and helped with the task, using a sharp two-pronged hoe.

Growing strawberries, not unlike growing crops of any kind, was a game of chance. Would a late frost damage the flowers? Would enough rain fall in the spring to produce plump berries? Would workers be available to assure that the juicy berries were picked at their peak? Would prices hold to ensure the grower a reasonable profit after expenses? The farm families, who had risked years of hard labor and a goodly amount of cash against the wily, unpredictable forces of nature, had much to worry about.

Ozark berries usually ripened about May 15. The average date for loading the first railroad car for shipment was May 15 to 21. At the peak of the strawberry season, an average of one to five railroad cars were loaded each day. When strawberry season began, workers arrived daily, seeking employment. Although local labor was sufficient to harvest the small individual patches, workers had to be recruited from a distance for the larger acreages. From all over the hills of Ozark Mountain Country, the pickers came, industrious and proud in their faded blue denim overalls and printed feed-sack dresses. Families often followed the strawberry harvest, living in tents or any available building. Many workers returned yearly to work for the same grower.

Pickers were provided with a durable wooden carrier called a "handie," which held six, one quart boxes. The handies were to be well-filled, with an extra handful of large, ripe berries placed on top to prove to the shed boss that he was receiving a full measure from the worker. For the effort, strawberry pickers in northern Stone County were receiving two cents per quart for picking in the early 1930's. Culling was done by shed hands who removed the over-ripe, under-ripe, small, or damaged berries, which were sold to local markets. Packing berries to be shipped was also done at the culling shed.

Growers delivered the day's yield of berries to the local receiving shed each afternoon or evening. While waiting for their cargo to be unloaded, they swapped yarns, discussed the best methods of growing berries, and caught up on the latest local gossip from their friends and neighbors.

The grower, well aware of the long hours of back-breaking labor performed by the worker as he stooped to gather the ever ripening fruit, showed his appreciation when the season came to an end. It was not unusual for workers to be loaded into a farm truck and transported to the banks of either the James or White River for a fishing outing. On these occasions, plenty of food was provided by the grower. As fish were caught—and many large fish were caught in those days—they were cleaned on the spot to be fried in a large, iron skillet over an open fire. Other frying pans held golden brown potatoes. Huge pots of steaming black coffee prepared from river water completed the meal.

Near the peak of the strawberry harvesting season, each small town played host to a traveling medicine show or carnival, or both. It was not by chance that the promoters of these affairs chose to visit the rural communities at this particular time. The managers were well aware that blue jean pockets would be jingling with strawberry money. If today's wages were spent tonight—no worry—tomorrow was another day. The long hours of hard, hot labor were forgotten in the spell woven by the carnival atmosphere, and a promise of a good time that night.

Fern Angus

Stills In The Depression Era

The Ozarks hillman contributed a great deal to the country's heritage. Like the Mountain Man of the West or the Frontiersman of Kentucky, he dealt with conditions as he found them, using his personal skills and wit. He was canny, frugal, and resourceful. He had his place in the building of a nation and should be understood for what he was—a man of his time.

During the Great Depression, it was illegal to manufacture and/or sell liquor. The law was represented by the ubiquitous presence of Sheriff Riley Thomason (a.k.a. "Two Gun"), dedicated to the eradication of all stills in his territory—Taney County. An impressive number of families whose names are prominent in the county's history had members who went to prison as a result of Thomason's zeal, men who under normal circumstances were law abiding, God-fearing citizens.

But years of drought and a rock bottom market made the depression years a disaster for farmers. The native became desperate in his efforts to feed himself and his family and turned his ingenuity to whatever method was at hand. The law of survival superseded that of man, represented by Thomason, who became a feared adversary.

One such area resident had lost his crop, seen his home burn to the ground, and was forced to live in a chicken house, his seven children sleeping on boards stretched across the rafters. They existed on whatever fish and game he could catch or snare.

Like many others, this hill farmer turned to bootlegging. There was always a market for liquor. Mostly the demand came from the tourists who visited the Ozarks to fish and hunt. They had money and a thirst for the forbidden product. With a trusted friend he set up a still in an innocent appearing cedar brake, and the two took turns watching the mash cooking. It was a dangerous operation, for the lawmen, always looking for telltale signs, were apt to shoot on sight.

Late one afternoon on his way to relieving his partner, the hillman thought it prudent to check out the whereabouts of the sheriff, stopping by the post office as part of the plan. A letter from his mother had arrived, and he made a big thing of its importance. Anything that broke the monotony of the day was of great interest then and bound to be remembered. As usual, he was wearing his old, worn leather jacket, the only outer garment he owned. In those days, an individual was easily identified by his clothing.

When he arrived at the still site, he removed his coat and hung it on a branch, intending to start another batch of mash while the present one was processing. Just as he got started, the sheriff and two deputies came crashing through the brake. The bootleggers dropped everything, the partner jumped and ran. As the hillman followed, Thomason opened fire on him and the blast of buckshot found its mark in his back. Nevertheless, he kept going and somehow managed to elude the lawmen.

Later that night he sneaked into his home, knowing it was the last place Thomason would look. By lamplight, behind covered windows, his wife washed the wounds with lye soap before patiently picking as much of the shot from his back as she could. It was during this session he remembered leaving his coat at the still—evidence that Two-Gun would surely use to identify him.

But the hillman's logic was at work and with the painful removal of each bit of lead, he formed a plan. Though he had but one coat, he did possess two shirts. When the operation was complete and the wounds saturated with tobacco juice as an antiseptic, he rolled up the bloody shirt, donned the second one, and woke the kids. Then, piling the whole family into his old car, he drove to his mother's home at Cassville.

The reunion was pleasant, and in due time the children were bedded down on quilts on the floor. The next morning the hillman rose early, burned the bloody shirt, then went into town and purchased a leather jacket. Styles didn't change as frequently then; his new jacket was identical to the one he'd left in the cedar brake.

After lunch, the visit came to an end and the family began the return trip home. Along the way the hillman turned off on a dusty side road that apparently saw little traffic. A short distance from the highway he stopped the car, got out, and taking the new coat by its collar, began beating it against the brambles until it was scarred and torn. Then he dragged it along the road where it absorbed enough dirt to look as though he'd worn it for years. Shaking the excess debris loose, he put it back on, smiled at his wife, and commenced an uneventful drive home.

After dropping his family off, he checked with his partner and learned that Two-Gun had been bragging that he'd got himself a moonshiner. Shot him he said, just hadn't located him—but he had the fella's coat proving his guilt.

On the surface it seemed the coat was damning evidence—there was no question who it belonged to, and that person hadn't shown since the shooting. Two-Gun was holding a pat hand.

But the hillman was about to play his hole card. He walked down the main street and paused in front of the sheriff's office to speak to a couple of friends, say-ing he'd just got back from a visit with his mother who'd been "feeling poorly." Of course they knew he'd received a letter from her so he seemed to have a logi-cal reason for the trip.

He'd expected Riley to be in the office—and when the lawman swaggered out, a smile of triumph on his face, ready to make an arrest, the hillman nodded as he would to any other acquaintance. Two-Gun took one look at that ragged leather coat and froze in his tracks. He just stood there for a minute while the hill-man continued talking to the amused audience. Thoma-son realized he was beaten and ducked back inside without a word.

Naturally, everybody in town knew the coat Two-Gun held belonged to the hillman, but they didn't understand anymore than the sheriff what had hap-pened. No one thought to look beneath the second coat for buckshot wounds. The hillman had counted on the sight of the coat being the right bluff. And he was right!

He understood the mind of his adversary; he was a man of his time.

Viola Hartman

The Moonshiner in Action

Then the long and lanky chemist
Sought his lair within the mountains
By the big spring in the hollow
Where the weeds and brush grew thickly
Built he there his moonshine factory
Skilled and cunning did he build it
That no eye could see the smoking
That no ear might hear the boiling
That no snoot might scent the scorching!
Mixed he then his mash with caution—
Purest corn and sparkling water
Waited then for the fermenting
Hoping, dreaming in the canyon.

Little did he mind the labor
Son of toil and son of sorrow
For he knew that this firewater
Clear as dew, and flowery scented
Would bring him a shower of dollars
Needed dollars this hard winter.
That men would rise up to call him blessed
Bless him for his skill and labor
Bless him for this pungent liquor
That he made down in the hollow
In the frosty, rocky hollow.

Mary Elizabeth Mahnkey

A World Filled With Music

With so much publicity being generated by today's country music boom, one might assume that music has only recently come to Taney and Stone Counties. However, in homes, school buildings, and community centers scattered throughout the White River hills, singers, fiddlers, and other musicians—from tots to octogenarians—carry on a musical tradition begun in pioneer days.

Despite the perils and difficulties of migrating to the Ozarks before the Civil War, many newcomers arrived with a musical instrument tucked among their belongings, a fiddle, a mouth harp (harmonica), sometimes even a pump organ. The settlers also brought ballads and folk songs passed down from their ancestors in England, Scotland, Ireland, or Germany. Those tunes and story-telling verses were sung, hummed, or whistled by pioneer housewives to speed the work of hoeing a garden, scrubbing clothes, or kneading dough.

Often frontier homes were temporarily emptied of furniture to make room for a party where young folks danced to traditional melodies or newly improvised tunes. At political rallies and community picnics, young and old would share the dance pavilion, circling in response to the caller's prompts, or individually clogging or jigging to the intricate folk tunes played by local musicians.

On school playgrounds, games with European origins often included traditional songs which became part of the heritage of all the children. Though the short school terms provided no time for music lessons, the school day frequently opened with a song, and box suppers and special programs always included singing.

The most popular music teachers through the first half of the twentieth century were the singing masters who traveled the area conducting well advertised singing schools. Songs were usually taught by "lining"; the instructor read each line, then sang it, and the students were expected to repeat what they heard. Students learned to sing gospel songs without reading standard musical notation or understanding key signatures.

Ozark hill music was passed from generation to generation. In the 1940's Coy and Lavoy Smith learned traditional Ozark tunes from George Baize.
(Photo courtesy of Betty Clark)

The singers had to learn only seven different shapes for the seven notes of an octave. No instrumental accompaniment was required. The teacher set the beginning note for each song with a tuning fork or pitch pipe.

Several companies published "shape note" song books, which the singing teachers sold to their students. Many of those song books, worn from much handling, survive in area homes, testimony to the popularity of the movement.

Sooner or later most shape note singers realized that they had actually learned to read regular musical notation, since the shape notes were printed on a standard staff. Of course shape notes were of little help to instrumental musicians or song writers, who had to read and understand the different musical keys.

Singing was also important in worship services, where hymns often inspired strong religious feelings. This was particularly true at the brush arbor revival meetings which were popular until well into the twentieth century. The popularity of group singing in Taney and Stone Counties can scarcely be overestimated.

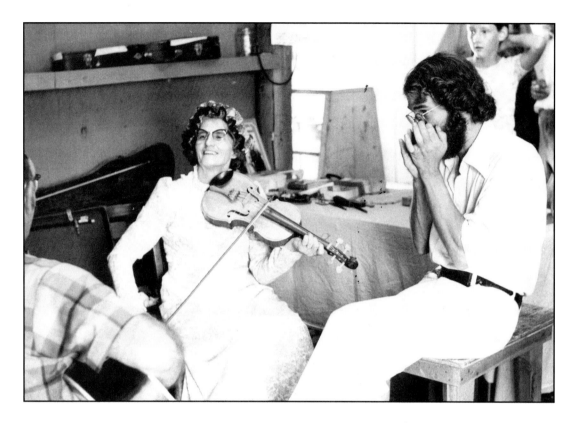

"The Fiddle Lady" Violet Hensley leads a modern jam session on one of the fiddles she made.
(Photo by Kathleen Van Buskirk)

Many groups and even whole communities set aside special Sundays for "an all day singing session with dinner on the ground," in other words, a picnic. Or small groups gathered to enjoy singing in some home on a regularly scheduled basis.

Similar gatherings of instrumental musicians were common in the region. Of all the instruments used in the Ozarks—fiddles, guitars, banjos, dulcimers, jews harps, and improvised instruments such as bones, saws, and spoons—the fiddle remains the most versatile and popular. It establishes the melody and rhythm for dances and is used to accompany singing. Without a fiddle a Saturday night Ozark jam session would not be complete.

Children at fiddling sessions who express an interest have traditionally been encouraged to pick up and saw away on an instrument, often with a minimum of instruction. Left to their own devices, talented youngsters sometimes become very adept at the finger-ing and bowing techniques typical of Ozark fiddlers. Fiddling competitions and conventions are still common. Particularly popular are the twice yearly gatherings of the State of the Ozarks Fiddlers' Association at the Compton Ridge Campground, and the many fiddling shows at Silver Dollar City.

Modern transportation, radio, and television have brought new musical influences to the area. Popular songs and country music styles have become a part of the traditional musical heritage of the Ozarks. This rich combination contributes to the success of the present country music scene in Branson, offering opportunities for talented local musicians. While today's growing commercial tradition is drawing national attention to the area, local musicians continue to entertain in living rooms, on back porches, and at community gatherings throughout the countryside.

Kathleen Van Buskirk

The One Room School

Among the memories dear to my heart are those of a one room country school which I attended as a child. Fond memories of a school? Yes, for the school was not only a place where we learned, but it was a location for church meetings and social occasions. Let's take a journey back and see what these simple yet marvelous buildings were like and how they served the needs of the community.

The first rural schools in Ozark Mountain Country were very crudely constructed of hand hewn logs and were called subscription schools. Each family paid according to the number of children attending. The school year began not at the end of summer but in July after the crops had all been planted; it ended around Christmas before the weather made getting to school difficult.

In the first one room schools, split logs served as benches for the children. The system of separating grades had not yet been implemented. At times twenty or thirty students would crowd into one room—with only one teacher.

After the turn of the century, white frame buildings generally came to replace the earlier log cabins. One student was usually assigned to a seat, but double seats were not uncommon. A podium was built at one end of the building for the teacher's desk. Behind the desk was a long blackboard. Nearby was a map of the United States and a world globe. The model of the modern classroom evolved from this early setup.

Somewhere near the front of the school building—the back of the classroom—was a room partitioned off as a place to hang the children's wraps. It was called a cloak room. A shelf in the cloak room held the tin buckets and boxes in which the children brought their lunches to school. On a Monday, the lunch pail might contain a piece of fried chicken and perhaps a piece of apple pie, left over from Sunday dinner. But otherwise the fare was rather basic. I remember having many a lunch of a cold biscuit and a piece of sausage.

By the late 1930's, a government program provided commodities to the rural schools. Although the staple items—beans, rice, flour, sugar, and the like—provided a rather bland diet, cooks improvised, often adding items from their own kitchens.

Drinking water in the early schools usually had to be carried from a nearby farm house or a hillside spring. Eventually, most schools had a deep well, operated by a hand pump. The speckled, blue granite water bucket sat near the front of the room. All students drank from the same long-handled dipper. Nobody worried much about picking up a "bug"; perhaps there were fewer germs lurking around in isolated areas in those days.

Before the days of indoor plumbing, the outside privies—one for boys and one for girls—held a seat with two holes and an old Sears Roebuck catalog.

A large bell, rung by the teacher, heralded the opening of school at 9 A.M. sharp each weekday morning. Students lined up outside the door and awaited the signal to enter and take their assigned seats. This procedure was referred to as "taking up books." Sometimes the day's activities began by singing patriotic songs. "The Star Spangled Banner" and "America the Beautiful" were favorites. In my school days, the "Pledge of Allegiance" had not yet achieved general currency: I do not remember repeating what later children would learn as a matter of course.

After the roll call of students, the teacher called each class up separately and heard their lessons. One advantage of the country school was that all grades could hear each class's recitations so that younger children could pick up concepts and store them in memory for later use.

In those days, incidentally, teachers who were recruited to rural areas commonly boarded in a home near the one room school. My parents, for example, boarded a young lady teacher, a cousin of mine, prior to my first year of school. Most families considered boarding a teacher a privilege because of the "good influence" the family's youngsters would receive. The setup was not always perfect, however. My mother retains an old newspaper clipping from 1917 which complained of a teacher who lacked table manners and who constantly cluttered her room and left it looking as if "a cyclone had struck it."

School in those days, after all, was not something separate from the rest of life. The school house was not just a center for learning; it was the focal point of the dispersed rural community and commonly served as a house of worship. Religious services were normally interdenominational. Nobody worried much about separating Church and state. In fact, the school directors would have hesitated to hire a teacher who was not considered to be a good Christian.

Christmas programs, pie suppers, and social activities also commonly took place in school buildings. The ever popular pie suppers brought together the entire community. Young men would compete for the privilege of eating with the teacher, especially if she were young and pretty. Boxes which held the pies were literally works of art, wrapped in crepe paper of brilliant colors. Often a colored, artificial flower blossomed in all its glory on top of the box. The pies were auctioned to the highest bidder. Young ladies made sure their beaus knew which box they had brought. Woe to the gentleman who forgot or who was reluctant to bid high enough!

Other traditions abounded: a jar of dill pickles was given to the most lovesick couple, a bar of soap to the man with the dirtiest feet, and a box of chocolate candy to the prettiest or most popular girl.

Christmas was a special time at the rural schoolhouse. Since Christmas trees were not to be found in every home then as they are now, the job of decorating the large cedar tree which graced the schoolhouse was enthusiastically taken up by all the children in the community. Paper chains, nuts wrapped in foil, and strings of popcorn were hung with care. Children of the poorer families would often receive no gifts except for those available at the schoolhouse. Santa Claus always managed to burst in the door at the right moment with a loud "Ho! Ho! and a Merry Christmas," his sack filled with goodies for young and old alike. Nativity plays, which had been practiced for days, were presented to an appreciative and responsive audience.

The one room schoolhouse was more than a place to learn ideas; it was the very heart of the rural community.

Fern Angus

Voice From the Ozarks
Mary Elizabeth Mahnkey

Almost from the time the Ozarks region was first settled by intrepid pioneers, hill people have been looked down upon and ridiculed by outsiders. The isolation and the rigorous demands of subsistence living have shaped Ozark culture, but from the perspective of the outsider, hill people are almost always depicted as uncultured and unsophisticated. It is for this reason that the people of the area treasured the writings of Mary Elizabeth Mahnkey. Beginning in the early 1890's, first in local papers and later for regional and national publications, she wrote about Ozark life in a simple, honest voice, helping both the local people and the nation appreciate the beauty of Ozark values and traditions.

A remarkable thing about Mary Elizabeth Mahnkey's writing is the influence it had, not only locally in Taney County, but in the larger Springfield area and even nationwide. Proud of her heritage, understanding of her neighbors and their problems, she presented a picture of the Ozarks that showed the pride, the beauty, the caring, and the work ethic of the people. She wrote of the ordinary, everyday activities of men and women. She wrote of dogs and horses, of family and children, of canning and gardening. She related the old stories she heard as a child, using the dialect of the hills when appropriate. She recorded the old medicinal cures, explained superstitions, and told about customs—from taffy pulling and dancing to rites of burial.

Her voice from the hills enlightened her readers to the real beauty of their native Ozark countryside,

the charm of the Ozark way of life, and the grace of living and being an Ozarker. She recorded the commonplace. She wrote, "I have found beauty in commonplace things, in a blue gingham apron with crisply tied strings…" It seems that her mission was to "…transform the commonest of commonplace things into silver and gold," so that her readers might see the beauty all around them.

The Ozark people, especially women, felt good about themselves when they read her writing. Outsiders reading her work saw a realistic, inside view of the Ozark people, free from the stereotype of backwoodsy hill people which was always imposed on the native population.

Hers was the voice of a sensitive and cultured woman, native to these hills. At a time when most writers who dealt with the Ozarks were outsiders, her authentic voice helped Ozark people appreciate what they had.

Mary Elizabeth Mahnkey was born in Harrison, Arkansas, August 16, 1877, to Alonzo and Ada Marie Prather. Though she lived the typical life of a rural and small town Ozark girl, marrying in 1899, and raising four children, Douglas (1901-   ), Roberta (1905-1983), Reggie (1907-1979), and Bill (1912-1920), her contributions were not typical.

Although she was not formally educated to be a writer, various influences encouraged her love of the written word. Her father was not only a lawyer and Union Army officer, but was active in education, agriculture, politics, and journalism. Though he lived in

---

Commonplace

I stick smart weed and beggar lice
In with my bouquet
And then I smile
When my friends say,
"How beautiful, how delicate,
What can these blossoms be?"
"O yes," I say, " O yes
But it takes one just like me
To show you all
That common things
Have beauty, charm, and grace,
But not until you see them
Stuck in a crystal vase."

Mary Elizabeth Mahnkey

Mary Elizabeth Mahnkey
(Photo by Townsend Godsey)

Taney County in the 1880's, he moved his family many times in northern Arkansas and southern Missouri, once even going to western Kansas for two years. From an early age Mary Elizabeth learned about the world outside her own neighborhood.

As was typical of many girls in the area, she attended only a few terms of school, but was self-educated through reading and family discussion. At 16, she obtained teaching certification and taught terms of school at the Ridgedale school (1894), Union Flat (1896), and the Old Branson school (1898).

In addition to the normal sunup to sundown work day of farm women at that time, Mary Elizabeth had the added responsibilities of postmaster and partner with her husband for many years in the crossroads stores they owned and operated at Mincy, Melva, and Oasis. In spite of these responsibilities, she found time

to write weekly rural correspondence columns for Taney County papers for 57 years, rarely missing a week from the time she was fourteen until her death in 1948. For 18 years (1930-1948), her monthly columns, "In the Hills," appeared in "The Waste Basket" section in the Springfield dailies. She contributed articles and poetry to *The Country Home* magazine in New York, to *Missouri Magazine,* and the White River Electrical Cooperative publications. She had special writing assignments to newspapers such as the *St. Louis Post Dispatch* and contributed poems and amusing tales to radio personalities such as Mirandy of Persimmon Hollow, *the National Farm and Home Hour* personality from Chicago, Illinois.

In 1934, the Taneyhills Study Club of Branson published a collection of her poems, *Ozark Lyrics.* Several editions of this book were printed, including two by the School of the Ozarks in 1972 and 1980. The most recent anthology of her poetry is *Marigold Gold: Verses of the Ozarks,* published by Bittersweet, Inc. of Lebanon, Missouri.

In 1935 she received a national award from Crowell Publishing Company of New York City as the best rural correspondent in the United States and Canada. Part of the award was a trip to New York where she was feted and interviewed by big city newspapers from all over the nation.

The volume of work taken in stride by an average Ozark wife and mother in the early 1900's would boggle the minds of modern women. How did Mary Elizabeth have time to do the usual tasks, then work in the store and write? She said in her journals that she just had to write. It was as necessary a part of her routine as was cooking or sewing. Rarely did she miss writing in her journals. Only during especially tragic times, such as when her seven-year-old son Bill was killed in the Melva tornado in 1920, did her urge to record daily events and thoughts desert her. However, even then she continued her weekly correspondent obligations.

She made time to write. During slack moments in the store, she would jot down ideas. In the evenings after the chores were done, she wrote. While pies were baking in the oven, she sat at the kitchen table, took the notes she had jotted down all week from the nail on the wall, and wrote her column.

Ideas would come to her while she was working, doing the commonplace tasks of women: churning, making bread, hanging out the clothes. She turned these thoughts into poems in her head, and then she would pause long enough to scribble them down.

While darning overalls, she would recognize the symbolism of her work and life:

Life's fabric has grown thin;
'Tis darned and patched and tied;
It has been turned so many times
To show the brighter side.

Or watching her neighbor cross the one-lane bridge over Long Creek, she would ponder on people's rights:

There's a twickety-twock on the bridge;
Uncle Andy is coming to mill
On his old gray mule, so steady and true,
From over yan side of the hill.
The old gray mule lays back his ears
At the sound of a motor horn,
And a rich powerful car whines down to a creep.

Serene, undismayed, Uncle Andy rides on,
Secure in his right-of-way.
"Let' em toot, let 'em cuss,
I'm fust on the bridge
An' I'm goin' to mill today."

Mary Elizabeth Mahnkey, though largely unknown today, was one of Taney County's outstanding women. She made a difference in her own time and helped Ozarkers appreciate themselves and the beauty all around them, while educating the rest of the world to the values inherent in the region and its people.

Ellen Gray Massey

Ellen Massey has written extensively about Mary Elizabeth Mahnkey and has collected an anthology of her poetry, *Marigold Gold: Verses Of The Ozarks* Mrs. Massey, who offers lectures to groups about Mary Elizabeth Mahnkey, can be reached through:

Bittersweet, Inc.
126 Maple Drive
Lebanon, Missouri 65536

Ozark Culture Saved in a Trunk
A Tribute to Vance Randolph

For roughly thirty years beginning in 1920, Vance Randolph combed the hills and hollers of the Ozark Mountains, collecting folk songs, tales, and beliefs. He would record the information on cards and store them in a trunk, utilizing a filing system which enabled him to put his finger on any given item at a moment's notice. Gradually, he published a significant portion of these folk materials. Largely because of Vance Randolph's efforts, the world at large knows about the lifestyle and speech patterns of the isolated Ozark hillfolk.

This section, dedicated to his memory, is divided into three parts: first, we offer two of the folktales he collected, then an essay about his contribution to preserving Ozark culture, and finally a reminiscence by an old friend and collaborator, Fern Nance Shumate.

Folktales

Three Dollars for the Bull

One time there was some folks lived on the old Sullivan place, just past the forks of Little Greasy. They had a Jersey bull, and a fine black stallion. Them two was the best male animals on the creek, and people used to fetch cows and mares from all over the country. The folks went to town one Saturday, and just left one boy at home to take care of any business that come along. "The main thing is not to get your figures mixed up," says the old man. "Remember now, it's three dollars for the bull, and five dollars for the stud-horse."

Soon as the wagon was out of sight, the boy set down on the steps, and he says to himself, "Three dollars for the bull, five dollars for the stud-horse. Three dollars for the bull, five dollars for the stud-horse." He kept saying it over and over, so as not to make no mistake. About four o'clock here come a man from the Hurricane Bottoms, with long red whiskers. There was a big gun stuck in his belt, and he acted kind of worked up about something. The boy couldn't make out just what was the matter, but he figured on doing the right thing. "It's three dollars for the bull, and five dollars for the stud-horse," says he.

"To hell with all that," says the man with the whiskers. "This here is a goddam serious business. Your hired man Elmer has got my daughter in the family way, and something's got to be done about it."

The boy just set there awhile, counting on his fingers kind of doubtful. "It's three dollars for the bull, and five dollars for the stud-horse," says he, "but I don't know how much they charge for Elmer."

The Oldest Inhabitant

One time there was a man in this county that says he is a hundred years old. The folks figured it was a lie, but they couldn't prove nothing, because everybody that knowed about it has died off long ago, and there wasn't no records in the courthouse. So when the fellow says he is a hundred years old the women-folks give him a birthday party, and people come from all over the country.

A fat woman from Little Rock was going to write a piece about him in the paper, because she is a reporter by trade, but the old man didn't like her looks. "Are you the oldest inhabitant?" she hollered in his ear. "No, I ain't," says he. "The Commercial Club offered me the job, but I turned 'em down. It looks to me like there ain't no future in it." The woman reporter mulled that one over for awhile, and you could see she was kind of bothered.

Pretty soon she hollered in the old man's ear again. "To what do you attribute your longevity?" The old fellow just shook his head. "How did you happen to live so long?" she asked him. "Poor health and whiskey is what done it," says he. "Smallpox kept me out of the Mexican War, and when the Civil War come along I had brain fever. My brothers was healthy, so they all got killed." The fat woman give him a sharp look, like she thought maybe he was kidding, and then she wants to know what has whiskey got to do with it. "I stay home and get drunk every Sunday," says he, "instead of riding around in automobiles. It's surprising how many people gets killed a-riding round in automobiles."

The newspaper woman wrote down what he said, but she looked kind of uneasy. Two fiddlers come along just then, and the old man got to showing how he could do the Buzzard Flop, which is a kind of buck-and-wing dance. "My goodness," says she, "you're mighty active for your age." The old man just laughed. "This ain't nothing," he says, "you ought to see my pappy!" The woman opened her mouth twice, but she didn't say a word. "He's nineteen years older than me," says the old man, "and just got married last week." The fat woman drawed a deep breath. "Nonsense!" she says. "What would a man a hundred and nineteen years old want to marry for?" The old fellow laughed right in her face, and he says, "Pappy didn't exactly want to get married. He had to!"

The folks all busted out laughing when they heard that, and the fat woman got pretty mad. She says a joke is all right in its place, but when a man is a hundred years old he ought to be thinking about serious matters. "Lady," says he, "it must be you never had no experience with things like that. If you think a shot-gun wedding ain't serious—" The whole crowd busted out laughing again, and the newspaperwoman just got in her car and drove back to Little Rock. She never did write nothing about the old man's birthday party.

These tales, used with the kind permission of Mrs. George Lott Jr., are reprinted from *Sticks in the Knapsack and Other Ozark Folk Tales,* New York: Columbia University Press, 1958.

Vance Randolph (1892-1980)
Friend and "Furriner"

Vance Randolph, right, in an early folk-music taping session.
(Photo from Townsend Godsey Collection, Lyons Memorial Library, College of the Ozarks.)

The two tales reproduced above demonstrate several qualities commonly found in Ozark folk tales. The first is a tendency of the hill people to make fun of their own foibles—the legendary problem with shot-gun marriages, for example. But Ozark story tellers took even greater pleasure in poking fun at outsiders—the central point of the second tale. In fact, Vance Randolph entitled one of his collections *We Always Lie to Strangers*. The title is not an overstatement; "always" means always. And Randolph probably chose the phrase as a title for good reason; he wanted to suggest that he was an insider and that only insiders could tell when a tale or folk belief was to be taken seriously or discounted as a humorous put-on.

The challenge that any outside collector—an academic folklorist or an anthropologist—would have faced is that the hill people were extremely suspicious of "furriners" and would not have shared their beliefs regarding sensitive issues: ghosts and witchcraft, pregnancy and childbirth, death and burial. Randolph said as much in one of his collections: "The man who wants to study the Ozark superstitions must live with the Ozark people year after year and gradually absorb folklore through the rind, as it were."[1] And that is precisely what Randolph did. Though he was born on the fringe of the Ozarks in Pittsburg, Kansas, he was lured into the area by its natural beauty and by a fascination with its people. He spent virtually all of his adult life living in the Ozarks—in Pineville and Galena, Missouri, and in Eureka Springs and Fayetteville, Arkansas. Though he worked as a journalist and a writer to support himself, often turning out hack materials, he put up with the drudgery of writing in order to have the the "freedom" to pursue his interest in folklore.[2]

Randolph managed to amass his encyclopedic folklore collections by befriending the natives. Everywhere he went, he sought out the best tellers of tales, and he had a truly remarkable array of informants, not merely in a few locations, but in town after town all over the Ozarks. Because he was well-known and conversant with the values and attitudes of the hill people, he was able to gain their confidence wherever he went. Where did he do his collecting? Listen to his own words—and to the prose rhythms of a writer steeped in oral tradition:

Such stories were told in lonely cabins, beside little stills in dark hollows, around midnight campfires on the ridges. I listened to story-tellers in taverns and village stores, on the courthouse steps, at the mill while our corn was a-grinding, beneath the arbors where backwoods Christians congregate. Several of my best pieces were recorded in

a house of mourning, when we sat up all night to keep cats away from the corpse.[3]

Perhaps the only wonder greater than the number of informants Randolph had was the breadth of his collections. Not only did he collect folktales and tall stories ("windies" as the natives called them), but he compiled a four volume edition of folk songs, a volume on superstitions, and a book on Ozark dialect.

Randolph recorded thousands of expressions and words which have lost currency and are now rarely heard. Language in the Ozarks was rich in metaphor and suggestion. A native might say that the weather was so cold that the wolves were "eating sheep just for the wool"; or a man might define himself as being so drunk "that I had to hold on to the grass before I could lean ag'in the ground!"[4] For the outsider who, at times, is confused by Ozark speech, Randolph's book on the subject can offer clarifications: the word "evening" means the time from noon to sunset in the Ozarks (and not "after dark" as in the rest of the country); or "I don't care to," used in response to an offer or request is often misinterpreted as a negative response by outsiders—though it means "I don't mind if I do," or to put it more simply "yes." And if an tourist hears a radio announcer say "the temperature has fell," Randolph's book offers general explanations of such unusual verb forms and their history.

It was Randolph's obvious down home qualities which enabled him to get so much information. And it is clear to anyone who studies his collections that his genuine love for what he was doing and for the people from whom he was collecting makes his material so valuable. He did not sit for hours on a porch just so that he could record a tale; he sat and chatted because he enjoyed the company. The friends he made just happened to be the great story tellers. Again, let us listen to his own words:

The Ozark Mountain region is a strange land, and few outsiders know anything about it. The people who live in the Ozarks are not like country folk elsewhere, and city dwellers do not understand them. Tourists who speed along our highways see men lounging about, so they say that the hillfolk are idle and shiftless. But the truth is that it does not require much time to make a living here. The hillman's material wants are few, and competition is not too keen. A backwoodsman can get everything he needs, and still have more leisure than townsfolk allow themselves for relaxation. When a city slicker takes a holiday, he goes somewhere and does something strenuous or debilitating. But the Ozarker just sits down, and talks with his neighbors. He likes to crack old jokes and tell old stories. It is a kind of recreation that urban people seem unable to enjoy nowadays.[5]

But how he became an insider is only half the story of Vance Randolph's success. However much he may have enjoyed relaxing on a porch or fishing and hunting with friends, lots of people did that in the Ozark hills without recording the folklore. Vance Randolph also had a burning desire to preserve something he knew would be lost if he did not make the effort. And that desire came from being a "furriner," an outsider.

Randolph received his training in the academic world. Ironically, being educated in the second decade of the twentieth century meant being influenced by thinkers who had little to do with the remote Ozark hills. On university campuses in those days, discussion and debates centered on the theories of writers like Freud, Marx, and Darwin—and Randolph was, to some extent at least, influenced by each.

Although Randolph never finished high school, he earned a bachelor's degree from the local college (now Pittsburg State University) before enrolling in a master's degree program at Clark University in Worcester, Massachusetts. Clark may seem to be a rather obscure name in universities now, but when Randolph attended, it had developed a national reputation for its graduate school. Part of its fame derived from the fact that it was the University to which Sigmund Freud (and his colleague Carl Jung) came to lecture in 1909, Freud's only appearance in the United States. Though Randolph attended the University several years later in 1914-15, he majored in psychology and wrote his master's thesis on

dreams; Freud, of course, had published his seminal work on the *Interpretation of Dreams* in 1900.

The Marxian influence shows in Randolph's attraction to socialism. In 1917, he began writing for the country's most widely read socialist publication, the weekly *Appeal to Reason*. While it is easy to assume now—with the collapse of Communism in the Soviet Union and eastern Europe—that putting faith in Marx or socialist ideas is ill-advised, one must remember that socialism had many adherents in the United States earlier in the century. Randolph always identified with the overworked and underpaid coal miners in the Pittsburg, Kansas area; and the abuses of the sweat factories of the nineteenth century—in which children might be required to work twelve or more hours a day—had not yet been forgotten. Randolph met and admired Eugene Debs, a socialist who was on the presidential ballot five times. In 1912 when Woodrow Wilson won the election with 6.2 million votes, Debs received almost 900,000 as a minor party candidate—an indication of just how widespread the attraction to socialism was.

And the influence of Darwin turns up too. In fact, one of the short books Randolph churned out was a volume entitled the *ABC of Evolution*, one of a series of ABC texts he wrote—the rough equivalent of modern Cliff's notes. The text is not important in itself, although it demonstrates that Randolph was conversant in a subject not central to his pursuits. What is important is that it shows how the study of science helped to develop his later diligent and thorough habits in collecting folklore. He wrote, "The painstaking methods of the laboratory man of today, his infinite attention to minute detail, are perhaps largely due to the evolutionary conception of the importance of little things."[6] From scientists like Darwin, Randolph learned of the significance of collecting seemingly unimportant details and recording them with a high degree of accuracy.

These disparate influences account in great measure for Randolph's achievements as a collector of folklore. Scientific study taught him to amass scores of specific details before making generalizations and enabled him to become a magnificent synthesizer: he could study a difficult and convoluted subject and reduce its complexity to clear, precise statements. From Freud, psychology, and anthropology, he not only developed a curiosity about human behavior, but he learned that "primitive" did not mean "simple."[7] And from Marx and the socialists, he found his identity with the common man, or perhaps it might be more accurate to say that he found the theorists appealing because he had already cultivated that sympathy for the downtrodden while a youngster in Pittsburg, Kansas.

By his own words, Randolph made it clear that he considered his work to be important; he did not simply record jokes because they were funny. He once said to Clay Anderson, editor of *The Ozarks Mountaineer* that "Everything that I wrote about the Ozarks, I took seriously."[8] In fact, one of the great disappointments of Randolph's life was not being accepted into a Ph.D. program at Columbia University in New York City. He applied, hoping to study under the anthropologist Franz Boas who had achieved worldwide fame for his work among Eskimos and northwest coast Indians. Boas was a pioneer who sought to treat social disciplines like the hard sciences by utilizing statistical methods. But Boas simply would not accept the idea that a study of isolated white hillfolk in the Ozarks merited the same scientific treatment as did "primitive" peoples.[9]

Randolph, therefore, never became the anthropologist he hoped to become. Though he eventually entered a Ph.D. program in psychology at the University of Kansas, he dropped out without earning the degree. The desire to do work which would be recognized as significant to anthropology, however, probably accounts for Randolph's selection of the subtitle of his first full length book on the hill people, *The Ozarks: An American Survival of Primitive Society*.[10] Despite his growing list of publications, Randolph's contributions were ignored by the academic community for years. But his collections were too good to be overlooked, and recognition did eventually come. In one of those strange ironies which seem to rectify injustices, Randolph was to have five of his major texts published by Columbia University Press, starting with *Ozark Superstitions* in 1947, then followed in the 50's by four collections of folktales. And in 1951 he was awarded an honorary doctorate degree of letters by the University of Arkansas at Fayetteville.

Randolph succeeded because he brought together two qualities: first and foremost, he was a friend and confidant to his informants, the hill people; but he also was a scholar, a prodigious writer who was profoundly influenced by the rigors of scientific scholarship. We owe the best and most extensive collection of folk materials ever made in the United States by a single individual to this extremely rare combination.

I think it is only a fair tribute to his contribution to give Vance the last word:

Well, time marches on, and you can't turn back the clock. Literacy has its advantages, electric lights are easy on the eyes, contact with tourists is profitable, concrete highways are convenient, and travel is broadening. A few years more and the younger hillfolk will be thinking and talking pretty much like conventional Americans elsewhere. To those of us who knew the old timers, the transition is not without a touch of melancholy and regret. We shall miss the storytellers. Their passing closes a romantic and colorful chapter in the history of our country.[11]

Frank Reuter

Notes:

1 Vance Randolph, *Ozark Superstitions* (New York: Columbia Press, 1947), p. 4. A Dover reprint of this book is available under the title, *Ozark Magic and Folklore*.

2 For information about Randolph's life, I am indebted to Robert Cochran's excellent biography, *Vance Randolph: An Ozark Life* (Urbana: University of Illinois Press, 1985).

3 Vance Randolph, *The Devil's Pretty Daughter* (New York: Columbia University Press, 1955), p. xiii. As Randolph pointed out in *Ozark Superstitions*, Ozark natives had a fear that if a cat "should so much as sniff at the corpse, some unspeakable calamity would overtake the whole family." p. 313

4 Vance Randolph and George P. Wilson, *Down in the Holler: A Gallery of Ozark Folk Speech* (Norman: University of Oklahoma Press, 1953), pps. 188-89.

5 Vance Randolph, *Sticks in the Knapsack and Other Ozark Folk Tales* (New York: Columbia University Press, 1958), p. xv

6 Vance Randolph, *The ABC of Evolution* (New York: Vanguard Press, 1926), p. 3.

7 In his Introduction to *Ozark Superstitions*, for example, Vance Randolph wrote that "The hillman is secretive and sensitive beyond anything that the average city dweller can imagine, but he isn't simple. His mind moves in a tremendously involved system of signs and omens and esoteric auguries." (p. 3)

8 Vance Randolph, *Vance Randolph in the Ozarks* (Branson, Missouri: The Ozarks Mountaineer, 1981), p. 3.

9 For an interesting treatment of this issue, see Cochran's biography, pps. 47-48.

10 The book was published by Vanguard Press in New York City in 1931.

11 *The Devil's Pretty Daughter*, p. xvi.

Vance Randolph

A Foster Son of Galena

I met Vance Randolph by chance in Galena during the early 1930's. A fellow newspaper reporter, Mildred Criger, and I were forced to take a week's unpaid vacation. It was, after all, the Great Depression. We decided we would spend the time—and very little money—in Galena, obtaining free transportation to and fro via the *Springfield Press* car which delivered papers there. We could rent a cabin cheaply with access to a small swimming pool. Mildred didn't swim, but the pool was the right size for my aquatic skill of one-two-three sink.

Congressman Dewey Short called us on the first day and said that Vance Randolph and his wife were boarders at the big white house just up the hill from the pool. Randolph had recently published *The Ozarks: An American Survival of Primitive Society*, generating considerable publicity in the big city newspapers—but not all that much in the local media.

Considering that in his later years Vance received an honorary doctorate from the University of Arkansas, had a state-wide Randolph Day and honors from here and there, it is hard to realize that in his early days, he was not exactly the idol of our area. Businessmen had not yet realized that there was money in folklore. Some folks, in fact, thought Vance was making fun of the local citizens and communities.

I decided to toddle up and interview Randolph at first opportunity. My motive was ulterior. If I could turn in a few stories, I might be able to collect part of my salary. As I was taking my dip the next morning, I noticed a tall, broad-shouldered man lugging suitcases from the big white house and stowing them in a Ford coupe. I climbed hastily out of the pool. My prey was about to flee in his coupe. My preparations for the interview were simple. Since the path was rocky, I slipped my shoes on, and I removed my bathing cap so I could hear any pearls that fell from Randolph's lips.

Using my basketball technique, I cut him off

neatly from the entrance to the house and said I was Nancy Nance of the *Springfield Press*; was he Vance Randolph? He admitted it but said, rather pointedly, that he was at the moment preparing to go to California to work for MGM on a screen version of The Shepherd of the Hills. At this moment a petite Jenny-Wren woman popped out the front door, and Vance introduced me to his wife, Marie. He added that this was the first time he had ever been interviewed by a reporter wearing a bathing suit. I did not reply, thereby probably giving the impression that this was my customary working garb.

I had to borrow a pencil and paper from Randolph so I could jot down his plans. The paper got a little soggy so I wound up with a very very short article. The Randolphs were obviously in a hurry but, hoping to improve my image, I remarked that I had heard a great deal about him and I was looking forward to reading his next book. I saw no point in telling him that I had not read his first, nor that my newspaper did not have a book review department. We shook hands. I handed back the pencil and, clutching my soggy slip of paper, trotted down the hill.

I only managed to write two paragraphs about that first interview so I was considerably surprised when I received a review copy of his next book, *Ozark Mountain Folks* in 1932. I wrote a small piece about it and sent him a note of thanks.

Soon after, the *Springfield Press* merged with the *Springfield News-Leader*, and along with virtually all of the Press staff I was, as they politely put it, "let go." I had been trying to do some free-lancing when Vance and Marie appeared at my door one day and invited me to lunch. Over the salad, he handed me a copy of his latest book, a boy's juvenile called *The Camp on Wildcat Creek*. He suggested I read it and write a juvenile for girls, which he would try to sell. He left me his book to read as an example.

With this expert, detailed advice, I sat down at

my typewriter and wrote *Girl Scouts in the Ozarks* in a month. The setting for my juvenile was Dewey Short's Camp Wawasse, a series of little cabins overlooking the James River. After all, Dewey had told me to use the camp any time I wanted.

When I informed Vance that the book was ready for him, he seemed surprised, not only that I wrote it, but that I did it in such a short time. Vance sold the book to Knopf. Shortly before he died Vance told me that he had never dreamed I would actually write the book. He had suggested writing books to a lot of people, but none had ever done it before.

Vance always referred to my venture into literature as "that awful time," and I can't think of a better phrase. It was the Great Depression and people just weren't buying books, especially juveniles. Everything that could go wrong did, so I finally left the literary field for the family business—trying to sell fresh flowers before they wilted. But not until after I had written *Camp Meeting Murders* for Vanguard Press, a novel which had both Vance's and my name on it. After I ceased writing, what had been a business arrangement turned into a lifelong friendship. I was never exactly sure why, but Vance once explained it to me in lucid terms. "A man's got to have someone to tell things to," he said, "and Gawd help me, I've picked you."

Of course, Vance had no outlet so he plugged away with his writing. Vance and his wife, Marie, had a kind of suite at the front of the second floor of Fannie Mathes' boarding house halfway up the hill overlooking Galena. Vance liked to tell people that Edgar Lee Masters had written a book on the big table he used as a desk. There was a bed in his study as well as one in the bedroom because Vance liked to write and correct his copy lying down. He had his papers stacked in piles all around him, and he propped a writing board on his stomach. He said that he had practiced writing slowly so that he would make less mistakes and write better. When I watched the turtle-like crawl of pencil or pen across the sheet of paper, each letter written carefully, I found it hard to see how he had turned out the volume of work that he did. Of course, he didn't have to rewrite anything.

His methodical style was perfectly suited to the Ozarks; in fact, Vance and Galena simply bonded. He liked the congenial easy pace of the town and county. He like the people and they liked him. The residents were proud of Galeny, as they called it, and of being Ozarkians. To them Vance was not a celebrity. He was just a fellow who wrote—like another resident, Otto Ernest Rayburn, author of a book about the Ozarks and publisher of monthly magazines filled with folklore.

Vance lived simply; he liked to boast that he could put all his worldly possessions in a suitcase, but he forgot to mention his precious tin trunks. One tin trunk contained his ballad collection. The other contained his store of Ozark folklore: jokes, superstitions, and folk stories, all neatly indexed.

In 1945 Vance developed heart trouble. Dr. Young managed to get him into the Veterans Hospital at Fayetteville, Arkansas. He improved and came back to Galena. Since his wife had died in 1937 and Fannie was unable to care for him, his old friend, Ralph Church of Pittsburg, and Church's wife, Frances, a nurse, came to his rescue. The Churches had recently bought a house in Eureka Springs and they took Vance there to share it with them. Vance's health improved again and in 1962 he moved to Fayetteville because he wanted to hear the lectures of a famous ballad collector. At the age of 70 he married Mary Celestia Parler, a professor at the University.

Meanwhile, the Galena he knew had changed. His old friends were nearly all gone. Fannie was dead and the comfortable big old white house had been destroyed by fire. But something of Vance remains. Years ago, looking at my small daughter, he once said, "I haven't got any children. But maybe on some dusty library shelf some of my books will be kept after I am gone."

There is a new library in Galena now. And there is a shelf of Vance's books, all autographed and not dusty. Nearly every one of these books contains names and material from Stone County. I think of them as Valentines to the town in which he lived—and to the people he loved.

Fern Nance Shumate

John G. Neihardt

A subdivision street name and a plaque in the parking lot of Koi Gardens Oriental Restaurant serve as small reminders that John G. Neihardt, nationally famous twentieth century poet, literary critic, and novelist, lived and wrote in Branson for more than two decades. Recognized through most of his lifetime as a literary giant, Neihardt's epic *Cycle of the West* continues to be admired and quoted by historians and well-known writers of the American West. In fact, when he was awarded an honorary doctorate by the University of Nebraska in 1917, others so honored at the same time included author Willa Cather and poet Ezra Pound—in addition to President Theodore Roosevelt and General John Pershing.

John Neihardt in 1923.
(Reproduction courtesy of Lois Holman)
The plaque in Branson which commemorates Neihardt.
(Photo courtesy of Kathleen Van Buskirk)

Born in Sharpsburg, Illinois, in 1881, Neihardt moved with his mother to Nebraska at the age of ten. An avid reader of classical literature—which would influence his own writing—Neihardt entered Nebraska Normal College in Wayne at the age of thirteen, taking a campus job to pay for his tuition. He graduated in 1897 but, for lack of a four dollar fee, did not receive a diploma.

In 1900, after two years of teaching school, John moved with his mother to Bancroft, Nebraska, a trading center for the Omaha Indian reservation and frontier farmers. While his mother took in boarders, John began his long career of writing and editing for newspapers. Here he developed his life-long interest in Indians, often camping out on the Omaha reservation where he shared Indian pastimes and studied their history, rituals, and language.

Through the next dozen years, while working for various Nebraska papers, Neihardt also wrote short stories and poems, many of which were published in national magazines. His first two collections, *The Lonesome Trail*, a book of short stories, and *A Bundle of Myrrh*, a collection of lyric poems, were published in 1907.

Though Neihardt was a small man—just an inch over five feet and slender of build—he was strong and agile and loved the challenge of adventure. In 1908 at the age of twenty-seven, he and a young companion traveled down the Missouri River by boat from its headwaters in Montana to the Mississippi. Neihardt was an excellent oarsman and swimmer, a dead shot with a rifle, a vigorous and tireless worker, and an enthusiastic hunter and outdoorsman.

Always intent on collecting material for his writing, Neihardt traveled the western mountains, plains, and rivers, listening to yarns of the old days spun by sons of the trappers and river men who were the first "pioneers" of the West. He sat by Indian campfires and heard ancient warriors and their womenfolk speak of their lost world, and of "the great wind" which many Indians, in the late 1800's, believed would miraculously sweep away the white intruders, allowing a resurgence of their tribal culture and dignity.

While collecting the lore of the Indians and frontiersmen, Neihardt also searched documents in state historical societies. He further acquainted himself with western locales from pictures, maps, and topographic materials, and sought out experts to learn of the geology of the region and of the native shrubs, trees, and grasses.

In 1908, while Neihardt was working for the *Omaha World-Herald*, he married Mona Martinsen, a young sculptress who had studied with Rodin in Paris and was also educated in voice, violin, and art. Having read his 1907 collection of poems, she initiated an extended correspondence with the poet. When she came to Omaha to see him, Neihardt met her at the train, a marriage license in his pocket. The couple had four children, three daughters and a son.

In 1912, Neihardt began to concentrate on *A Cycle of the West,* a work he estimated he could complete by the time he was sixty. He also moved his family to Minnesota, where he had been offered fifty dollars a week by the *Minneapolis Journal* to write literary criticism. Though he held this job for eight years, Neihardt, soon realizing that the city contained too many distractions and that his work on the Cycle was not progressing satisfactorily, took his family back to Bancroft. There, within three years, he completed the first book of the Cycle, *A Saga of Hugh Glass,* a tale of the famous mountain man who, after being mauled by a grizzly bear, saved his own life by crawling two hundred miles across the high prairie.

Increasing recognition brought Neihardt many lecture requests, leading to a new facet of the poet's career, one which would help provide for his family through the many years he worked on the Cycle. On the lecture stage, Neihardt's mop of unruly golden hair, startling blue eyes, expressive face, and resonant baritone voice held audiences spellbound—whether he lec-tured on poetry or read from his dynamic, often haunting epic verse. He always lectured to packed houses.

By the time *The Song of Three Friends*, the second book of the Cycle, was published in early 1919, the Nebraska climate was causing recurring respiratory problems for Neihardt. In the fall of 1920, a few months after the Neihardts' third daughter, Alice, was born, the family moved to Missouri, to a hilltop house an easy walk from downtown Branson.

The following year, the Nebraska Legislature passed a bill naming John G. Neihardt "Poet Laureate of Nebraska and the Prairies." The poet returned to Nebraska to accept the honor, but declined offers which would have taken the Neihardts back there to live. Whether lecturing, researching, or traveling, Neihardt always felt drawn home to Branson for the quiet which allowed him to write. Although he became famous as a writer, he was always a family man. Despite long absences on lecture tours, Neihardt loved the companionship of his children. He taught them to swim in Roark Creek down the hill behind the house. He romped with them in the woods and took them camping.

By 1925, Neihardt had *The Song of the Indian Wars* ready for publication. However, his writing slowed on the fourth part of the epic, *The Song of the Messiah*, because of the hard days of the Depression. To support the household, he made extended lecture trips, and spent considerable time in St. Louis where the *Post-Dispatch* welcomed his literary criticisms and book reviews.

Neihardt made two trips to the Pine Ridge Reservation in South Dakota in 1930, with the permission of the Secretary of the Interior and the Indian Commissioner. On the first trip (with son Sigurd as his companion) he learned more about the Oglala Sioux and the Battle of Wounded Knee; on the second (with daughters Hilda and Enid, who served as stenographer) he recorded the memories and philosophy of Black Elk, the aging leader of the tribe.

The materials he collected provided the information and insights Neihardt needed to complete the

Messiah, which was published in 1936. The poet was sixty in 1941 when *The Song of Jedediah,* the last work in his Cycle, was published. Though the last volume received much critical acclaim, Neihardt's goal of seeing all five epics collected in one volume was postponed because of World War II.

During the war years, the publishing business was at a standstill, and the lecture circuit was dominated by war and politics. Faced with a mounting financial crisis and plagued by respiratory and eye problems, Neihardt, with his wife Mona, moved first to St. Louis and then in 1943 to Chicago where Mona took a job with *Time* magazine and John became Director of Information for the Bureau of Indian Affairs.

In 1944, the Bureau sent Neihardt, accompanied by Hilda, back to the Pine Ridge Reservation to collect more stories and lore for a cultural history of the Oglala Sioux. Before Neihardt could do anything with the information he collected, however, his work with the Bureau was reduced to standby status. The materials he collected became his personal property and served as the basis for his last book, a novel called *When the Tree Flowers,* published in 1952.

Rather than return to live in Branson, which had grown and no longer offered the solitude and peace the Neihardts had treasured, the couple bought a farm north of Columbia, Missouri in 1948. Neihardt began a new career as Poet in Residence and lecturer at the University of Missouri, where recently he had been awarded an Honorary Doctorate. His classes were phenomenally successful: Advanced Poetry Writing, Critical Essay Writing, and Epic America, a course intended to acquaint undergraduates with *A Cycle of the West.* The latter course dealt with the focus of Neihardt's writing

career—the heroic spirit engendered in the pioneers who had been cut loose from their social roots, and the agonies of the native American people as they were subdued by the westward encroachment on their lands. Neihardt's lectures and poetry readings were filmed and still educate and enthrall classes today.

John and Mona Neihardt have been gone for many years now; she died in 1958, he in 1973 at the age of 92. But *A Cycle of the West,* which earned the poet recognition as "an American Homer," and many of Neihardt's other books of poetry and prose, are still to be found in book stores and libraries all over the world.

Kathleen Van Buskirk

Rose O'Neill

Rose O'Neill maintained homes in New York City, Connecticut, and Italy, but Bonniebrook, the rustic mansion she built for her family in a secluded valley north of Branson, was the place she called home. Here, among the tangled woods along a spring-fed brook, her fertile imagination made up Kewpies, elves, and friendly monsters.

When asked where she got her artistic talent, famed artist and illustrator Rose O'Neill, replied, "All I know is that when I picked up my pencil, there it was!" Although she achieved a measure of success as a writer and sculptor, Rose is best remembered as the designer and creator of the cherubic Kewpie dolls.

Cecelia Rose O'Neill was born June 25, 1874 in Wilkes-Barre, Pennsylvania, daughter of William Patrick and Alice Asenath Cecelia Smith O'Neill. In 1877, the O'Neill family moved west to Battle Creek, Nebraska, and then to Omaha, where her father operated a bookstore for several years.

While still a school girl, Rose entered a drawing contest sponsored by the *Omaha World-Herald* and won a five dollar gold piece. The judges, questioning whether a child of fourteen could have produced the drawing she submitted, were amazed when she again drew parts of her entry as they looked on. Shortly after that contest, several of her illustrations were bought by local newspapers.

Rose was nineteen when her parents sent her to New York City where she lived at the convent of the Sisters of St. Regis and studied art. Through the following three years, her illustrations were purchased by *Harper's Weekly, Collier's,* and other magazines.

In 1893, shortly after Rose went to New York, the Patrick O'Neill family moved to a secluded tract of land on Bear Creek in Taney County, Missouri. An abandoned two-room "dogtrot" cabin became the home of Patrick, his wife (affectionately called Meemie), and

Rose's brothers and sisters: John Hugh, Mary Illene (Lee), James, Callista, and Clarence.

The following year, Rose visited her family in Taney County. In an illustrated story which appeared in the *St. Louis Post-Dispatch* on December 5, 1937, she described her introduction to the place which became her lifelong sanctuary. She was met at the train in Springfield by her father and her two sisters. The fifty mile journey by wagon to their Bear Creek home took two days. Rose, newly affluent, wore a plumed hat and boa, and carried a parasol. Her dress had an enormous bell skirt which repeatedly tangled with the wagon's wheel. Beneath the dress were a silk ruffled petticoat, lacy chemise, panties, and garters, and a tightly cinched pink corset and corset cover.

The driver of the rough, horse-drawn wagon was a crusty hillman. Rose wrote, "The horses were old and unimpassioned. The driver caressed them once in a while with a fragile branch, but relied mainly on the power of verbal persuasion. And oh, such verbs! And other parts of speech! And that gentle casual drawl.

"'Buck, you low-lookin' crawlified son of a terbacker worm! Scat! Get along thar! Pete, you fluffy fly-blown, tough-hided ornery critter! I'll pull up a tree in a minute an' wa'r ye to a shoe-string!'"

An overnight stop was made in the Riverdale-Highlandville area at the cabin of Maw McNabb, two rooms with a covered dog-trot porch between. During the night, Rose awakened to see Maw and her daughter creep into the room being occupied by the O'Neill girls to examine, by the light of a candle, the citified clothes heaped on a chair.

Deeply impressed by the wild countryside, Rose wrote of her journey's conclusion, "The next day we went deeper and deeper into the woods. I called it the 'tangle,' and my extravagant heart was tangled in it for good. After crossing Bear Creek thirty-two times we found ourselves on the same side (as the feller said). The Forest Enchanted closed us in, and suddenly ahead of us stood Meemie and the other children by the brook." The delighted artist immediately began planning a large new house for her family in the little valley. That house, built between 1904 and 1910, was named Bonniebrook by the O'Neills.

In 1896, two years after her first stay in the Ozarks, Rose married Gray Latham, a marriage which ended in divorce in 1901. A year later she married editor and popular writer Harry Leon Wilson. With Harry, Rose lived in New York City and Connecticut, traveled extensively in Europe, and rented the Villa Narcissus on Italy's Isle of Capri, where they entertained Booth Tarkington and many other famous writers. However, in 1908, after much emotional turmoil, Rose fled to the Ozarks and divorced Leon Wilson.

In the tranquillity of Bonniebrook, she met "in a dream" the elf-like babies she named Kewpies. Rose O'Neill's illustrations of children had long been popular. When the first Kewpie drawings appeared, in late 1909, many well-known editors approached her to draw the cunning creatures for their magazines. She was hard pressed to keep up with the increasing demands. Little did she dream that people all over the world would take her precious Kewpies to their hearts and cherish them for a lifetime.

Rose O'Neill created, in clay, the first Kewpie dolls in 1912. These dolls, carefully protected by copyright, went on the market a year later, manufactured in Germany. Rose's younger sister Callista, who had been studying art in France and Italy, took on the task of overseeing and managing the business of making Kewpie dolls in Germany, Belgium, and France. The earliest Kewpie dolls came in nine sizes, each doll made of high quality bisque.

In the early 1920's, cloth-bodied, cuddly Kewpies were being made in American factories; in 1925, Rose created a second elfin character, Scootles, a lovable tot dubbed "the Baby Tourist."

Royalties from Kewpie doll sales poured in and her illustrations were always in demand. Whether residing in a renovated mansion she called Carabas Castle, at Westport, Connecticut, a studio on New York's fashionable Washington Square, or the Villa Narcissus, which she bought in the late 1920's, Rose took her work with her. Frequently she visited Bonniebrook. On one such visit she wrote in her diary, "I love this spot better than any place on earth. Here I have done my best work, and here I want to live out the rest of my life, to die and be buried next to my brother in the little cemetery."

During the time Rose was associated with writers and artists, she adopted a mode of dress which set her apart from her Ozark neighbors, a one-piece Greek style mantle, always flamboyant in color, and complemented by sandals and a long golden chain or necklace. Her clothes contrasted strangely with those of small town women and the farm wives who came to Branson on a Saturday for weekly shopping. Yet here most people accepted her as she was, an attractive woman, warm and caring, a free spirit.

In 1937, Rose O'Neill came back home to stay. In her papers she described her return to Bonniebrook: "On a moonlight night a wolf howls on the back ridge, an owl hoots in the deep timber and the brook gurgles its song of peace. This is a good place to unbutton."

Always energetic, imaginative, and full of new ideas, when she was sixty-five Rose designed the Chinese elf, Ho Ho. "Year by year," she said, "as the world gets less and less funny, the thought gets clearer in my mind. So he is a little clown Buddha, the wisdom of ages, finding its last words in the supreme wisdom of laughter." Ho Ho was molded, cast, and painted at Bonniebrook, and was shipped by the boxcar load to destinations throughout the nation.

Rose suffered a stroke, and recovered from it, sometime before she wrote her last words for an autobiography in the fall of 1943. (The book was never published.) The final entry speaks of springtime:

It is raining on all the roofs at Bonniebrook. In my tree-high studio there is a great clatter. The hills and the thick trees with their swelling buds seem to press closer. The brook is full and roaring. There has been lightning with thunder—my kind—metallic. ...It is Spring. Even where the grey limestone skeleton of the earth shows through, there are wild flowers. And there are wildflowers beginning all down the valley and on the hills. Sap is running in the branches.... I oddly regret that

> There are few who live, alas
> And they are far from here—
> Who knew how young and dear I was
> When I was young and dear.

Rose laid her pen down and slumped back in her chair, overtaken by another stroke, the first of a series that would claim her life. Taken to a Springfield hospital on November 15, 1943, she died five months later, on April 6, 1944 at the Springfield home of a nephew. Rose O'Neill was buried in the tiny plot by the stream at Bonniebrook. A redbud tree was beginning to show pink, and yellow cowslip and other wildflowers bloomed beneath the greening trees. Only a low, hand-laid wall marked her grave, between her mother and brother Jamie.

The cemetery where Rose is buried has, in recent years, been cleared by Bonniebrook Historical Society volunteers, who have built a stone wall and placed a wrought iron fence around the family graves.

In 1947, while Clarence O'Neill was still living at Bonniebrook, fire destroyed the house and its contents. For decades the foundation lay crumbling, hidden by tangled weeds and bushes. In the mid-1970's, the Bonniebrook Historical Society was formed by Rose O'Neill admirers, with the intent of rebuilding the house. The owners of the O'Neill property, Clay and Jean Cantwell, leased it to the Society so the house could be rebuilt; and in 1984 the homestead was placed on the National Register of Historic Places. The reconstruction is well underway.

The house exterior, completed in early 1992, faithfully follows old pictures and descriptions of the original. A caretaker now resides on the premises. The inside has been altered somewhat to meet modern construction standards for buildings open to the public. Much support for the building effort comes from the hundreds of members of the International Rose O'Neill Club, formed in 1968. The club's three-day Kewpiesta,

The reconstructed Bonniebrook.
(Photo by Kathleen Van Buskirk)

held each April, brings to Branson Kewpie collectors and Rose O'Neill admirers from all parts of the nation and several foreign countries.

The renewed Bonniebrook will serve as a museum, with Rose's drawings, writings, and memorabilia on display, surrounded by furnishings and decor as much as possible like those the O'Neill family enjoyed. The third floor studio and the library crammed with classics will again greet visitors as they did when Rose and her family lived there.

Bonniebrook will keep museum hours. For an appointment, large groups will need to contact:

The Bonniebrook Historical Society
P.O. Box 263
Branson, MO 65616

To reach Bonniebrook from Branson, follow U.S. 65 north approximately 10 miles, turning off to the right (east) just north of the Bear Creek bridge. Follow the two lane county road a half mile, and turn left at the Bonniebrook parking lot sign.

Fern Angus

Section IV
A Thread of Violence

For over a century the lawlessness of the frontier has been an integral part of America's "western" literature. Normally, we think of such violence as taking place in the untamed cattle towns of the high prairies or the gold camps of the Rocky Mountains. But much of the violence associated with the frontier originated right here in Southwest Missouri. What is generally thought to be the first street shootout, for example, took place not in Dodge City, Kansas, or Tombstone, Arizona, but in Springfield, Missouri, when in 1865 Wild Bill Hickock killed a man named David Tutt over a dispute dealing with a watch. The date is significant because the shootout occurred in the year the Civil War ended. And it was the Civil War which made Southwest Missouri a lawless no man's land.

Pre-Civil War violence started in bloody Kansas as pro and anti-slavery advocates used intimidation and bloodshed to try to drive off settlers who opposed their views. Once the war started, the hatreds spilled over into continuous border violence in southern Missouri and northern Arkansas. Although a number of major battles took place in the two states, neither side wished to expend their limited resources on the frontier. Because of this, irregular armies began operating in the area. The most notorious perhaps was Quantrill's Raiders, a group of cutthroats who terrorized Missouri and Kansas during the Civil War. In fact, they were so violent and unscrupulous that the Confederates, after originally encouraging Quantrill, would not formally commission him or support his activities. Though Quantrill was killed, others members of his gang went on to lives of violence after the war was over—characters like Frank and Jesse James and the Younger brothers.

In the southwest Missouri and northwest Arkansas area any number of unscrupulous characters used the war as an excuse to prey on the defenseless women and children who were left behind when their men went off to fight. These ruthless gangsters, who came to be known as bushwhackers, used the chaos of the war as a cover for their crimes. Of these, the infamous Alf Bolin, the subject of the first essay in this section, was one of the worst.

It is almost impossible for us to imagine the total devastation which prevailed in the no man's land of the Arkansas-Missouri border during the Civil War. Family loyalties were commonly split, passions ran high, and murder and thievery were commonplace. As the war dragged on and towns on both sides of the border were occupied by alternating armies in succession, the devastation to the region accelerated. Towns like Forsyth, Missouri and Berryville, Arkansas were put to the torch. Families left the area by moving further north or south, seeking shelter not only from the opposing armies but from the bands of outlaws.

The war created radical dislocations even for years after it formally ended. In the vacuum of authority which followed the end of the war, many unsavory men seized control of civil authority. Justice was virtually non-existent, with a resultant lawlessness which plagued the area. When murder after murder went unpunished, vigilante organizations like the Bald Knobbers came into existence to impose law and order— and quickly established their own new brand of lawlessness.

While the years finally healed most of the wounds associated with the rift between Yankee and Reb, the Ozark region has continued to be a place which because of its relatively remote and inaccessible nature has lured individuals escaping from the law. Therefore, we include essays on visits to the area by the infamous outlaws Bonnie and Clyde, and the notorious gangster Jake Fleagle, who attempted to hide away from the law here in Southwest Missouri after being involved in several bank robberies and murders. The section ends with the ironic story of Stone County's only documented legal hanging.

Alf Bolin's Reign of Terror

During the Civil War, civilians struggling to survive in the "no man's land" along the Missouri-Arkansas border cowered in fear of the onslaughts perpetrated by outlaw gangs. Victims of these gangs called the gang members "guerrillas" and "bushwhackers." Guerrillas were irregulars who usually sympathized with either the Confederate or the Union cause. Bushwhackers were less likely to be driven by patriotism; they were usually nothing but bandits who used guerrilla tactics to plunder the unprotected—the elderly or the wives and children of men who had gone to fight on one side or the other. Some bushwhackers were out to wreak vengeance, punishing individuals or groups who had injured or simply crossed them at some point. But most were driven by greed.

Historians claim that the White River Valley's most vicious bushwhacker was Alfred Bolin. Those who lived to describe Alf Bolin said he sported a chest-length red beard and wore a coonskin hat over his long red hair. He was a tall, slim man with a quiet, somewhat anti-social personality. A psychiatrist might diagnose Bolin's personality as psychopathic.

Early in the Civil War, Bolin left his home in Stone County and went down to the Big Bend area of the White River in southern Taney County where he organized a gang of cutthroats. At times, his band ranged in size from two to a rumored fifty, although the number was probably closer to twenty.

Bolin led his men on a reign of terror that cut a swath from Ozark and Sparta in Missouri to the area around Crooked Creek, Arkansas. When he came in contact with frightened citizens, Bolin often bragged about how many people he had killed personally—at times he claimed to have murdered nineteen, at other times he said he had killed forty. Because record-keeping was almost non-existent with the region in the grip of the Civil War, historians have difficulty verifying whether he was merely fantasizing or if he killed as many as he claimed.

Most of Bolin's victims seem to have been hapless individuals who wandered across the brigand's path. One, an eighty-year-old man, was shot to death as he forded the White River enroute to Christian County with a wagonload of corn for starving women and children. Another, a twelve-year-old Roark Creek boy, did nothing more provocative than climb a fence to feed his own horse.

Although Bolin supposedly embraced neither side in the war, he did boast once that he had killed thirty Federal soldiers. Union officials alleged that Bolin and his gang assassinated seven members of the Sixth Missouri Regiment. Two Union soldiers Bolin killed supposedly lie in unmarked graves under a small clump of cedars near the base of a mountain about a mile and a half north of Murder Rocks, Bolin's favorite ambush site.

Murder Rocks, sometimes referred to as Bolin's Rocks, stand along the west side of the old Carrollton-Forsyth Road, now designated as Taney County's JJ Highway. The rocks are visible today, but because the roadbed has been raised, they look less menacing. In 1863, Murder Rocks loomed above the road, high enough to conceal a lurking bandit on horseback. Their location also afforded a broad view of the valley, allowing Bolin and his highwaymen to spot approaching travelers. From this vantage point, Bolin's gang surprised unwary soldiers heading home, relieving them of their weapons, ammunition, and probably their horses, too. The gang ransacked wagons filled with household goods, driven by women seeking sanctuary for their families across the Missouri-Arkansas border.

Finally, the federal government offered a five thousand dollar reward for the capture of Alf Bolin, dead or alive. By publicizing the reward, the government fed the greed of individuals foolhardy enough to try to capture the outlaw.

Shortly after the announcement, a stranger appeared at Murder Rocks. Bolin robbed the man, then invited him to join the band. That night, Bolin and his gang went to sleep, wrapped in blankets and sprawled around their campfire. Bolin awoke to find his new recruit bending over him, holding a large hunting

The Murder of Calvin Cloud

Most visitors to Ozark Mountain Country are introduced to the name Alf Bolin on the train ride at Silver Dollar City. Members of the "notorious Bolin gang" stage a mock holdup and entertain passengers with witty skits. What most visitors probably do not realize is that Alfred Bolin was a real outlaw, one of the most brutal in history. While he is known to have killed old men and young boys, perhaps the most dastardly act he ever committed was murdering a man by the name of Calvin Cloud.

Alfred Bolin's background was not ideal. Neither his troubled childhood nor his abandonment by his mother could have foreshadowed his life of crime. At the age of eleven, he was taken in by Calvin and Mary Jane Cloud who opened their hearts and home to him and reared him as one of their own. Bolin would eventually repay Calvin's charity with murder.

Calvin Cloud's death certificate attributes his murder to "brushwhackers," but in the oral tradition of Stone County the bloody act is ascribed directly to Bolin. Bolin and his gang, at the height of his vicious, blood-thirsty career, sought refuge one day at the home of Calvin and Mary Jane Cloud near McCall Bridge in Stone County. Alf, wearing a mask, demanded that Calvin supply him with food and guns. Calvin denied the request, an action which cost him his life. Bolin drew his gun and shot his surrogate father through the head. He then threatened to kill Mary Jane Cloud (who was pregnant) and her four children.

An important component of this story is that Calvin's wife, Mary Jane, could identify her husband's murderer, in spite of his mask, because she was familiar with his voice. Her familiarity with him also caused her to later be ordered to Ozark to make a positive identification of the deceased Bolin's head after it had been severed from his body by one Colbert Hays. According to tradition, she rode thirty miles on horseback though a winter storm to confirm the identification.

There are other traditions and stories: that Bolin was raised by a man named Bilyeau, for example. Perhaps he was taken in by several different families at different times, but the conviction in Stone County is that Bolin was the lowest form of an ingrate—a man who, without compunction, killed his benefactor.

Fern Angus

knife. Bolin kicked the stranger in the face. Then he stripped him and branded a message on the man's bare chest with a hot poker. Bolin tied his attacker onto a burro and sent him back to town, his naked chest bearing this message: "I found Alf Bolin."

For safety, Bolin started sleeping in a cave, a site he kept secret even from his men. One night, the wily gang leader suspected that one of his troops was tracking him, probably looking for the loot that Bolin allegedly stashed in the cave. Bolin ambushed his pursuer and killed him. The next morning, his men awoke to find their *compadre* hanging from a tree by his own belt.

The five thousand dollar reward offer eventually triggered a successful effort. One of the prisoners in the stockade at Springfield was Robert Foster, a

Confederate sympathizer. Foster and his wife lived in a double log cabin in the Layton Pinery, three miles southwest of Murder Rocks. Since he was in jail and Bolin and his gang were operating so close to his cabin, Foster worried about his wife. Living so near the bushwhacker's hideout, the Fosters felt constrained to be neighborly to Bolin. On several occasions the gang leader had dropped in and "invited" Mrs. Foster to prepare him a meal.

Foster approached Union officials. If they would parole him and bring his wife up to Springfield, he would reveal Bolin's whereabouts. The Federals jumped at the chance and ordered Zachariah E. Thomas, 22, of Keokuk, Iowa, to capture Bolin.

Zack Thomas, a corporal from the Iowa Volunteer Cavalry, saddled his horse and rode to Forsyth. He slept that night in the tent of another Iowan. The morning of February 1, 1863, he donned a confiscated Rebel uniform and rode fourteen miles south to the Foster home.

Thomas convinced an uneasy Mrs. Foster to ride over to Bolin's hideout. Mrs. Foster was to tell Bolin that the Union had paroled her husband to the Springfield city limits and she would be permitted to join him. To lure the gang leader to her cabin, she offered to sell him some of their goods and make him a good deal on their cattle out on open range.

Three hours later, Mrs. Foster returned home. Bolin would stop by at 10 o'clock the next morning.

Early on February 2, 1863, Thomas dressed in the Rebel uniform, tucked his Colt army pistol in an inside jacket pocket, and climbed the ladder to the Fosters' loft. He heard Bolin rap on the door. Through a crack in the floorboard, Thomas saw Mrs. Foster open the door. Bolin cautiously scrutinized the cabin before entering. Once inside, he stashed his rifle in a corner.

Bolin and Mrs. Foster conversed until Thomas accidentally made a noise. Bolin leaped to his feet and demanded to know who was upstairs. Mrs. Foster explained that a Rebel soldier, on his way home to Arkansas, had fallen ill and was up there in bed, recuperating.

At Bolin's insistence, Mrs. Foster called Thomas down. Bolin stood within reach of his weapon as he examined the stranger. Then, apparently satisfied, he walked over and shook Thomas's hand.

While Mrs. Foster fussed with pots and pans, the two men sat, discussing the war. At one point, Bolin got to his feet and picked up his rifle. He brought it over and showed it to Thomas. His weapon, he boasted, had killed thirty blue coats plus a lot who didn't wear the blue.

Mrs. Foster placed food on the table and the two men started to eat. Thomas, sitting opposite Bolin, watched for a chance to pull his weapon and shoot the guerrilla. A noise outside distracted Bolin's attention, and Thomas reached for his revolver. But Bolin turned back and Thomas drew a handkerchief from his inside pocket instead. Soon Thomas saw another opportunity, but Mrs. Foster was standing behind Bolin's chair and the corporal feared he might injure her.

Thomas finished his meal, got up, and walked to the fireplace. He picked up an iron tool propped in a corner. Bolin came over and asked about it. Thomas said he wasn't sure but thought it might be part of a plow. Bolin took the tool, examined it, and handed it back. It was a plow coulter, he said.

Then Bolin leaned toward the hearth, searching for a hot coal with which to light his pipe. Thomas raised the coulter and smashed it down against the back of Bolin's head. The guerrilla fell to the floor. Thomas struck the outlaw's head two or three more times.

When Mrs. Foster and the corporal were convinced Bolin was dead, they carried him into an attached shed and threw an old carpet over his body. The woman fetched a bucket of sudsy water and started to scrub the blood off the floor. Thomas was outside saddling his horse when he heard Mrs. Foster scream. She could hear Bolin stirring, she said, trying to rise. Thomas ran into the shed and, seeing Bolin on his hands and knees, drew his pistol and fired a shot, killing the bushwhacker.

Thomas left for Forsyth, and Mrs. Foster started packing. Several hours later, the corporal returned with a Major and twenty-five troops of the First Iowa Cavalry. They brought two wagons pulled by six-mule teams.

In one wagon the soldiers loaded Alf Bolin's body; in the other they packed the Fosters' household goods. The caravan reached Forsyth before dawn, February 3, 1863.

Word of the detested bushwhacker's death spread like wildfire. By morning hundreds of hillfolk jammed the streets of Forsyth. They had traveled from throughout the countryside to celebrate Alf Bolin's demise, to exult over the end to a reign of terror. Among the celebrants were his victims' families, grieving survivors with bitterness in their hearts, and dozens of Missouri soldiers who had chased the bushwhacker.

In his diary, an Iowa soldier recorded his impression of the frightful corpse: "He was a large sinewy man and must have been of great strength and endurance. His hair was matted with blood and [blood was] clotted over his face, rendering him an object of disgust and horror."

Later that morning, a squad was mustered to escort the wagons of Mrs. Foster and the one containing the bushwhacker's body to Springfield. Less than a mile north of Forsyth, along the road that still skirts the east bank of Swan Creek today, a man named Colbert Hays halted the procession. Before the guards could stop him, Hays raised an axe and chopped off Bolin's head. The soldiers buried the body a short distance up a wooded slope by a tree that grew near Spencer Cole's spring. Wrapping Bolin's head in a gunnysack, they

placed it in a pine box and headed north again.

That afternoon, the contingent arrived at the town of Ozark. Someone unwrapped the head and stuck it atop a pole on the courthouse lawn. Adults, and children pelted the macabre relic with stones.

After retrieving the head, the entourage got underway. Reaching Springfield, the soldiers delivered Mrs. Foster to her husband and presented Bolin's head to the provost marshal of the Union troops—"evidence" of the bushwhacker's demise. Later, after the skull was taken to Jefferson City, Corporal Thomas received the five thousand dollar reward. He gave the Fosters three thousand. On March 24, 1863, young Thomas was commissioned a second lieutenant and made a scout in the 11th Missouri Cavalry.

While he lived, Bolin corrupted the people of Taney and Stone Counties with such strong, enduring hatred that its energy has survived the dilution of six generations. Remnants of that hatred can be found today. Casual mention of the name "Alf Bolin" can cause tempers to flare. There are descendants of Civil War survivors who, no matter on which side of the issue their ancestors' sympathies lay, still tell of some ancestor—a great grandaunt or uncle or a great grandfather—whom Alf Bolin robbed or killed. Some local folks remain convinced that on dark, still nights, more than a hundred years later, one can hear screams coming from Murder Rocks.

Mary Hartman

Taney County's Night Riders
The Bald Knobbers

Today's visitors to the Branson area's lakes, music shows, and theme parks speed along Highway 65, oblivious to the rich fabric of history that transpired in these hills and valleys long before U.S. 65 or a town called Branson existed. As cars and motor homes cross the concrete bridges over Bull and Bear Creek, Bee and Roark Creek, their passengers are unaware of the frightening, often bloody, scenes that occurred over and over again in the nearby woods during the reign of the Bald Knobbers.

Let's hop into a time capsule, reverse the years, and create an imaginary scene at an isolated log cabin in the hardwood forests of central Taney County. We're at Shoal Creek, an hour on horseback from Kissee Mills, but we could be at any of a multitude of places, for such horrendous events occurred frequently. We're observing the macabre business conducted night after night by companies of Bald Knobbers. Except for the young farmer, Walter Adams, who represents a composite of dozens of victims, the characters are real. Although this particular incident is fictional, it has been compiled from the unpublished memoirs and oral histories of men and women who lived in Taney County during the years 1885 through 1889. Rarely did these victims leave behind a documented trail, for few came through their ordeals with the stamina to file formal complaints.

Picture a full moon, casting light and shadows on the cleared field around the farmyard and its forty acres of corn, ears tasseling out on the stalks. Inside the cabin, a young farmer is awakened by the stomp of horses' hooves and the rustle of brush as a group of riders moves through the thick stand of trees. He jumps out of bed and hurries to the door. Lifting the bolt, he yanks the plank door open and stands frozen, his heart pumping with fear, his eyes wide with the effort to see into the night.

Then the forms of men on horseback take

Nat Kinney, leader of the Bald Knobbers
(Photo belonging to Mary E. Parrish of Forsyth; presented by Lucile Morris Upton to the Christian County Library, 1983)

shape as the intruders emerge from the forest. A staccato bark of gunfire erupts. The homesteader flinches and ducks behind the door frame, even though he realizes that the snipers are holding their rifles high, aiming toward the moon.

The leader kicks his horse in the sides and the animal breaks into a gallop. At least a dozen riders pull up behind him as he reins in by the front stoop.

"Get on out here, Walter Adams. We got a message for you."

The speaker has tied a kerchief across the lower half of his face, but Adams recognizes the muffled voice as that of his neighbor. He glances at the others. All wear disguises: bandannas, pillow cases, or flour sacks with eyeholes cut in them; socks are pulled over their boots, coats turned inside out. Still, he recognizes several horses: Joe McGill's bay, the pinto that Charley Groom bought for his oldest boy, the big ugly roan of his neighbor.

"Walter Adams, you chose to ignore our warning ten days ago when we tossed a bundle of sticks on your porch," shouts the man on the pinto. On his head is the light-colored ranchman's hat that Groom brought back from St. Louis last spring. "We told you to tear down that barbed wire you strung across your neighbor's claim."

The young man finds courage to voice his objection. "Mister Groom, I've had that land surveyed twice now, and my fence runs true to the markers."

"Grab him, boys," shouts the neighbor, sliding off his roan.

Adams hears his bride's wail as four masked men rush in and drag him out the door. They shove him ahead of them, poking rifle barrels into his back and kicking him in the buttocks. They steer him through the corn patch and into the woods behind his barn. Out of sight of the house, they tear off his night shirt, force his arms around a hickory tree, bind his wrists.

Adams hears the snap of a blacksnake whip whistling through the air. He feels a sharp pain across his back. The lash bites into skin and muscle, and the warm wetness of blood trickles down his spine. Again and again the whip sings through the night air and cuts into his flesh. He loses count, loses track of the blood spurting from the wounds. And then he loses consciousness.

Before dawn, his wife, seven months pregnant, finds him and cuts the rope that binds his arms around the tree. Leaning heavily on her, he stumbles home. Before she can finish swabbing his raw wounds with lye soapsuds, he pulls on his trousers.

"Hurry," he orders. "We got to get going. Pack only what you absolutely need."

Within a few hours, the young couple leaves, their plow horses pulling the farm wagon as it creaks and groans up the road toward Kissee Mills. The wagon is loaded with belongings with which they'll start again someplace else: boxes of quilts and blankets, jars of canned pickles and peaches, plates and bowls wrapped in wool skirts and longjohns. The plow wobbles next to the flour barrel.

As soon as the neighbor sees the wagon go by, he saddles his roan and heads for the county courthouse at Forsyth. He's already checked the status of young Adams' property taxes. They're in arrears, for cash is a scarce commodity among all but the most established farmers in this Ozarks community. He pays the tax bill, and before sundown the land, the house, and the barn belong to him. He will harvest the ripening corn, dig the potatoes, and round up the few head of cattle that roam the woods on open range.

Full responsibility for the terrors that routed families like the Adamses during those years, total blame for the disasters that beset a majority of Taney County's seven thousand inhabitants, rests on the shoulders of one man. The man who single-handedly organized and masterminded the fearsome night-riding vigilantes known as the Bald Knobbers was a newcomer named Nathaniel N. Kinney.

When Nat Kinney settled in Taney County in 1883, he found a deplorable state of affairs. Outlaws and renegades ruled, most of them holdovers from the bushwhackers and guerrillas that rampaged through Southwest Missouri during the Civil War. After the war, the lack of even minimal law enforcement afforded outlaws free reign. Clans elected and controlled the local sheriff, whose authority it was to subpoena jury panels. If outlaws or their relatives didn't sit on the juries, they bribed those who did. As a result, although thirty to forty murders occurred in Taney County between 1865 and 1885, not a single suspect was convicted.

Unlike the county's officeholders, Kinney

feared no man. He stood six feet six and weighed more than three hundred pounds. After his discharge from the Union Army in West Virginia, he took a job as a railroad detective in Topeka, Kansas. With the proceeds from the sale of a saloon he later owned in Springfield, Missouri, he bought 267 acres of land along the White River. (Today, part of his property lies under Lake Taneycomo; the rest is along Lakeshore Drive across from downtown Branson where Camp Kanakuk is located.)

The murder of merchant Jim Everett on September 22, 1883, prompted Kinney to consider forming a law and order league patterned after other vigilante groups that were a national fad between 1865 and 1900. After a biased jury acquitted Everett's murderer, Kinney called together twelve of the county's leaders—lawyers, county officials, mill owners. They drew up resolutions and a loyalty oath, designed secret grips and passwords, and went out to recruit one hundred of the county's finest men.

On April 5, 1885, two hundred showed up at the League's organizational meeting on Snapp's Bald, the highest peak along what is now Taney County's T Highway. Kinney chose the "Bald," a hilltop devoid of vegetation, because the barren slopes allowed sentries to detect interlopers. Almost immediately outsiders dubbed the league's members "Bald Knobbers."

Kinney, a golden-tongued orator, was unanimously elected chieftain. He exhorted his vigilantes to keep the oath and the roster secret. Then he sent his men out to recruit others. The membership doubled and redoubled, and before long, there would be between five hundred and one thousand Bald Knobbers.

The Bald Knobbers burst upon the public a few days later when one hundred broke open the door of the Taney county jail, kidnapped, and then lynched the Taylor brothers, rapscallions who had wounded a storekeeper during an argument over credit for a pair of boots.

Such violence appalled several founding members and they dropped out. The community split into two factions: those who adored Kinney and would follow him to the ends of the earth, and those who hated his tyrannical attitude and wished him dead. There was no in-between.

From what we discern of Nat Kinney's personality, it is not surprising that most of the emotional responses focused on him. Kinney could be convivial one minute and angry as a black thunderhead the next. His detractors considered him ruthless, intolerant, violent, and wicked. His devotees noted that he treated animals and children with tenderness and evinced a passionate commitment to religion.

Kinney organized a popular Sunday school at Oak Grove, a white frame country school that still stands on T Highway with a front-door view of Snapp's Bald. The former saloonkeeper and railroad detective taught Bible lessons and led hymn singing. As threats against his life intensified, he preached sermons with his two six shooters on the table before him.

At first, after they had lynched the Taylors, Kinney's Bald Knobbers rode out at night to scare drunks or gamblers or "loose" women into changing their ways. They frightened wife beaters and couples "living in sin" and men who failed to support their families. They even called on some whom they simply considered "ornery." They began to scare off or flog or brand suspected thieves, arsonists, robbers. They hanged or beat to death men they accused of assault or disturbing the peace or destroying property. And then some Bald Knobbers started to use the menacing power of the group for greedy and selfish purposes; they went after men who owed them money or who owned a farm one of them coveted; they "settled" feuds over fence lines or roads or property deeds; they whipped men for disrupting services in their churches or for supporting the wrong candidate in an election.

But the Bald Knobbers saved their harshest punishment for those who talked against their organization. A few victims who resisted the Bald Knobbers disappeared. Several turned up in the woods, beaten to death. Some who lived to tell the tale claimed that Kinney's followers killed more than thirty men and at least four women. A more realistic estimate is that between fifteen and eighteen men (including some Bald Knobbers) died in the conflict, and many more men and women suffered severe injuries from brutal beatings. During the strife that Nat Kinney called "a war between civilization and barbarism," there was such turmoil that officials—not necessarily competent record keepers in the first place—failed to provide accurate tallies of the casualties.

As the Bald Knobbers grew in numbers and their violent acts escalated, a vehement resentment festered among a small group of men who became known as the Anti-Bald Knobbers. But the vigilantes thwarted every Anti-Bald Knobber's effort to mitigate the situation. When a judge called for a state audit to ferret out corruption among the county's officeholders, an arsonist—allegedly a Bald Knobber—burned down the courthouse. The anti-vigilantes organized a local militia; but the Bald Knobbers convinced Gov. John S. Marmaduke that the existence of a semi-military body would thrust the county into open warfare. The governor ordered the militia to cease and desist.

The nation's newspapers published stories about the bloody war in Missouri. An embarrassed Governor Marmaduke sent Adjutant General J.C. Jamison to look into the situation. (The Forsyth that Jamison visited was situated on the flats beside the White River where Highway 160 runs past the city park today. The current location of the city was established when Bull Shoals dam was built.) On April 10, 1886, Jamison met with both sides of the conflict and informed each that they were illegal, since they were not state-chartered institutions. He then took Nat Kinney aside and threatened to throw him in jail if he did not disband his Bald Knobbers. Kinney called five hundred of his men together and gave the requested order. A resolution was drawn up, signed, and forwarded to the governor.

But the Bald Knobbers disbanded on paper only. Nothing changed, except that Kinney no longer advertised vigilante meetings in the local newspaper. He still spent nearly every waking hour directing Bald Knobber activities, and the beatings and killings and banishments continued as before. Bald Knobberism

flourished to the extent that historian Richard Maxwell Brown described the group as one of the nation's largest, fiercest, longest-lasting vigilante movements.

But then a series of incidents took place at Oak Grove School that built a fire under the Anti-Bald Knobbers. Among the families attending Kinney's evening prayer services were the Coggburns. Andrew Coggburn, a cocky youth, badgered Nat Kinney. He poked fun at Kinney's Sunday school and at his Bald Knobbers. He composed doggerel verses that ridiculed Kinney and his men, and he sang "The Bald Knobber Ballad" loud and clear. A gang of Bald Knobbers took out after Andrew and his brother one night, but Coggburn brandished a knife and stood them off. Kinney ordered the sheriff to arrest Coggburn for carrying a concealed weapon.

Coggburn put up a twenty-five dollar bond but neglected to show up for trial. Kinney asked that he be deputized to serve the warrant for Coggburn's arrest for failure to appear.

The next time Kinney and Coggburn crossed paths was Sunday night, February 28, 1886 when Andrew and his friend Sam Snapp showed up at Oak Grove's prayer meeting. Kinney approached Coggburn, intending to take him into custody. "Throw up your hands," he shouted. Though Coggburn obeyed, Kinney shot and killed him. At the coroner's inquest Kinney swore that Coggburn had tried to draw a revolver.

Sam Snapp, the only Anti-Bald Knobber present at the scene, did not testify, and the jurors declined to indict Kinney. But the Bald Knobbers worried that if some future prosecutor decided to reopen the case, Snapp might swear that Kinney killed an unarmed man and that a Bald Knobber planted a revolver in the dead Coggburn's hand. So the Bald Knobbers decided to do away with Sam Snapp; the man assigned to the job was Kinney's bodyguard, George Washington Middleton.

On May 9, 1886, Wash Middleton goaded Sam Snapp into an argument in front of Kintrea's Store in Kirbyville. Middleton pulled his revolver and shot Snapp three times, killing him. A jury convicted Middleton, but the night before he was to be sentenced he escaped through a mysteriously unlocked jail door.

The Snapp family paid bounty hunter Jim Holt fifty dollars in gold to track down Middleton. It took Holt two years, but on July 4, 1888 he killed Sam Snapp's murderer at Mount Parthenon, Arkansas. Holt collected fifteen hundred dollars in rewards from the Snapps, the governor, and county officials.

More than any other disaster, the murder of Sam Snapp roused the Anti-Bald Knobbers. They drew up a "hit list" of Bald Knobber leaders, with Kinney's name at the top. The anti-vigilantes calculated correctly that without the big chieftain to lead them, the Bald Knobbers would fall apart.

Then five Anti-Bald Knobbers rode their horses to the farm home of Almus "Babe" Harrington, a prominent lawyer. Harrington lived where the James River crosses the southern extension of Springfield's Campbell Street, the present-day Highway 160.

Asked what constituted a valid defense against first-degree murder, Harrington replied, "Self-defense." His visitors paid the lawyer a five hundred dollar retainer in case one of them might be charged with murder someday. Then the five retired to Harrington's barn and played a bizarre game of poker. The "loser" would be designated to kill Nat Kinney. Billy Miles, a young farmer from Taney City (now Taneyville), tossed away enough good cards to lose the game. Matt Snapp, Sam's half brother, won the right to back Billy up.

On Monday, August 20, 1888, Billy Miles found Nat Kinney inventorying merchandise in a store on the Forsyth square. Kinney had been appointed receiver in the storeowner's bankruptcy.

Bald Knobbers loafing outside heard four pistol shots reverberate from the store's windows. Billy Miles walked out on the porch, his .44-caliber Smith & Wesson revolver in his hand.

"I have just killed Nat Kinney in self-defense," he announced.

The building had already known violence. Four years and eleven months earlier Jim Everett was murdered in the same two-story, white frame building. It was the acquittal of Everett's murderer that compelled Nat Kinney to set out on a fiery, devastating, murderous mission to reform Taney County. In fact, Kinney first met with the twelve founding members of the Bald Knobbers in the store's back room.

The ultimate irony, however, was that a Greene County jury, hearing the trial on a change of venue, found Billy Miles not guilty of Kinney's murder.

The impact of Bald Knobberism on Taney County has diffused with the passage of time. None of the participants on either side of the conflict is alive today. However, numerous descendants of the Bald Knobbers and the handful of Anti-Bald Knobbers who brought them down still live in the area. Strong feelings surface when the topic arises, and arguments flare up occasionally. It's clear that those affected either believe that the Bald Knobbers were either knights in shining armor or devils in disguise. As their ancestors did in the 1880's, everyone takes a side. No one is neutral.

Mary Hartman

Mary Hartman has also co-authored a book on the Bald Knobber era: *Bald Knobbers: Vigilantes on the Ozarks Frontier* by Mary Hartman and Elmo Ingenthron (Gretna LA: Pelican Publishing Co., 1988).

Two Against the Bald Knobbers

Nowhere in the United States was vigilante-connected violence more brutal than in the Ozarks during the post-Civil War era. Should laws be enforced by elected officials or should a band of self-appointed night riders capture, sentence, and punish those they deemed guilty of crimes? Should righteous men use violence to quash violence? In Taney County, Missouri, passions ran so high over these questions that a man found it impossible to remain neutral.

A small band of Bald Knobbers lived in extreme eastern Taney County, as did two of the vigilantes' most outspoken critics. One of these opponents was Jim Cobble. Had the Bald Knobbers invited Cobble to join he would have refused, for he loathed the vigilantes.

Up Turkey Creek a mile or so from Cobble's cabin lived Burden H. Barrett, an Irishman born in New York State, a shoemaker who, with his wife and five sons, followed the lumber camps to Michigan and wound up in Missouri. Barrett excelled in binding wheat and in making boots for lumberjacks and shoes for farmers. He was five feet five and weighed only one hundred ten pounds. But he had muscles as tough as the saddle leather he fashioned into winter brogans. He feared nothing and would fight any man, no matter how big.

Barrett also excelled in swearing and ran the gamut of his colorful language whenever he expressed his vivid opinions about whatever displeased him. He hated the Bald Knobbers—singly and en masse—and often said so. Although the vigilantes whipped others for saying less, they wisely left Barrett alone.

The Tree Accurst

Whene'er I passed that grim old oak
  I felt a sense of dread,
It spread its arms so wildly-
  It tossed its blighted head.
The shade it cast was black and still,
  The earth was bleak and bare;
No flowers, no birds, no nestlings,
  No sweet winds lingered there.

Then someone told the story
  Of this piteous cursed tree,
And then I went another way
  For fear that I might see
The helpless wretches dying,
  Swinging from that oak,
Victims of the savage mob
  In sable hood and cloak.

Mary Elizabeth Mahnkey

One spring night in 1886, the Bald Knobbers decided to punish Jim Cobble. Fifteen horses carrying masked riders rode up to Cobble's house and caught Jim sitting in front of his fireplace, chewing tobacco. Before he could put on his shoes, the Bald Knobbers grabbed him, dragged him out to the yard, and tied him to a tree. Slowly and deliberately, various vigilantes called his attention to acts they considered out of keeping with the community's social mores. Jim denied these allegations until one of the Bald Knobbers produced a bundle of switches and flogged his bare back unmercifully. They warned him they would be back to see that he had left the countryside. Before a week passed, Cobble and his family moved away.

Jim Cobble had lived a long time in that neighborhood. He recognized the horses and the voices and could identify most of the fifteen who called on him.

Within three weeks, members of the Bald Knobber band started receiving personal letters from Texas. The outside of the envelopes bore crude drawings of coffins, skulls and crossbones, men hanging from trees, and other gory illustrations.

"Before the leaves fall," each letter said, "I will come back, and when I do, ill fortune will befall you." Jim Cobble signed his name.

A few weeks later, odd catastrophes started to befall the men who had whipped Cobble: Fires of mysterious origin consumed barns and sometimes houses. Some Bald Knobbers found their stock lying dead on the range. As others plowed their fields, the roar of a shotgun resounded from the brush, and fine birdshot peppered their plowhorses from head to tail.

Ten days following each occurrence, a letter signed by Jim Cobble would arrive from Texas, asking the victim how he liked it.

Naturally, this treatment began to scare the Bald Knobbers. No one knew when his barn would burn or when he would have to spend the day picking buckshot out of his horse. Finally, the vigilantes decided to do their farmwork together. Instead of plowing alone, five or six would join forces and travel from field to field. It was not uncommon to see four or five men in a five-acre cornfield, going down the rows between the handles of double shovel plows, Winchesters strapped to their backs, revolvers in their belts.

They finally hired Burden Barrett to do their work. Since everyone knew how much Barrett hated the Bald Knobbers, no one would believe he'd go to work for them. But that summer, the shoemaker laid aside his shoe last, picked up the handles of a plow, and trudged behind a mule, earning flour, bacon, corn, tobacco, and other produce to feed his family. That didn't stop him from holding forth against the Bald Knobbers, however.

We don't know what eventually happened to Cobble. But we do know the Barrett story had another chapter. In the fall of 1886, Barrett and his entire family came down with malaria and the chills. None of them could leave the house, even to do chores. His corn stood in the field uncut, his woodyard lay bare. No hams hung in his smokehouse, and his prospects for the oncoming winter looked bleak.

Then one day a dozen Bald Knobbers, led by little George Adams, appeared at the Barrett cabin. They filled the lard can, hung hams and shoulders in the smokehouse, cut great ricks of wood and piled them in the woodyard. They gathered and reaped his corn, then solemnly marched away. From that day on, Barrett never uttered another bad word against the Bald Knobbers.

Mary Hartman
Adapted from *Bald Knobbers, Vigilantes on the Ozarks Frontier*, by Mary Hartman and Elmo Ingenthron.

"Jake Fleagle Was Our Neighbor"

When Jake Fleagle, alias Walter Cook, and his "brother" Lee rented a cottage near the Arkansas border on Highway 65 in the fall of 1929, Jake was wanted for bank robbery, murder, and assorted other crimes.

To their neighbors in the loosely knit community of Ridgedale the Cook "brothers" were peaceful farmers, primarily concerned with the setting of eggs for their white leghorn hens. Walter "had lung trouble and had to rest a lot." He fed and watered the 160 chickens, sunned himself on the porch, and walked in the forested canyon which ran along the back of the house under a protecting ridge. Lee, who it was later noted did not look much like his brother, had a ready smile and did most of the talking. He worked a little on the new highway being built past the place.

The two never seemed to lack for money, but they never "showed much money" either, except in the poker games played in their cottage when rain halted work for the road crew.

During one of the games Walter pulled his .45 from under his shirt, then put it back and grinned. One road worker, who spent a night at the house, later said he was shown a revolver kept under the mattress. Another visitor discovered a machine gun, but was told it was a World War I keepsake. Neighbors were well aware of the savage police dog kept chained to a long steel "clothesline" in front of the cottage. However, no one thought much about such displays. Everyone in the hills took precautions to protect themselves.

On May 23, 1928, eighteen months before the Cook brothers moved to the cottage, Jake Fleagle, his real brother Ralph, Howard Royston, and George Abshier had held up the First National Bank in Lamar, Colorado. As employees and customers looked on with hands held high, the gangsters stuffed $290,000 into money bags. The bank president, A.M. Parrish, pulled a pistol from his desk and shot Royston in the face, then was gunned down before he could fire again. Bank employee J.F. Parrish rushed to his fallen father—and paid for his concern with his life.

Taking a cashier and a teller hostage, the gunmen fled in a waiting car. Once outside of town, they slowed to shove the teller from the crowded car, enabling Sheriff L.A. Alderman and his deputy to almost catch up with them. However, before the lawmen got close enough to use their pistols, the sheriff's car was disabled by rifle fire from the fleeing men. None of the witnesses—the lawmen, the terrified bank teller, onlookers in the bank—could give a usable description of the outlaws' faces.

The robbers drove to Fleagle's ranch near Garden City, Kansas. In response to Royston's anguished pleas, Abshier was sent to get medical help. He returned with Dr. W.W. Weininger of Dighton, Kansas, who quickly realized that the "injured ranch hand" he was summoned to treat had been shot. After Royston was treated, Weininger was driven to a lonely canyon, blindfolded, shot in the head, and pushed over a cliff in his own car.

While posses searched the entire region, Sheriff Alderman, scouting western Kansas in a low-flying airplane, sighted Weininger's wrecked automobile. The doctor's death was linked to the bank robbery after the kidnapped cashier also was found shot in the head. Weininger's car had been wiped clean of fingerprints, but Jake Fleagle accidentally left a bloody print on a window as he helped push the car over the cliff. The fingerprint was sent to the FBI in Washington and to police all over the country.

In June, 1929, after $17,000 in cash was taken from a mail train near Pittsburg, California, a suspect who gave his name as William Harrison Holden was arrested at Stockton, fingerprinted and then released. His prints, forwarded to the FBI, matched those of convicted robber Jake Fleagle, who in 1916 had served a year in the McAlester, Oklahoma, penitentiary. An FBI fingerprint expert also linked the print of Fleagle's right index finger to the one found on the slain physician's car. Postal inspectors, railroad detectives, and the California police joined in the search.

As the "Cook" brothers were establishing themselves at Ridgedale, Garden City police visited Fleagle's ranch. His parents and brother Fred were found with large sums of cash and sizable bank accounts. Fred revealed that Ralph Fleagle had been sending mail to Garden City, and postal inspectors soon apprehended him at the Kankakee, Illinois post office.

After many weeks in the Colorado Springs jail, Ralph admitted his part in the Lamar holdup and agreed to identify his companions if authorities would not request the death penalty. Royston was arrested in San Andreas, California, and Abshier in Grand Junction, Colorado. All eventually confessed and were tried. Despite the fact that the prosecutor did not ask the death penalty, the jurors decreed hanging for all three. The sentences were carried out in July, 1930. None of the men would give any information about Jake Fleagle.

At Ridgedale, the Cooks tried to be as unobtrusive as possible. Walter Cook saved magazine and newspaper reports of the Fleagle gang. He took care to deface all pictures of Jake Fleagle. Lee Cook, appearing to have no concern about being identified, sometimes went to both Hollister and Branson to shop. He also caught the passenger coach which passed through both those towns to visit communities farther away. And both Lee and Walter shopped at the Ridgedale store a mile or so from their house. The storekeeper, William Cary, who usually picked up mail in Hollister for his neighbors, never received any for the Cooks.

Cary's daughter, Blanche, helped out in the store. In later years she remembered the Cooks coming in for gasoline and groceries. "I sold Jake a french harp. When he came in one evening to look for one, I said, 'Aren't you Walter Cook?' and he said 'Yeah.' I said, 'Well I never know you.' I guess that was exactly what he wanted to hear! He looked different every time he came in the store."

In the summer of 1930, Harry Lee Watson, arrested while operating a plush hideout in the wooded hills of nearby Texas County, revealed that Fleagle was in the vicinity and might be mailing letters on the White River line between Carthage, Missouri and New-

port, Arkansas. Samples of Jake's handwriting, obtained from the Kansas ranch, were circulated to postal employees all over the region. On July 30, after Ralph Fleagle's execution, the governor of Colorado received a letter in Fleagle's handwriting, an unsigned plea for clemency for Ralph.

A second letter, found among mail posted on the rail line, was addressed to a man in California. Postal officials delivered the letter and waited while the recipient, a known associate of Fleagle, opened it. Jake wanted to meet his friend, and asked him to insert an ad in a Wichita paper if he agreed. Prompted by the postal inspectors, the friend inserted the ad and received an answer from Fleagle asking for a meeting in Yellville, Arkansas on October 14, 1930.

Several weeks before the proposed rendezvous, Mrs. Cary, wife of the owner of the Ridgedale store, had a visit from postal inspectors with some pictures. "Do you know any of these men?" they asked. When she said one looked like one of the Cook brothers, she was told they were looking for the bank robber, Jake Fleagle, and she was advised not to mention the conversation to anyone. Badly frightened, Mrs. Cary did not even mention the visit to her husband or daughters.

On October 13, 1930, some 25 lawmen were deployed along the White River Line. Several were at the Branson station when the passenger train passed through town before noon. No local law officers had been asked to be on hand.

The Cook brothers arrived in Branson that day between 10 and 11 a.m. They bought one ticket to Hollister, then waited in their automobile. When the southbound train arrived, Walter, clean-shaven, shabbily dressed in blue overalls, blue serge coat and a felt hat, and wearing heavy, dark-rimmed glasses, walked up the platform.

On the train with Jake's old friend were three postal inspectors, two police officers from Kansas City, two from Los Angeles, and one from Colorado Springs. Fleagle climbed aboard and started to take a seat in the first row where he could see the entire length of the car. A policeman ordered, "Put 'em up," but Fleagle reached

Thirteen law officers involved in Fleagle's capture posed for a Branson photographer.

(Photo by Payne, courtesy of Kathleen Van Buskirk)

for his gun. One shot was fired. It went through the outlaw's stomach, then lodged in a window sill.

Fleagle, struggling fiercely, was handcuffed, put in leg irons, and taken by ambulance to the local office of Dr. Guy B. Mitchell. Later he was taken, under heavy guard, to a Springfield hospital where he was operated on. By the next morning, however, he was dead. He never admitted to any crimes, but in delirium alternately called for his mother and cringed in fear of officers "still pursuing him."

Did Jake expect to leave the train with his friend at Hollister and be picked up there? Lee Cook had been waiting in a Hollister store when reports spread of the Branson capture. The storekeeper reported that he got in the old car and simply drove away.

There was no one at the Ridgedale cottage when officers sped there after Fleagle's capture. They did find tools for tapping telephone wires, a pile of newspapers and magazines, a closet full of very expensive suits, and quantities of tacks which the editor of the Branson paper theorized would have damaged the tires of pursuing cars. No money was found and Fleagle had only some small change when he was shot.

Inside the house, wall studs were covered with building paper under which was found an arsenal of guns and ammunition. By simply poking a hand through the paper the Cooks would have been able to grab a gun. After the police left, neighbors tended the chickens and the anxious dog, and tore off bits of the tar paper for souvenirs.

Jake's mother claimed his body for burial beside his brother Ralph. His father arranged an auction of the animals and household effects, minus the guns, which were confiscated.

Postal inspectors dropped by to thank Mrs. Cary for confirming Fleagle's identity. Only then did she tell her family of her fearful ordeal. Months later the Carys were told that Lee Cook had been caught, but they never learned what crimes he was wanted for, nor who he really was.

Mrs. Cary told her family to forget the help she had given the police with those photos. By that time the story had been told and retold by neighbors, and many seemed to disapprove of all those policemen coming in and killing "their neighbor, Walter Cook."

Kathleen Van Buskirk

Bonnie and Clyde

The rat-a-tat-tat of a machine gun in the hands of Bonnie Parker, or her lover, Clyde Barrow, spelled death and destruction throughout the southwest during the 1930's. Newspapers carried headline articles of the atrocious crimes committed by the pair of outlaws. But the notoriety of the Barrow gang seemed far removed from the hills of Ozark Mountain Country until a day in February, 1934 when the startling news that Bonnie and Clyde had kidnapped an area man began to circulate in the small towns of Reeds Spring, Galena, and Cape Fair.

Clyde Barrow, born March 24th, 1909, was one of eight children born to Henry and Cumice Barrow of Telice, Texas. An incorrigible child, he was committed to the Harris School for Boys when he was nine years old. In his early teens he began a career of robbery and murder with his older brother Marvin (Buck) Barrow. In January, 1930, he met Bonnie Parker, a slender blonde who was living with a friend in West Dallas, Texas. Emma Parker, mother of Bonnie, once said, "I knew there was something between them the first time I saw them together. I could see it in Bonnie's eyes." Clyde, already a fugitive from the law, paired up with Bonnie and traveled the country, robbing and killing at will.

On February 12th, 1934, Stone County officers had been warned to be on the alert because "some kids" in Springfield had stolen a car and were headed south. At the time, no one suspected that the car thieves were Bonnie and Clyde and another member of the Barrow gang, Henry Methvin.

A roadblock was set up by Constable Dale Davis and his men near the Missouri Pacific Railroad underpass north of Reeds Spring. When Clyde Barrow saw the roadblock, he spun his car around and headed back up Highway 13. Because he had already eluded pursuit in that direction, he turned off onto a rural road to make his escape. Lacking a knowledge of the area's roads, the fugitives forced a local man, Joe Gunn, into the car and ordered him to help the gang escape by guiding them through the back roads to Berryville, Arkansas.

In making their get-away, the gang encountered another roadblock south of Reeds Spring, set up by Deputies Earnest Hayes and Sam Thompson. Trapped, the outlaws opened fire and shot their way through the roadblock, careening into a ditch and out again, all the while showering the officers with a hail of bullets as the car sped down the dusty road.

Upon reaching Berryville, Arkansas, the desperadoes gave Joe Gunn twenty dollars and released him unharmed. Joe was so scared that he made his way home through fields and wooded areas, never traveling on the main road and only arriving back in Reeds Spring the following day. Joe Gunn's harrowing experience with Bonnie and Clyde is still related in the Reeds Spring area today.

This shootout was not the only visit of the Barrow gang to the southwest Missouri area. In 1933, Buck Barrow, W.D. Jones, Bonnie Parker, and Clyde Barrow had robbed a jewelry store in Neosho, Missouri and raided a Federal Armory in Springfield. But their time was running out. Bonnie and Clyde were killed by a Texas posse on May 23rd, 1934 on a country road between Sailes and Gibsland, Louisiana.

A number of books have been written about the lives of Bonnie Parker and Clyde Barrow; most picture Bonnie as a gun-toting, cigar smoking moll. Bonnie always emphatically denied that she smoked cigars. She maintained that pictures of her had been altered to create the impression. "Nice girls don't smoke cigars," she said.

Fern Angus

A Stone County Hanging

A loud—Zing!—rang out from the gallows rope. The slack tightened with a sickening thud. Roscoe (Red) Jackson, convicted killer, paid with his life for the murder of a man he scarcely knew, Pearl Bozarth.

The residents of Stone County, particularly Galena, had been disgusted by plans for a legal hanging on the lawn of the County Courthouse in Galena. They had good reason to be; the murder had not been committed in Galena, or in Stone County. Neither the murderer, the man murdered, nor the judge who meted out the sentence were residents of the county.

Pearl Bozarth, the owner of a poultry medicine company in Evansville, Illinois, spent a part of his time on the road selling his products. Traveling from Springfield to Forsyth, Missouri in 1937, he picked up a hitchhiker, Roscoe Jackson. Jackson was on his way to Howard's Ridge, south of Gainesville, to visit relatives there. At the small community of Forsyth, the two spent the night, Bozarth paying for meals and lodging.

The following morning the two men left Forsyth for Ava, Missouri. Near Brown's Branch in the northeast corner of Taney County, Jackson shot and killed the man who had befriended him, threw his body out on a side road in the hot August sun, took his car and billfold, and drove away. A farmer in the neighborhood found the badly decomposed body of Pearl Bozarth a few days later.

Roscoe Jackson, apprehended in Oklahoma a short time later, took a change of venue to Stone County, Missouri, rather than be tried in Taney county. A jury of Stone County men found him guilty of first degree murder; the penalty for this crime—death by hanging—was assessed on December 11, 1934, by Judge Robert L. Gideon.

After his conviction and sentence, Jackson was taken to the state penitentiary where he remained in solitary confinement for twenty-nine months before being returned to the Stone County jail in Galena, Missouri.

The gallows.
(Courtesy of Doal Yocum)

In spite of objections which had been raised to the hanging in the county, curiosity seized the small town. On the day of the hanging, May 21, 1937, some four hundred people surged into the enclosure built for the purpose. Fully that many, and perhaps more, waited outside the gate to get a glimpse of the convicted killer. Sheriff Coin mounted the gallows and asked for quiet. Jackson's spiritual advisor, Father Ahern, read the rite of contrition which was repeated by the man about to be hanged. A black hood was drawn over the convicted man's face; Sheriff Simmons of Taney County placed the noose about his neck while other officers strapped his ankles and knees together. The crowd was silent as Sheriff Coin pulled the lever, and Jackson plunged ten feet to his death. The lever was pulled at three minutes past six o'clock. Ten minutes later Jackson was pronounced dead by Dr. H.L. Kerr of Crane and Dr. L.S. Shumate of Reeds Spring.

Thus, as the result of a crime which had nothing to do with the county itself, Stone County witnessed the only legal hanging in its long history

Fern Angus

Section V
Indians

Far more than most of us realize, the American Indian had a great deal to do with shaping the values and attitudes of the Europeans who settled the "new world." It took only a few generations for British ideals to be modified in the new American nation. Frontiersmen like Daniel Boone and Davy Crockett became heroes because they adopted a distinctly Indian temperament: they learned to find their way through trackless wilderness, steal upon prey without detection, suffer deprivation stoically, and not cower before overwhelming odds.

Indians in the Ozarks, as elsewhere, had an important influence on the white settlers. Many of the first commercial roads in the Ozarks—such as the Wilderness Road between Springfield, Missouri and Carrollton, Arkansas—followed old Indian trails and traces. Contact for the purpose of trading was extensive, and considerable intermarriage took place between the pioneers and native Americans.

Even though all Indian tribes were eventually removed from the upper White River Valley, many Indians remained behind by hiding out in the hills. Quite often these native Americans had married whites and, consequently, descendants of early families in the area often discover that they have some Indian ancestry. Thus, though the Osage, who inhabited the area in the early nineteenth century, and the Cherokee, Delaware, and other tribes that were here for a while have moved on, their influence remains—not only genetically, but in local practices. What would fall in the Ozarks be, for example, without the men going off to a hunting camp to bring home a deer?

Indians of the Upper White River

Before the old White River channel disappeared under the newly formed area lakes, archeologists specializing in Indian culture searched fields along the river and its tributary creeks. Almost everywhere they looked, they found Indian artifacts.

Though certain archaic spear points suggest that small groups of hunters may have utilized the upper White River as long as ten thousand years ago, the Ozark Bluff Dwellers, who moved into the area roughly two millennia ago, were the first inhabitants to leave extensive physical remains. Their name derives from the fact that they used cave-like bluff overhangs—especially south facing ones—as protection from the elements. Normally their shelters were situated above flood danger, near springs and creeks. From bones, tools, bits of clothing, and other debris found in caves, archeologists know that they hunted (depending heavily on deer, but utilizing a wide variety of animals) and grew corn, beans, and squash. Later the area was also settled by small numbers of Hopewellian Indians—gardeners, gatherers, and hunters who lived in clan groupings and made primitive pottery.

Archeologists theorize that after these cultures declined, the Osage tribe moved into the Ozarks and began using the White River hills for their hunting grounds around the 13th century. In 1803, when the Ozarks became part of the United States, the Osage, having bartered with French and Spanish traders for at least a hundred years, were living in villages around the edge of the Ozark plateau so that they could do business with white traders and protect their rich hunting domain—the woodlands of the Ozarks—from other tribes.

The Osage Indians left a particularly strong impression on early white explorers. Washington Irving call them "the finest looking Indians I have seen in the West," and George Catlin, the famous painter of Indians on the western frontier, wrote:

The Osages may justly be said to be the tallest race of men in North America, either of red or white skins; there being very few indeed of the men, at their full growth, who are less than six feet in stature, and very many of them six and a half... They are at the same time well-proportioned in their limbs, and good looking.[1]

Catlin painted one Osage chief, Black Dog, whom he estimated to be seven feet tall and to weigh between 250 and 300 pounds. But it was not merely their size which impressed the settlers. Osage men shaved their heads in the same style as the Mohawk, leaving only a central lock, often spiked with feathers or deer hair. In their deerskins, and wearing earrings and necklaces, they were a formidable sight. Their strength, too, was legendary. The naturalist Thomas Nuttall was so impressed by the endurance of the Osage that he found their "activity and agility ...scarcely credible. They not uncommonly walk from their villages to the trading houses...in one day, a distance of about 60 miles."[2]

Historically, the white men who first came in contact with the Osage registered mixed feelings about the tall and impressive Indians. While the Osage were often known to be both gracious and generous, they also had a reputation for being menacing and savage to their enemies. These handsome people, the white men found, were fearsome protectors of their land and beliefs. The Osages' reputation for being fierce warriors developed after "foreigners" began encroaching on their lands, especially tribes of eastern Indians, driven west into the lands which the Osage had inhabited historically.

Of course, few white men really understood or even made an effort to understand Indian culture; they judged the native Americans by their own standards. For example, in 1818 Henry Rowe Schoolcraft reported seeing a deserted Osage hunting encampment at the mouth of Swan Creek near present-day Forsyth. He described the lodges as looking like large, inverted birds' nests. Demonstrating a lack of appreciation for the Indian culture, he reported that the villages were built in random order, a totally erroneous description since Osage villages had a meticulous order based on social customs.

Indeed, the Osage had developed an elaborate and complex culture which reflected their own beliefs regarding "natural order." Their tales told them that, at one time, their ancestors had resided near the stars, and had been sent by Wah'Kon-Tah (the Great Spirit) with the special responsibility of being the caretakers of the earth. They were so in awe of Wah'Kon-Tah that, in spite of their size, they called themselves Little People.

Because they established their villages near rivers and streams, the tribe called themselves Ni-U-Ko'n-Ska, Children of the Middle Waters. As with many Indian tribes, they felt that all life was sacred and that the Great Spirit could communicate to them through the natural world. The knowledge they had of their surroundings—the animals and plants—was extensive, not only because they depended on such knowledge to feed themselves, but because they believed that they were related to the animals of their domain. Their songs, dances, and chants, especially the haunting dawn chant, were all associated with maintaining the harmony of the natural world and with promoting health and longevity.

Their villages were rigidly ordered into various clans, separated into two major divisions, the Tzi-Sho or Sky People and the Honga or Earth People. Their permanent villages also included a Mystery Lodge where the chiefs and elders of the tribe performed their sacred rituals and tended to matters of government.

Although the Osage grew corn, squash, and beans, they largely depended on game for their survival. They hunted not only in the Ozark mountains, but also in the nearby plains to the west, which abounded with large animals, especially buffalo. Over the years, the Ni-U-Ko'n-Ska had learned to make bows and arrows for hunting and protection and obtained horses which the Spanish had introduced to the western hemisphere. The use of horses made their lives much easier, allowing them to greatly expand their hunting range, especially

into the great plains. Because other tribes utilized these hunting grounds as well, their enemies also increased in proportion to the distance they roamed from their lodges.

When white men, with their vastly superior technology, came upon the Ni-U-Ko'n-Ska, they were oblivious to the Indians' values. To them, the tribe was just an impediment to western expansion.

Change for the Osage was being generated by the political forces in Washington, D. C. and other capitals around the world. The United States, during the presidency of Thomas Jefferson, purchased the Louisiana Territory from a war-weary France desperately in need of money. President Jefferson, in sympathy with the eastern Indians, developed a policy that he thought would settle the Indian "problem" permanently. He would remove all Indians east of the Mississippi River to new homes in the newly-acquired Louisiana Purchase. But, before he could do this, tribes already west of the Mississippi would have to cede certain of their lands. To fulfill this purpose a treaty between the Osage and the United States was signed in 1808 whereby the Osage relinquished much of their land in the southern Ozarks for additional land and protection in the western part of Missouri and eastern Kansas. As was typical in such treaties, only a portion of the important Osages actually signed the treaty, and the tribe always contended that they had not given up hunting rights to their ancestral lands. When other Indians and white men began encroaching on their lands and depleting the wildlife, the Osage exacted brutal vengeance. Since the government favored the claims of the transplanted eastern "civilized tribes," the Osage eventually were forced to sign another treaty granting them land in southern Kansas—and removing them permanently from their ancestral homelands.

Once the Treaty of 1808 between the Osage and the U. S. government had been signed, other tribes from east of the Mississippi River began moving into the White River Country. Groups of Shawnee, Peoria, and Miami Indians constructed villages along the river during this time. The largest tribe, 2,100 Delawares, arrived in 1821 and established villages along the James River, with the largest settlement south of Springfield. From 1821 to 1833 Indian Trading posts existed on the White River at Swan Creek, at Turkey Creek (across from present day Branson), and at the mouth of the James River, in addition to a post at Delaware Town up the James River, south of Wilson Creek.

Life for the Delawares in the region proved to be difficult as is attested by this letter from the tribal chief to an Indian agent:

Last summer a number of our people died just for the want of something to live on.... We have got in a country where we do not find all as stated to us when we was asked to swap lands with you and we do not get as much as was promised us at the treaty of St. Mary's neither... Father—we did not think that big man would tell us things that was not true. We have found a poor hilly stony country and the worst of all no game to be found on it to live on. Last summer our corn looked very well until a heavy rain come on for 3 or 4 days and raised the water so high that we could just see the tops of our corn in some of the fields and it destroyed the greatest part of our corn, punkins and beans and great many more of my people coming on and we had to divide our little stock with them. Last summer there was a few deere here and we had a few hogs but *we was obliged to kill all of them and some that was not our own* but this summer there are no game nor no hogs and my old people and children must suffer. Father—You know its hard to be hungry, if you do not know it we poor Indians know it...[3]

In 1829, another treaty again "conveyed and secured forever" to the Delawares a 2.5 million acre tract of land north of present-day Kansas City. The Delawares moved there immediately, only to be moved again—for a final time—to Oklahoma. The moving of the Delawares opened up Ozark Mountain Country to further white settlement.

By 1840, the Osage and Delaware Indians who had resided in the area, and the Cherokee Indians who

David Sample, of Crane, helps young people of the area appreciate Indian culture.
(Photo courtesy of Dale Kesterson, Las Animas, CO)

had passed through on their forced migration to Oklahoma, were gone. The only reminders of their presence were the few towns and rivers which retained their Indian names (e.g. Neosho), and the stone tools and arrowheads which could be found in old campsites.

The Indian heritage was not totally exterminated, however. Many of the long-established families in Stone and Taney Counties have long known that their lineage includes Indian blood. A few members or small groups from each of the tribes in the area resisted going with the main body and hid away in the hills. Often these Indians had already intermarried with the new settlers. Many area family have old pictures which show family members with Indian features: high cheek bones and glossy black hair. The identity of the people in the pictures is often difficult to determine, for they had been shunted into their families' backgrounds. There were good reasons for this anonymity. In the early decades of the nineteenth century, it was dangerous to speak of being of mixed Indian blood. Such an admission might cause an individual to be forced onto an Indian reservation. By mid-century, the social stigma against individuals of Indian or mixed blood was so strong that few would willingly admit to being part Indian.

In 1966, David Sample, an area resident from Crane and injured Viet Nam veteran, began to piece together his native American heritage and the heritage of other Indians in Southwest Missouri. In learning about his Indian origins, he collected Indian lore, learned the skills of living off the land, and, in turn, taught others what he discovered. Now he travels across the country, giving talks and programs about the Indian heritage of America. His efforts have helped people understand the culture and values of the American Indian, especially the reverence native Americans have for the rest of nature—a lesson which we are all coming to realize is essential to the well-being of all future generations.

Frank Reuter
Robert McGill

1 George Catlin, *Letters and Notes on the Manners, Customs, and Conditions of the North American Indians* (New York: Dover Publications, 1973) Vol II, p.40. (Originally published: 1844).

2 Thomas Nuttall, *A Journal of Travels into the Arkansas Territory During the Year 1819* ed. Savoie Lottinville (Norman: University of Oklahoma Press, 1980), p. 207.

3 C.A. Weslager, *The Delaware Indians* (New Brunswick, New Jersey: Rutgers University Press, 1972), p. 364.

The Trail of Tears, 1838-1839

Footsore and weary, often with nothing to protect their bare and bleeding feet, thousands of Cherokee Indians made their way westward over the hilly, rough terrain of Ozark Mountain Country during the Forced Indian Removal of 1838-39. Because the march was conducted during the winter months, sickness and suffering plagued the travelers along the eight-hundred mile journey. Death was common, especially among the most vulnerable: the elderly and children. Since burials could only be made in the evening, mothers whose children died during the day were forced to carry the lifeless corpses until they reached the next campsite. After breaking camp the following morning, the survivors would be forced to abandon the grave sites of their loved ones forever. To the Indians, therefore, the march came to be called "the trail where they cried."

The irony of the forced eviction of the Cherokees from their lands in the southern Appalachians is that the tribe had made a conscious and continuous effort to adapt to the white man's ways and culture. They had reason to be proud of their accomplishments. The renowned Indian Sequoyah had developed an alphabet which enabled the Cherokee to write their language and produce their own newspaper. The Cherokee Nation even modeled its own constitution and government on that of the young American nation. And the tribe took great pains to get along with the white settlers. From 1785 to 1835, numerous treaties had been negotiated between the United States government and the Indians. In more than three quarters of these treaties, Indians ceded lands. While the vast cultural differences between the native Americans and the pioneer settlers played an important role in the forced Indian removal, the main factor was the white man's greed. Gold was discovered in the northeast portion of the Cherokee Nation in 1828. Prospectors rushed in and took up claims without regard to Indian ownership. Although pleas for intervention were sent to officials of the United States government, they fell on deaf ears. All hopes for assistance crumbled when Andrew Jackson became president in 1829.

The treaty of New Echota, Georgia, which was signed by some notable members of the tribe though it was not supported by the Cherokee at large, ceded the territory of the Cherokee Nation to the United States government in return for lands in the west. Under this treaty, the government would pay the cost of removal of the tribe and provide one year's subsistence to the Indians upon their arrival in the west. When Martin Van Buren became president in 1837, he ordered General Winfield Scott to remove the Cherokee by force without delay.

By June, 1838, General Scott reported that nearly all Cherokee had been taken prisoner. The Indians were seized as if they were criminals: men were taken from the fields, women from their homes, and children from play. The captives were marched away under rifle and bayonet to stockades where they were placed in a crowded, deplorable environment. Many died of exposure, malnutrition, and starvation even before the journey began. It has been estimated that four thousand native Americans, or roughly one fourth of the Cherokee Nation, died either before, during, or as a result of the forced removal.

Another bitter irony of the Indian Removal is that some Indians, seeing the handwriting on the wall, had already migrated to lands in the west. One of the best records of the Indian experience as they passed through Ozark Mountain Country comes from one of these earlier groups. In 1837, B.B. Cannon, Indian Conductor, led a detachment of three hundred and sixty-five Cherokee along a route which passed through southwest Missouri.

According to the Journal of Occurrences, Conductor Cannon's hand-written diary, on the night of December 20th, 1837, the group camped at Mr. Allen's, a farm situated five miles west of the present town of Crane, Missouri. The journal, of course, emphasizes the Indians' pain and suffering. Several days earlier, on

December 16th, 1837, the group had stopped at Springfield, Missouri. Cannon noted that it snowed that night, and that Elijah's wife, and Charles Timberlake's son, Smoker, were buried. The weather was extremely cold; sickness prevailed to a considerable degree; and all were very much fatigued. On December 18th, the group was detained because of sickness and Dr. Townsend was forced to go back to Springfield to obtain medicine. Dreadful Waters was buried that evening. On December 19th, the group was also detained because of sickness and intense cold.

From such entries, we can see that the hills of the Ozarks, being near the end of the exhausting journey, must have been especially hard on the Cherokee. The one consolation undoubtedly would have been that they were nearing the Indian Territory. For Cannon's group, they would reach their goal on December 30th, 1837 after a grueling journey of seventy-eight days.

Fern Angus

"We always lie to strangers"
Vance Randolph

(Photo by Kathleen Van Buskirk)

Section VI

Historic Places

Although Ozark Mountain Country shares a common heritage and history which is reflected in the earlier sections of this book, each community also has a special character of its own. Therefore, in this final section, we offer histories of the area's communities. As the reader will see, some of the once prominent communities are now almost forgotten while some of the big name towns were late in developing. Because of their historical importance to the area, we also offer essays on the old Wire Road, the College of the Ozarks, Skaggs Community Hospital, and the Kanakuk Kamps.

This section is organized in alphabetical order for ease of reference.

Branson

The men who founded the town of Branson in 1903 were planning an industrial center in the Ozarks that would generate trainload after trainload of logs, lumber, and manufactured products for the outside world, thereby generating steady income for area residents. Today, as country music theaters, motels, and restaurants mushroom across the surrounding hills, an industrial boom has indeed come to Branson, but it is based on drawing tourists to the town's entertainment industry, not exporting the area's resources.

The logging industry near the mouth of Roark Creek on the White River began about the time the first steam engine of the St. Louis and San Francisco Railroad arrived at Springfield in 1870. In the next fifty years, millions of ties would be needed for the thousands of miles of railroad tracks which were to bring growth and industry to the midwest. In the 1870's, farmers along the upper White River began earning hard cash by hacking out ties and floating them to collection points like the waterfront near Roark Creek. From there, the ties were either loaded on freight wagons and hauled to Springfield or lashed into rafts and guided on downstream to the nearest railroad.

Despite that logging activity, when Reuben Branson, a young school teacher and storekeeper from Gasconade County in eastern Missouri, opened a store and established the Branson post office near the mouth of Roark Creek in 1882, all his neighbors were farmers. By the turn of the century, a water-driven mill for grinding grain and sawing lumber, a cotton gin, a tobacco barn, and a handle factory had been built near the Branson store. In 1886 Reuben Branson moved to Forsyth, the county seat, to take a political job, and William Hawkins became the Branson postmaster and storekeeper.

When Missouri Pacific building crews began preparing a railroad right of way across the Branson waterfront in 1903, railroad planners realized that the cost of establishing the White River Line through the rugged Ozarks Mountains from Carthage, Missouri to the

The Town Called "Lucia"

The Town of Lucia (the old timers pronounced it "Loo'sha") is one of Branson's early mysteries. The significance of the name seems to have been lost, but between May 2, 1901, and June 11, 1904, letters mailed at the Branson post office were cancelled with the name Lucia. Thomas Berry, who owned the farm where the post office was located, was determined not to sell his land to the Branson Town Company, a railroad backed group which was planning a plat for a town. Early in 1902, twenty months before a plat for a town of Lucia was filed, Thomas Berry died under questionable circumstances. His son Henry, named conservator of Tom Berry's estate, ordered the platting of Lucia in the spring of 1903, but a short time later he also died.

Conservatorship then passed to Tom Berry's son-in-law, who filed the plat, then relinquished most of the townsite to the Branson Town Company, still leaving the Lucia post office outside the town limits of both Lucia and Branson. The rest of the Berry farm was bought by a nearby rancher, Charley Thompson, who, in 1904, moved the post office to his new general store "in Branson" and changed the post office back to its original name.

Mississippi River at Helena, Arkansas would be very high.

To make the rail line profitable, the Missouri Pacific encouraged modern farming and marketing methods on the fertile uplands southeast of Carthage, and the clearing, draining, and farming of the rich swamplands in the Mississippi River delta region of east central Arkansas. The backers invested in orchards and cattle ranching, and planned industrial centers to tap the tremendous timber resources of the upper White River region and to exploit the new lead and zinc finds along the Missouri-Arkansas border. Not overlooked, of course, were the hundreds of miles of scenic valleys and bluffs which were sure to attract vacationers to the long inaccessible region.

When work on the railroad began, land agents had been in Taney County for several years, acquiring property for the planned railroad and for Charles Fulbright, president of the Branson Town Company. Fulbright was also the Missouri Pacific's immigration agent, hired to draw settlers, industries, and businesses to Branson. First he had to get control of enough land to plat a town.

Much controversy attended the acquisition of the needed land, and adjacent plats were filed in 1903; for a competing Town of Lucia on October 2nd, and for the Town of Branson, on October 26. By the end of November, Fulbright's Town Company owned both townsites but the two plats, with different block lengths and disconcerting jogs in streets, continue to puzzle motorists even today.

At the end of 1903, woods still covered many of the platted streets of Branson. The town's only business establishment, Henry Sullenger's two-story gabled saloon was situated several blocks up the hill from the center of today's downtown. The saloon had only recently opened when the railroad workers, who had no equipment to compact the built-up right-of-way, left the rail bed to settle for several months while they worked elsewhere on the White River line. Six months later, when workers returned to lay the tracks, Branson had become a modest town, with a hotel, a second saloon, two buildings belonging to doctors, and two general merchandise stores (one of which housed the Branson post office). All were located near Sullenger's saloon.

Early in 1905 the Branson Hotel, built by the Town Company, began providing comfortable lodgings for businessmen arriving to look over the town's prospects.

On June 10th that year, though the railroad bridge across the White River and the tunnel at the top of Turkey Creek were not finished, freight trains from

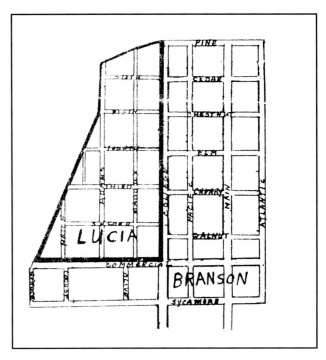

Plats filed for Lucia (Oct. 2, 1903) and Branson (Oct. 26, 1903).
(Plats courtesy of Karlene McGill)

the north began bringing supplies to Branson's growing population and returning north loaded with ties and logs.

Other area merchants and entrepreneurs began buying lots from the Town Company and moving their businesses to Branson, but the men who then were guiding the town's development, recruiting new industries, and underwriting much of the civic expenses were Springfield or St. Louis businessmen working with or directly for the railroad. Some of those men had been in the area for several years, involved in mining ventures and developing the Maine Fishing and Hunting Lodge and experimental orchards at nearby Point Lookout.

Vernon Todd, one of those St. Louis businessmen, ran a lumber yard a block from the railroad tracks and operated a small banking facility nearby. Early in 1906, as soon as the rail line was completed, Todd built a two-story, brick bank at Main and Commercial, the heart of the Branson Town Company's planned business district. When the bank opened its doors that

April, it was surrounded by empty lots and poorly defined streets—but not for long. Soon a hardware store, furniture store, and several smaller businesses appeared, all built by R.O. Whelchel. Nearby was a two-story, frame Commercial Hotel, and a large concrete, stone and brick business block with shops on the first floor and hotel rooms above, equipped with electric lights powered by a gasoline-run generator, and bathrooms with running water.

Through the next four years ten new industries came to Branson's waterfront: a cedar factory, wagon factory, foundry and machine works, wood products factory, box factory, a mill where wood veneer was made, a spoke factory, a tie and timber yard, a feed and flour warehouse, and a cannery.

Visiting newspaper editors toured the area and informed their readers of its beauty, its hunting and fishing pleasures, and Branson's industrial possibilities. Their news stories described the bustling Branson scene. Trains were bringing hundreds of visitors who filled local hotels, camped near farm homes in the vicinity, or tramped the hills for a day. On the White River at the end of Main Street, the Branson Boat Company had boats and fishing equipment for rent. Locally-built, gas-powered boats and motor launches were, by 1907, taking passengers up and down the river, their passage somewhat hampered by hundreds of floating logs. On the Branson waterfront, piles of logs lay at every turn. Bales of cotton awaited shipment beside the railroad tracks, and up Roark Creek, cattle were crowded in pens at rail sidings, about to be sent to market.

For the Fourth of July celebration in 1907, Branson's Commercial Club, anticipating many excursionists as well as local families, organized lakeside festivities: swimming, boat races, a picnic, a baseball game, dancing, fireworks, and political and religious speeches. It was an exciting celebration, though the boat races were cancelled, probably due to all those floating logs.

Branson's initial growth and industrialization were less spectacular than its founders had hoped. In October, 1907, Charles Fulbright, who had invested four years and much money promoting industry in "his

town," sold the remaining Town Company properties to a St. Louis company headed by Willard P. Heath, who two years before had supervised the building of the Maine Lodge at Point Lookout. Vernon Todd became the new president of the Town Company; his primary responsibility over the next several years was to get the businesses up on Third Street to move their wooden buildings to Commercial Street or Main.

By 1909 these buildings, formerly on Third Street, had been moved to Commercial.
(Photo by Kathleen Van Buskirk)

The consolidation of Branson's business district was an accomplished fact in 1910 when a surveying team for the Ambersen Hydraulic Construction Company began locating a site to build a hydroelectric dam across the White River.

The building of the Powersite Dam twelve miles downstream near Forsyth brought prosperity to Branson and began shifting the town's emphasis to tourism, though even today the maintenance of a manufacturing base continues to undergird many civic decisions. Most of the materials used in building the dam came first to the Branson depot, to be transported to the construction site on large, shallow-draft barges built on Branson's waterfront. Through the two years of construction, a continuous train of wagons delivered food, clothing, and other necessities for the thousand or more workers and their families housed temporarily near the damsite, as well as smaller items needed in the building process.

The cost of impounding Lake Taneycomo was $2,250,000. Every facet of the project brought dollars

The railroad helped consolidate the town of Branson. Railroad officials encouraged both industry and tourism in the White River Valley.
(Photo courtesy of Chloe LaRue)

and jobs to Branson's work oriented residents. When the dam was completed, enough local property was in taxpayer's hands to support the incorporation of Branson as a fourth class city.

When incorporated, on April 1, 1912, Branson had 1,200 residents. Its boundaries were Roark Creek on the north, the White River on the east and south, and, on the west, the original plat lines beginning at Roark Creek and extending to the White River. There

was a big indentation in that western boundary, however. The hillside acreage south of the platted town of Lucia became a part of Branson in 1916. Although platted as a housing subdivision in 1912, it was still being farmed by owner Charley Thompson.

C.H. Nichols, the first mayor of Branson, was still trying to organize his responsibilities on August 29, 1912 when the town's residents were wakened in the early morning hours by the frantic pealing of the bells

On August 29, 1912 Branson residents awoke to learn that a fire had broken out in a downtown hotel. Before the fire burned itself out, 21 businesses had been destroyed.
(Photo courtesy of Kathleen Van Buskirk)

in the Presbyterian Church tower. A fire had started in the Commercial Hotel. The town had no fire department. Even though every able-bodied man turned out to fight the blaze, by sunset twenty-one business buildings, including most of the wooden buildings that once stood on Third Street, were in ashes. The few businesses left standing—the Branson Hotel, Todd's lumber yard, the Bank of Branson, the railroad depot, and the saloon building (then a boarding house)—were far enough away to escape the flames.

In earlier years such a loss might have been the end of the town, but now the community went to work to reconstruct its business center.

A year later, all the buildings had been rebuilt, larger than before and now of bricks or cement blocks, and the downtown district's wooden sidewalks were now cement. But Branson's resilience was to be tested again. At 2:10 a.m. on October 17, 1913, gunfire and shouts alerted the newly trained volunteer firefighters to a blaze in Whelchel's "new, modern fireproof business block." Six businesses were destroyed, but much equipment and stock was carried to safety. The insured building was quickly rebuilt.

In the midst of the reconstruction following the 1912 fire, the first issue of the *White River Leader*, published May 9, 1913, announced that the dam near Forsyth had been completed. Within thirty-six hours torrential rains brought the waters of the new Lake Taneycomo to the top of the overflow dam. The river road to Forsyth was inundated. Creek crossings near the river became lake coves, rendering many roads unusable. However, overland roads, which followed old freight routes north and south of the lake, carried traffic to the county seat, and by mid-June the "Sammy Lane Passenger Boat" had been put into regular service, carrying people and the U.S. mail between Branson and Forsyth and to resorts along the lake.

That summer a steel bridge was completed across the White River at the end of Main Street, and a long "wagon bridge" allowed farmers to cross the newly widened mouth of Roark Creek, which could no longer be forded. Coon Creek, on the far side of Lake Taneycomo, also was bridged, and a road was cut along the base of the bluff so wagons could get to Hollister.

The unpaved road to Hollister continued south to the Maine Clubhouse and orchard, which became The School of the Ozarks after that boarding high school was burned out of its dormitory-classroom building at Forsyth in 1915.

A cooperative two-county road was built, leading west over Dewey Bald to the popular Shepherd of the Hills Farm and on to Reeds Spring in 1914.

Such roads were built for wagons and horses; for early automobiles they were a nightmare. Not until the 1920's did gasoline-powered road vehicles become commonplace in Branson, their purchase made reasonable by new Highway 3 (later U.S. 65) leading north from Branson to Springfield, and south by way of the Main Street bridge to Hollister and the Arkansas border. Nonetheless, between 1913 and the mid-1920's, thanks to the railroad and the new lake, tourism grew in the Branson area, even as the logging industry began to dwindle along with the supply of hardwood trees.

The idea of Branson as a resort town was taking root in 1914, spawning a commercial ice plant, a soft drink bottling plant, and candy and ice cream factories near the waterfront. The town's three hotels—the Commercial, Branson, and Malone (the latter renamed the White River Hotel in 1937)—were catering to vacationers, and neighboring factories and businesses were encouraged to stack their logs, lumber, and bricks so they looked more tidy.

Hobart McQuarter, who had a boat factory and a bulk gasoline business on Branson's waterfront in conjunction with his passenger service up and down the lake, built Branson's first vacation cabins—the Sammy Lane Resort—just upstream from the Main Street bridge. The cabins stood on stilts and were anchored with cables to keep floods from washing them away.

The women of Branson, many of whom were employed or helped operate family businesses, organized a Civic League in 1914 and began what would be a decades long effort to beautify the streets, establish parks, and make life better in their community. They paid off the debt on the old community building and in 1936 supplied the land where a new community building was built. They planned community celebrations and activities and provided the town a well-equipped municipal bathing beach and picnic ground on Lake Taneycomo.

By the 1930's Lake Taneycomo had become an inexpensive vacation spot easily accessible to distant or nearby cities by car or train. Visitors drawn by street fairs, parades, community picnics, and boat races, as well as by the scenic lake and hills, helped the town's businesses survive through the Depression and bank failures.

WPA projects acted as replacement for failed local industries in the 1930's. New bridges were built across Roark Creek and Lake Taneycomo; Highway 65 was realigned to the present Business 65 route and paved. Before the decade ended, a hard surface highway stretched from the Arkansas border to Springfield.

A municipal airport (a short grass landing strip) was built west of town in 1935 when Jim Owen was Mayor of Branson. Owen was an outgoing young man who in 1933 came to Branson to help his father go into business as a druggist. The town needed young Owen's enthusiasm. The local logging companies had dwindled to one, the American Cedar Pencil factory which, through the 1940's, continued shipping out cedar oil, fence posts, telephone poles, and cedar from which pencils would be made. The only other factories still operating were a stave factory, installed in the old tobacco warehouse in 1933, a box factory, and two canneries that bought produce from farmers and provided seasonal employment.

Jim Owen installed the town's first movie theater in 1934 in the Civic League's Community Hall, and soon thereafter began operating a fishing service out of an old factory just west of the railroad tracks. In 1936 he built the rustic Hillbilly Theater on South Commercial Street, thereby encouraging a local interest that had begun in 1906 when, the *Branson Echo* reported, "standing room only crowds enjoyed still pictures projected by light created by oxylithic gas." In 1916, an

Jim Owen, western actor Smiley Burnette, and Steve Miller in the 1940's when movie stars frequented Branson.
(Photo courtesy of Jim Gibbs)

"electric theater" opened in Branson, the first in the county; and in 1924, dreams of movie stardom were fostered in Branson when Professor Oscar R. Gleason of Kansas City set up a temporary studio downtown and bought acreage west of Branson for "a permanent movie studio and location work." For several weeks, comedian Lindsay Wilson was photographed by day and, in the evening, entertained in the community hall.

Local people again felt a personal interest in the movie industry in the 1930's and 1940's as they followed the career of Ned Mann, a director and special effects man who had grown up in Hollister. For a time Mann operated the Hollywood Hills Hotel, on a bluff overlooking Lake Taneycomo north of Branson, where many well-known motion picture celebrities stayed as his guests.

At Jim Owen's invitation, movie stars posed in front of the Hillbilly Theater, were guests of honor at extravagant festivities for local high school graduations, and enjoyed fishing expeditions on Lake Taneycomo. One even purchased a hideaway ranch in the nearby hills.

When inviting such celebrities to Branson, Owen always hoped that the White River would behave for the occasion. Though he had missed the famous flood of 1927, such events were all too frequent in the 1930's. Owen, like other Branson folk, came to a new understanding of the river in 1945, shortly before the end of World War II, when rampaging water covered the railroad tracks, flooded his warehouse, and tore the Main Street bridge from its mounts, sweeping it downstream and over Powersite Dam.

After World War II, many artists, craftsmen, and retirees came to the area, along with returning servicemen and war industry workers. One of those returning workers was artist Steve Miller, who took a job managing Jim Owen's Hillbilly Theater. In the late summer of 1949, he and businessman Joe Todd dreamed up the idea of putting a huge lighted Adoration Scene on the Mount Branson bluff, across Lake Taneycomo from downtown Branson. With help from local carpenters, the creche scene's figures, up to 28 feet tall, were in place for lighting on the first Sunday of that December, in front of thousands of awe-struck visitors.

In 1953, with more people coming for the lighting each year, the sponsoring Chamber of Commerce took a leaf from Branson's long history of Santa Claus parades, pet parades, and costume competitions, and added an Adoration Parade to the lighting ceremonies. The parade and ceremony, kept free of commercialism, today draws crowds as large as 30,000 people.

Preparations for the construction of Table Rock Dam began the year after the first Adoration Parade, and continued through most of the 1950's. When the dam was completed in 1959 and water rose to its expected average level, Branson's citizens were relieved that

floods no longer threatened their waterfront. Tourists came in growing numbers to enjoy the big new lake, the Herschends' fledgling 1890's Silver Dollar City theme park, and the Trimbles' new outdoor theater at the Shepherd of the Hills Farm. Resorts near Branson and on downstream were encouraging their guests to fish and to visit the area's new attractions. Lake Taneycomo was too cold for swimming now that it was fed by the deep cold waters of Table Rock Lake.

Branson's merchants welcomed the increasing number of tourists. However, the local cheese factory, which the Chamber of Commerce had encouraged to go into business in 1948 and which was buying milk from hundreds of area farmers—providing employment for truck drivers and for many workers in its processing plant—found it increasingly difficult to keep its trained workers during the summer tourist season.

The number of visitors to Branson and Taneycomo, Table Rock, and Bull Shoals Lakes has increased steadily over the thirty-three years since Table Rock Lake was completed. Each year has brought additional attractions designed to draw even more vacationers.

In 1960, just as tourism began to increase rapidly in the area, the Missouri Pacific cancelled all passenger service on its White River Line. With so many visitors arriving by automobile, traffic on winding U.S. 65 to Springfield often slowed to a crawl. To shorten and straighten that route, dynamite crews and earth moving equipment blasted a road through the limestone hills between Springfield and Branson. When the modern road surface was laid between the deep dramatic cuts and across more than a dozen new bridges, that driving distance was reduced from seventy-five miles to forty.

In the mid-1970's, a four-lane bypass was completed, rerouting U.S. 65 away from Branson's congested downtown business district and providing interchanges at Highway 76 and at Highway 248, and a new bridge across Lake Taneycomo. At that time, businesses were just beginning to develop along 76 west of Branson. Beyond the newly opened Wal-Mart store there were only a few scattered shops and five music shows.

The oldest existing commercial building in Branson was built around 1903. Today the building houses a memorabilia shop which caters to tourists.
(Photo by Kathleen Van Buskirk)

A decade later, eleven more music shows and many restaurants, motels, and tourist attractions had extended the built up area three miles further west, engulfing the city's old airport. The latter was no longer in use after 1970 when the recently developed college at the School of the Ozarks built a modern general aviation airport. Today most of the old airport land, owned by the city of Branson, is leased—to White-Water, the Factory Merchants' Mall, and other tourist businesses.

The Branson city limits now stretch west on Highway 76 to the old airport site, and north to include the high school and a large housing area off north U.S. 65. Though Highway 76 has been widened, and several traffic signals installed, congestion problems have not yet been overcome. In the 1990's, with continually increasing traffic buildup and the population in and around Branson probably twice the town's official "under 4,000," a network of by-pass roads is being developed, and there is talk of circle highways, and passenger trains, trams, and trolleys to move the ever-increasing number of visitors more efficiently.

The quiet little town of Branson has developed urban sprawl. Several years ago an Ozark Mountain Christmas season extended the tourist year to nine months; motels and tourist related shops multiply so fast it is hard to keep track of them; and the number of music shows, which started with the Baldknobbers in 1957 and increased to sixteen in the 1980's, now exceeds thirty.

In the first decade of this century, Branson's citizens and the Town Company worked very hard to turn Reuben Branson's country village into a prosperous industrial town and still attract sightseers and vacationers. Today those two aims are one, and Branson residents and their mayor, city council, the Chamber of Commerce, and the Downtown Branson Betterment Association face many new challenges as they go about the business of welcoming and entertaining more than a hundred thousand visitors each day in their overgrown small town in the Ozarks.

Kathleen Van Buskirk

Cape Fair

Nestled like a jewel amidst the lakes and trees of the Ozark hills, the quaint village of Cape Fair has become a mecca for fisherman from all walks of life. Tourists come by the thousands to the little community for a relaxing vacation in the heart of Ozark Mountain Country.

Most visitors do not realize that Cape Fair is one of the oldest settlements in Missouri's Stone County. In 1835, the John B. Williams, Zachariah Henson, and Elijah McLain Todd families made their way overland from Kentucky and Tennessee to Missouri. Legend ascribes the naming of the town to members of this party. A young man, his sister, and his sweetheart were bound for what is now the Cape Fair area. They became friends with some Delaware Indians and pushed on ahead of the rest of their own group. When the Indians led them to a high hill, a vantage point at the confluence of the James River and Flat Creek, one of the girls exclaimed over the beauty of the scene. She then asked the Indians what they would call such a cape. The Delaware responded with a term which, when translated, was Fair Cape, so the area became know as Cape Fair.

The Williams, Henson, and Todd families, traveling by oxen drawn, two-wheel carts, arrived in the area on Christmas Day. They lost no time in constructing log dwellings for themselves. Zachariah and Armala Henson, newly-weds, resided in a log cabin for many years until Zachariah went up Flat Creek, cut large pine logs, and rafted them downstream to build a new house. This house, still standing at the turn of the century, had a great stone chimney with the date 1850 inscribed on it. In addition, Zachariah built a water-powered mill, which he operated for many years. As did all the new settlers, he farmed, but he also ran a big wool carding machine.

John B. Williams, in partnership with Elijah Todd built a powder mill on Flat Creek near the settlement. A heavy log frame was first built in the water course with a huge sycamore log as a cross beam. A depression was hewed in the log to accommodate an undershot water wheel, which provided the power. Ingredients used in producing the powder were saltpeter, sulphur, and charcoal. The saltpeter was obtained at Bear Den Cave on the James River. Three grades of powder were made: coarse musket powder, a medium grain for shotguns, and a very fine powder for squirrel rifles. In addition to the Williams' mill—the first powder mill west of the Mississippi River—the small village boasted a sawmill, gristmill, general store, blacksmith shop, distillery, and cotton gin.

In organizing Stone County's government, meetings were held in the homes of Cape Fair's early families. However, when Stone County began operation in 1851, Galena became the county seat.

A devastating flood on the James River and Flat Creek in 1885 destroyed much of the small town and the powder mill. Residents, fearful of rebuilding on the flood plain, moved their homes to higher ground, two miles south of the original site. Business establishments followed.

Now, more than a century later, Cape Fair is experiencing rapid growth and has a stable economy—thanks to the coming of Table Rock Lake. The population is comprised of both the descendants of the early settlers and newer arrivals, drawn to the attractive and thriving location. Although Cape Fair has experienced a boom, life still flows along at a leisurely pace—which makes it especially attractive to the tourist.

Fern Angus

Working for an Education
College of the Ozarks

Visitors to the College of the Ozarks often comment on the beauty of the campus—the white stone buildings, the gem-like lake and sparkling fountain, and the colorful flower beds. But why, they ask, are cows grazing in the field beside the entry road? The answer helps explain the purpose and character of the college. To pay for their education, the school's 1,600 students work—they tend cows, maintain campus buildings, cook and serve meals, help run an airport, man the campus fire trucks, and fulfill dozens of other work assignments.

Mitchell Hall, the first building on the campus at Forsyth, was built with much volunteer labor in 1907. It was destroyed by fire in 1915.
(Photo courtesy of Walker Powell)

The school's goal of offering an opportunity to work for an education goes back to its origin. At the turn of the century, area students attended school only three or four months a year and seldom were educated beyond the eighth grade. Even their teachers normally had only an elementary education. Eager to improve this situation, the Reverend James Forsythe, a Presbyterian pastor, proposed the establishment of a boarding

school in the town of Forsyth. In 1902, he challenged church leaders to develop a mission high school where youngsters could meet most of their educational expenses by working.

Help came from many directions: Masonic Lodge members and the Reverend A.Y. Beatie, a Presbyterian evangelist in the area, collected enough money to purchase 160 acres on top of the hill east of town. Two businessmen in St. Joseph, Missouri pledged funds to build and equip a fifty by seventy-five foot stone building. The Presbyterian Synod of Missouri set up an educational corporation and appointed a Board of Trustees.

With the help of volunteer labor, Mitchell Hall was built, and on September 24, 1907, the School of the Ozarks opened in Forsyth with 128 students. Sixteen were boarders and 112 were children from the Forsyth

The College of the Ozarks began as a work-study school (above); but friendships have always been held dear by those who attended. At right are early students Miss Ray, Miss Wright, and Miss Myteler Bonebrake.
(Photos by Harrison Powell)

school, ranging down to the first grade. Voters in the local school district, anxious for their children to participate in the nine-month school year, had agreed to share the educational expenses.

The director of the School of the Ozarks faced the daunting task of organizing a curriculum for grammar and high school students, supervising the boarding students' work, study, and leisure activities, and making sure the boarders and staff were adequately fed and housed. The matron, four teachers, and the farm supervisor saw their work as a mission and their motivation was high. Though they were paid little more than their room and board, they ran the school as a self-sustaining family. Along with academic subjects such as mathematics and history, students learned manners and morals. The boarding students interspersed their lessons with cooking and cleaning, washing and ironing, plowing, planting, and harvesting; tending and butchering cows, hogs, and chickens; and chopping endless stacks of firewood for the school's thirty stoves.

In 1913, the Forsyth school board learned that tax money could not be paid to a church related school, and beginning that year the School of the Ozarks taught only eighth grade and high school students. Eighth grade instruction, used to remedy weaknesses in students' preparation for high school, was eventually discontinued when nine-month school years became common in the region's public schools.

Had the commitment of the school's faculty and backers to educational opportunity not been as strong as it was, the institution might easily have been forced to close its doors in 1915 when Mitchell Hall—the major building on the campus at that time—was destroyed by fire. In mid-January, with the teachers and thirty-five boarding students all asleep in the second story dormitories, fire broke out in the building. Everyone escaped without serious injury, but few belongings and little equipment was saved. Through the remainder of the academic year, while President John Crocker and the Board searched for a new location for

When fire destroyed Mitchell Hall, students moved from Forsyth to the Old Maine Building (renamed Dobyns Hall) near Branson. In 1930 the log building was also destroyed by fire. Abernathy Hall, below, was the first building constructed by students on the new campus.
(Photos courtesy of Charlene Cox)

the school, classes were held in the Forsyth grammar school and boarding students were placed in private homes in town.

The School of the Ozarks reopened the following September in the Maine Lodge, a sprawling log building on 207 acres at Point Lookout, overlooking the White River. The property, developed by the St. Louis Fishing and Hunting Club, was purchased with the $15,000 insurance check for the loss of Mitchell Hall. Along with the lodge, the school acquired a dormitory, kitchen, and dining room in a two-story building, several farm buildings, and eighty cultivated acres, mostly planted in fruit trees.

The lodge became Dobyns Hall, with the upper floor used as dormitories for the girls and the women teachers. On the first floor, the large central hall became a living room and the north wing a chapel. The dormitories offered more student housing than Mitchell Hall, and from hills and hollows all over the region, youngsters enrolled, anxious to get a high school education by working for it. Monday was a work day. From Tuesday through Saturday students attended classes and did their chores, while on Sunday students attended church and a strictly supervised afternoon social hour.

The new president, Reverend George Lucius Washburn, searched for funds to operate and enlarge the school. More dormitory space was high on the list of needs. In 1917, H. T. Abernathy, a wealthy Kansas City sportsman, provided $11,000 for a modern dormitory. Students built the structure under the direction of a work supervisor. The stone for Abernathy Hall was quarried and dressed on campus. The building housed manual training shops, a print shop, classrooms, and housing for forty boys. Despite the added dormitory space, in 1919 the school had to turn away fifty applicants. Mr. Abernathy, pleased with the industry of the students, donated another $10,000 for a second dormitory, Stevenson Hall, with space for sixty girls, a kitchen, dining room, and laundry.

Twenty-seven year old Robert McGowan Good, the superintendent of schools at Lexington, Mississippi, came to the School of the Ozarks as president in June, 1921. For the next thirty-one years, Good led the school, bringing it up to accreditation standards by 1925, and enlarging the institution's scope with a dozen or more new buildings, all built by the students with donated funds. During those years, Good and his wife Lyta Davis Good, who had been on the staff of the school since 1912, educated the minds and molded the characters of over two thousand youngsters, many of whom became teachers, doctors, lawyers, and businessmen.

When Good first arrived, many of the youths who came to the School of the Ozarks had little prior contact with religion. To compensate for this shortcoming, Good instituted a Bible Assembly each morning before breakfast, and prayers were said at every meal. In 1922, the campus chapel became a Presbyterian Church, and four years later almost a hundred students were on its membership roll. In the mid-1930's the school brought a minister on staff as chaplain and religious instructor. Today's chaplain is responsible for the spiritual life of the students, who are required to attend a specific minimum number of the chapel's non-denominational Christian services and religious convocations each semester.

In the difficult days of the Depression and the shortage-filled years of World War II, feeding the school's 200 students was a constant concern. A cannery donated in 1927, and a larger 1938 replacement allowed student workers to preserve the fruits, vegetables, and meat grown on campus, ensuring an adequate diet every day of the year. The sale of surpluses added to the school's operating funds.

The days of the boarding high school were numbered, however. By 1946, nine-month school years could be found in most Ozark towns of any size, and school consolidation and busing brought twelve years of education within the reach of most area children. Dr. Good and the board of trustees were well aware that the need for the boarding high school would one day disappear, despite the fact that there were 240 boarding students at the School of the Ozarks, most on full work scholarships.

Dr. Good, overloaded with work, welcomed to his staff energetic M. Graham Clark, a thirty-seven year old Atlanta insurance man, and former major in the Air Corps. For the next six years Clark worked as vice president, becoming familiar with the school's operation and the student body, helping to raise funds, and preparing for the day when the school would become a college.

In 1952, Dr. Good retired to emeritus status, and Clark, recently ordained as a Presbyterian minister, became president. Dr. Good, however, remained on the staff through the next twelve years as the school evolved into a four year liberal arts college. The two men worked together, maintaining a viable accredited high school for the younger students, and also inaugurating a two-year college in 1956. The junior college received tentative accreditation in 1958, enabling the first of the school's junior college graduates to transfer

Dr. Good and Dr. Clark—their combined terms as president spanned sixty years.
(Photos courtesy of Lois Holman)

course credits to the University of Missouri and other four year colleges. Full accreditation followed in 1961.

The school's leaders and the board of directors faced many challenges in shifting the school's emphasis to post-secondary education. A well-qualified college faculty had to be assembled, and the process of restructuring the work program to fit more mature students began. Rules of behavior and curfew, which had served well with high school students but seemed dictatorial and childish to young people in college, had to be amended. To meet the spiritual needs of the growing student body, an imposing Gothic chapel was completed in 1958 near the spot where the old log Dobyns Hall stood before it burned in 1930.

In 1967, the last nineteen high school students graduated, along with the first sixty-nine students receiving bachelor's degrees. At that time, Dr. Good, after 15 years as president emeritus, retired again. However, for the next eight years until his death in 1975, he could be found at his desk every day, answering his portion of the mountain of mail received at the school and encouraging each student who came his way.

By the early 1970's, a thousand college students studied and worked on campus, taught by thirty-four full time professors and instructors plus nine who worked part-time. The school's farm, which had from the beginning provided food for the campus and work experience for students, was developing a modern agribusiness curriculum under the guidance of Dr. Howard Doane, a pioneer developer of systematic agricultural business practices at the University of Missouri. An airport was built north of the farm complex and an aviation science department was established. And on the stages of the Beacon Hill Theater (since destroyed by fire) and Jones Auditorium, music and theater students put on performances before tourists, townspeople, and fellow students.

Today, in every course of study, the faculty works to provide hands-on experience which complements the students' learning and prepares them for the business or profession they seek to enter. Work assignments on campus are learning tools, taken seriously by the seventy to seventy-five work supervisors. First year assignments are designed to instill responsible work habits, and are assigned randomly. By the students' senior year, many work in situations directly related to their chosen career field.

Over the past twenty-five years, the faculty has more than doubled, with a high percentage holding doctorates. The growing college curriculum and supporting services have brought more than forty new buildings to the campus—dormitories, classrooms, auditoriums, a fieldhouse, the airport, and a modern cafeteria and student center. Several new agricultural buildings have been built, and land acquisitions have increased the campus to 2,000 acres.

The college president is continually on the move, dealing with his campus responsibilities and cheering on the thousands of alumni and local friends who contribute to the college. He must also find benefactors to finance campus growth, provide scholarship funds for the students, and support the growing campus payroll.

The president dealing with today's challenges is Dr. Jerry Davis, who came to the School of the Ozarks in 1988, after eleven years as president of Alice Lloyd College, a similar institution in Kentucky. One major

Beautiful Memorial Chapel on the College of the Ozarks campus is visited by thousands each year. The chapel signifies the importance of religion and values in the education of young people at the school.
(Photo by Kathleen Van Buskirk)

change greets visitors at the gate today. In 1991, the school's name was changed to the College of the Ozarks.

In recent years, the College of the Ozarks, "the school that works for a living," has been rated a "Best Buy" among midwestern liberal arts colleges, but that is something the school's neighbors in Taney and Stone Counties have known about since 1907, when the parents of Forsyth helped build Mitchell Hall so their children could have the benefit of a nine-month school year.

Kathleen Van Buskirk

Crane

For many years, Crane claimed the distinction of having the largest population of any community in Stone County. Since the town had a railroad depot, it served as the center of a trade area which extended north to Marionville and south to Galena and the James River. As the importance of the railroad waned and tourism increased, Kimberling City on the shores of Table Rock Lake replaced Crane as the economic and population center of Stone County.

The town of Crane and the creek which runs alongside it both derived their names from the wading birds which frequent the stream. Though the birds are actually herons, locals have always called them "cranes." Of course, the first inhabitants of Crane Creek valley were Indians. Traces of Indian culture have been found along the stream east of the present town of Crane as well as in the many caves along the banks of the stream's sparkling waters.

The small town of Crane had its beginnings on the south bank of Crane Creek, near the location of the present city. At first, the settlement was called Hickory Grove, taking its name from an early school which was located in a grove of hickory trees. This school stood directly north of the present Christian Church on Highway 13. When the school was destroyed by a tornado, its replacement was erected directly across the creek to the north. Later, still other schools were built. One was erected in what was called South Town, or Old Town; then in 1911-1912, a brick school building went up in North Town. Finally in 1920, after voters approved a bond issue, the present school was built.

In early years, the community was drawn together and found its identity largely through the schools. But the growth of the area from a scattering of settlements to a real town can be attributed largely to the coming of the Missouri Pacific Railroad in 1904. With the influx of new business, the town advertised itself as "on the map with both feet."

The tomato growing and canning industry helped to support the community for many years. The hills and rocky soil of Stone County were not conducive to many types of farming, but were especially suited for growing tomatoes. In fact, Porter Lucas of Crane owned canning factories in Crane, Elsey, Quail Spur, Hurley, and Abesville.

From 1940 to 1960 a large percentage of the farms in Stone County had sizable chicken sheds. The farms were diversified, and the extra income from the chicken production boosted the economy. However, when the large feed companies began supplying the broiler industry, production costs increased and the average farmer could not generate enough profits to continue to produce broilers. Though the demise of the broiler industry in Stone County was a blow to the local economy, the industry's influence still survives. Crane, once acclaimed the capital of the area's broiler raising industry, still sponsors a Broiler Festival begun in 1952 by the Southwest Broiler Association. This event is held annually on the last Friday and Saturday in August. Thousands of broilers are barbecued and served to visitors who come from far and near. Revenues generated by the Festival are used to help local charities.

Fern Angus

A Town Of Many Courthouses
Forsyth

The fortunes of Forsyth, Missouri, have fluctuated with the status of Taney County's courthouses. Since 1837, when the Missouri Legislature set boundaries for the new county and named Forsyth as its seat of justice, inhabitants of the town have seen nine courthouses go up. These courthouses range from the log farm home that hosted the county's first grand jury hearings and administrators' sessions to a one and a quarter million dollar second-story addition completed in 1990.

Prior to 1835 when legislators decided to split Taney County from southern Greene County, before 1821 when the state of Missouri entered the Union, and before 1812 when the Territory of Missouri was formed, the future townsite at the mouth of Swan Creek had been populated by more than wildlife. For hundreds of years before the white man arrived, Osage Indians favored the fertile land on the banks of the White River as their winter hunting grounds.

Legends, persistent but never confirmed, suggest that French and Spanish explorers trekked through the area, trading with the Osage for pelts of bison, bear, and elk and seeking lodes of gold and silver.

Henry Rowe Schoolcraft put the area on a map in 1818 when he explored along the shores of Swan Creek and found three abandoned Osage hunting camps. Seven miles downstream, near the mouth of Beaver Creek, he stumbled onto two white men, James Fisher and William Holt, building cabins. A few years later, the lands along the river held thousands of Algonquin Indians, displaced from their homelands in the east. But the land and its wildlife could not support so large a force, and the Indians soon faced starvation. In 1830, the federal government removed the Indians to northeastern Kansas where they would have access to the huge buffalo herds.

After the Indians left, settlers from east of the Mississippi River pushed into the Ozarks, first poling crudely constructed flatboats up the White River, then

A street scene in early Forsyth when the town was located on the flood plain at the mouth of Swan Creek. (Photo courtesy of Chloe LaRue)

driving wagons along wilderness roads hacked through the forests.

When the Legislature officially organized Taney County in 1837, population density was 1.5 individuals per square mile. The governor appointed three county administrators and a sheriff. The administrators organized and named townships and designated county roads; they recruited justices of the peace and provided for civil and criminal courts; then they established voting precincts and arranged for elections.

These administrators also adopted the double log, clapboard shingled home of Jesse Jennings as Taney County's first seat of justice. Jennings' cabin was located on the north bank of the White River, a short distance upstream from what is known today as Cedar Point. The historic point is situated a few hundred yards down Highway 176 from its junction with Highway 160 in north Forsyth.

The governor also appointed a committee to select Taney County's seat of justice. But arguments over the location raged between the governor's commission and local citizens. At that time, there were no settlements in Taney County that could be identified as villages or towns. Wherever the courthouse was located, a town would undoubtedly spring up.

Finally, the competition came down to two sites: the mouths of Bull Creek and Swan Creek. Proponents of the Swan Creek location erected a log courthouse there. The governor's men chose Bull Creek instead and built a cedar log courthouse near the old Renshaw Cemetery.

In 1841, Taney County voters selected the Swan Creek site, but a lawsuit was filed, and officials continued to hold court in the Bull Creek courthouse. For three years, Taney County had two functioning courthouses. Finally the Legislature settled the argument by designating the mouth of Swan Creek as the official site for the county seat. The log cabin on the banks of Swan Creek became Taney County's legitimate courthouse. A flood swept away that log cabin in 1844 so another went up in its place. However, the dispute over the Legislature's decision would continue.

Several years before Missouri's legislators mapped out Taney County, a merchant named David Shannon operated a trading post at the mouth of Swan Creek. His customers were the Indians and, later, the white settlers.

In the autumn of 1837, John W. Hancock established a post office alongside Shannon's trading post—the only post office between Carrollton, Arkansas and Springfield, Missouri. Hancock registered the post office as Forsyth, in honor of his friend, John Forsyth, a former Georgia governor and Andrew Jackson's secretary of state.

In 1843, John W. Danforth, ancestor of longtime Missouri senator, John C. Danforth, bought Shannon's trading post. Two years later, Danforth acquired title to the fifty acres of land that comprise the peninsula between Swan Creek and White River. Today that land is the Forsyth City Park. Danforth and his wife deeded the land to Taney County for the county seat's townsite. When the town was platted, officials dedicated a square block for a new courthouse. Surrounding the courtyard were streets named for political figures: Jefferson Street for Thomas Jefferson, Jackson Street for Andrew Jackson, Benton Street for Thomas Hart Benton, a popular state senator.

During the next few years, farmers settled in and around Forsyth. They came mainly from slave-holding states in the east—Virginia and the Carolinas, Kentucky and Tennessee. Many brought Negroes to work their cotton fields, although farming and logging proved to be the most profitable businesses. Water-powered gristmills and sawmills operated, subscription schools opened, roads were extended, and two steamboats even made it up the White River to Forsyth.

By 1855, with the expanding population and a healthy economy, the log courthouse became inadequate. The Legislature gave county officials authority to finance construction of a new courthouse by selling half a million acres of government lands, issuing bonds, and levying taxes. Soon, Forsyth had a new three-story brick courthouse, reputedly one of the finest buildings in the White River Valley.

Six years later, the Civil War wreaked havoc upon the nation and no less upon the Ozarks. Forsyth became a pivotal arena in the bitter conflict between the North and South. Early in the fray, a company of Rebels seized the courthouse for their headquarters and a storage depot. On July 22, 1861, twelve hundred Union troops arrived to drive the Confederates back to Arkansas. Cannonballs from the Union's twelve-pound howitzers tore gaping holes in each of the building's three stories. Their mission accomplished, federal troops retired to their Springfield headquarters. The Confederates moved back in. Nearly a year later, Union soldiers returned, and the Rebels again vacated the courthouse. Before the last blue uniform had disappeared, the Rebels came back. This seesaw of occupancy occurred so many times that Union commanders finally dispatched several units to set up an outpost at Forsyth. These soldiers, fearing a Confederate attack, tore down houses and built breastworks and a stockade around the courthouse.

But on April 22, 1863, federal troops were called elsewhere. To keep the fortifications out of enemy hands, they fired the town. All that remained of Taney County's seat of justice was the burned-out shell of the once proud brick courthouse. From then until the end the conflict, there was no courthouse; there was no need for one as there were no elections, no county officials, and no county business to conduct.

In fact, for eleven years after the Civil War ended, Taney county did without a civil government. Those few inhabitants who returned to rebuild their homes lived in extreme poverty amid devastation. And they suffered under a state of anarchy, for the outlaws who had preyed on civilians during the war were still around, bullying the unprotected citizens.

Finally, the governor appointed new officials and charged them with reorganizing Taney County and reconstructing the courthouse by erecting new walls inside the old brick structure. But weak law enforcement and demoralized courts did little to halt the vengeful cycle of violence between neighbors—some of whom had fought for the Union, others for the Confederacy. Criminals turned into scofflaws and escaped across the border into Arkansas or Indian Territory.

The disarray gave birth to renewed petitions to relocate the seat of justice. Elections to award the county seat to Kissee Mills or Taney City, now called Taneyville, failed to garner the necessary two-thirds majority vote. The dissension also spawned the Bald Knobbers, one of the nation's fiercest, largest, and longest-lasting vigilante groups. In 1885, a ruckus over political corruption prompted an arsonist to set fire to the courthouse. The building was utterly ruined and its records destroyed. Because the fire was strongly suspected to be arson, the county's insurer refused to cover the loss. For the next five years, county officials operated out of rented office space in various Forsyth buildings.

The Bald Knobbers rampaged across the county until 1888, when a handful of citizens known as Anti-Bald Knobbers killed the vigilante group's leader and put an end to the fearsome reign.

In 1890, Forsyth was incorporated as a town, and the Missouri Legislature, calling the courthouse fire a public calamity, appropriated five thousand dollars

toward construction of a new building. The new two-story stone building, forty by fifty feet, was the county's seventh courthouse in fifty-three years.

Peace and a semblance of prosperity descended on Forsyth at last. Famous visitors were soon drawn to the area. In 1896, after losing the presidential election, William Jennings Bryan selected Forsyth for a

Forsyth's seventh courthouse was built in 1890.
(Photo courtesy of Chloe LaRue)

rest. Learning of his presence, the citizens of Forsyth insisted that he address them, which he did—from the steps of the courthouse.

In 1906, the completion of railway tracks brought trains to the new towns of Branson and Hollister. The mail arriving there by rail then came by riverboat to Forsyth. Before long, tourists from Kansas City, St. Louis, Chicago, and other cities discovered the peace to be gained by vacationing in the Ozarks. Because there were few roads, the visitors boated over to Forsyth from the train depots.

Then in 1913, the construction of Powersite Dam, upriver from Forsyth, created Lake Taneycomo (the name is an abbreviation of Taney County, Missouri). At that time, Powersite was one of the nation's largest dams used exclusively for the generation of power.

Lake Taneycomo attracted more tourists than ever. An isolated resort near Forsyth became a favored watering hole of insiders from Kansas City's Pendergast regime, including a fledgling politician named Harry S. Truman. The resort, with its broad verandas overlooking the lake, still stands, operating as the Plantation Hills nursing home.

Newly paved roads in the 1930's and rural electrification in 1941 enticed an ever-increasing number of tourists and new residents to Forsyth and the surrounding area.

Then in 1947, the U.S. Corps of Engineers announced its plans to construct Bull Shoals Dam north of Cotter, Arkansas. The huge dam would control floods on the White River and generate hydroelectric power. The result, Bull Shoals Lake, earned fame for its walleye and its largemouth, spotted, and white bass.

Water backing up behind the dam would inundate the town of Forsyth, which was located on a flood plain. Federal officials offered city fathers two options: they could either relocate Forsyth, accepting reimbursement to rebuild their waterworks, streets, and city hall; or the town could cease to exist, forcing its inhabitants to accept payment for the assessed value of their homes and establish themselves elsewhere. The city opted for the high ground west of the cliff called Shadow Rock. The new townsite had originally been a large farmstead and in later years a golf course.

The federal government started acquiring land in 1950. Farmers, homeowners, and businessmen from the drainage basin resented the forced eviction. The heartbreak of giving up long-held family homesteads, of reinterring coffins in new cemeteries, of envisioning old landmarks inundated by seventy feet of water caused much confusion and dismay.

Since the building of additional high dams upstream, the ravaging waters which once flooded old Forsyth have been controlled, but prolonged rainy seasons cause scenes like this at Old Forsyth Park and the County Fairgrounds. (Photo by Kathleen Van Buskirk)

In 1911 the Ozark Power and Water Company began construction of Powersite Dam, a privately owned dam on a public waterway, the White River near Forsyth.

A new town, Camp Ozark, was created to house workers at the dam site. A power plant, (left) was constructed. Building materials arrived by rail at Branson, then (below) were moved to the construction site.

The gates of Powersite Dam were closed on May 9, 1913.
The dam, with its 546 foot wide spillway and 70 foot face,
creates the 22 mile long Lake Taneycomo.
(The photos on these pages were taken by the Hall Photo Co.
and are courtesy of Chloe LaRue.)

In the midst of the confusion came renewed debates about establishing the county seat at Taneyville or Branson. But Forsyth's officials granted land to Taney County on which to build another new courthouse, and the seat of justice remained in the new Forsyth. The federal government awarded the county $75,000 for construction of a Spanish style, one-story building with an inner courtyard. That courthouse remained a Forsyth landmark until 1989, when the courtyard was closed and a $1.25 million, second story addition was erected above the first.

Yet, despite all the hubbub surrounding each of the nine different courthouses that for more than a century and a half dominated the heart of Forsyth, the community remained imperturbable. Amid fervent battles over relocating the county seat, despite the demolition of its courthouses by cannonballs, arsonists, floods, and the government's God-like usurpation, the town of Forsyth has continued to grow and excite the interest of an unusual combination of inhabitants. The present-day population of Forsyth represents a congenial diversity: men and women descended from early-day homesteaders; retirees from all corners of the country—some whose careers took them around the globe and who plan to spend their twilight years fishing or golfing; and tourists seeking a slower pace and more peace than is available in the busier tourist areas.

Mary Hartman

Forsyth

When I go back to Forsyth
I'll go across the hill;
I'll not go by the water
Nor near the old red mill.

When I go back to Forsyth
I'll go the mountain trail;
I'll keep my eyes from turning
Down Swan Creek's pleasant vale.

For should I go the valley road
Bright shadows there I'd see
Lovers gaily roaming
The lass I used to be.

Mary Elizabeth Mahnkey

Galena: The Tenacious Town

Galena as it appeared after the turn of the century. The fortunes of Galena have always been closely tied to the James River and, later, Table Rock Lake.
(Photo courtesy of Chloe LaRue)

Galena, the county seat of Stone County, had its origins almost 150 years ago, but at another site and with another name. Galena's early history can only be garnered from fragmentary comments in old county history books, from references in old diaries, and from information passed down orally. During the first half of the nineteenth century, a town by the name of Jamesville was established on the James River in Mack Spring Hollow, about five miles southwest of the current town site. In 1844, one of the ravaging floods which roar down the James River washed the town away. The town's residents, in the search of a safe haven, moved up the river to the present site of Galena. For another ten years, the town retained the name of Jamesville.

When the county was formed and Jamesville became the county seat of Stone County in 1851, the town was still little more than a peach orchard. The first three commissioners, appointed by the governor to serve until a general election could be held, met in the cabin of John B. Williams on April 7, 1851.

Stone County's close ties to Taney County were evident from its formation. Not only was much of Stone County carved from Taney County, but it was named for Judge William Stone of Taney County. The Taney County Collector was authorized to collect Stone County's revenue the first year of its existence, and the representative to the state General Assembly served both Stone and Taney Counties.

During the first decade the county was in existence, the commissioners dealt with a variety of issues that affected the town and county. The first year, the commissioners approved the building of a courthouse for $375. In 1853 the minutes of a commissioners' meeting refer to the county seat as Galena—the first indication of the name change. They also built a double-walled log jail. Funds were then expended to build roads. An east-west road across the county to connect Galena with Cassville, the county seat of Barry County, and Forsyth, the county seat of Taney County, became a high priority.

Animals, too, were within the jurisdiction of the commissioners. In 1854 the commissioners set a $1.00 bounty on wolf scalps, although thereafter the bounty fluctuated from year to year. Today one can only wonder at the stories of wolf hunts which must have flourished around Galena each time a scalp was brought to the courthouse. Commissioners were also required by state law to find the ownership of stray animals. Early court records give detailed descriptions of stray horses, cattle, oxen, and a few hounds. The descriptions were posted prominently at the courthouse and at trading centers. If the rightful owner could not be found, the animals were sold at half of their established value.

Within a few short years, the Civil War played havoc with Galena and all of Stone County. Even though no major battle took place in the county, the county was ravaged. Southern troops from Arkansas, marching to Springfield for the battle at Wilson Creek, passed along the Wire Road in the northern part of Stone County. These troops foraged the countryside as they passed through—as did other units from both sides over the next four years. In addition, the conflicting loyalties of the county's residents, who often made war on each other, caused much chaos.

Because the terrain was rough and hiding easy, outlaws, desperados, bushwhackers, and deserters from both sides sought out the area to prey on the defenseless population. Criminal deeds were perpetrated by such men as Alf Bolin and his gang in the northern part of the county and Ike Bledsoe in the southern part. Most of the county was terrorized. Homes were burned, crops destroyed, and livestock plundered and killed— all at a time when many of the men in the county were away fighting for the side of their choice.

One vivid account of plundering during the Civil War tells of a band of desperados from Arkansas who, marauding in Stone County, took several cows belonging to residents in and around Galena. The band then fled southward down Railey Creek on its way back to Arkansas. But members of the Home Guard—middle-aged and older men who banded together to protect the community—pursued the bandits, caught them south of present-day Reeds Spring and took the cattle back. Though the desperados escaped, they were still trailed by a few members of the Home Guard. When the bushwhackers bedded down for the night a few miles fur-

ther south, members of the home guard attacked and killed many, or perhaps all, of the thieves and threw their bodies into a nearby pond. For many years thereafter men and boys would go to the pond south of Reeds Spring—a pond which came to be called Ghost Pond—and retrieve human bones and skulls from its murky bottom.

In time, the gruesome acts of the Civil War faded into the past, and the county began to heal. By the turn of the century, optimism, generated by the building of a railroad, prevailed in Galena and Stone County. Work gangs traveled up and down the county, building the railroad tracks that ran through the town. An article in the weekly county newspaper, *The Stone County Oracle*, published in Galena, chronicled the building of the railroad. The major addition in Galena was the construction of the railroad bridge over the James River which was completed in 1904. The railroad stimulated various forms of economic development: a railway station and stock yards were built, and the railway expedited the export of timber products and farm produce.

For the following thirty to forty years, Galena flourished as a trading center for the area. For a while, railroad ties were the most important export. Meanwhile, buildings began to spring up around the square. A tomato canning factory was established. In 1915 the second bridge across the James River, a wagon bridge, was completed. Electricity was introduced to the town in the early 1920s when two brothers, Leonard and Ray Schultz, installed a water wheel and generator in the James River and wired the homes in Galena. When heavy rains and a swollen river washed out the water wheel, the brothers installed a petroleum-driven generator in the back of an auto repair shop on the town square. Electricity was supplied to town residents from 6:00 a.m. until midnight, daily. In 1927 the third bridge (known as the "Y" bridge) was built across the James River. Dewey Short, who would shortly become a nationally famous congressman, spoke at the dedication ceremonies of this automobile bridge.

The town's history was not all progress; several

infamous events also occurred. Leonard Short, well known and liked resident and the congressman's brother, died violently after escaping from prison in Oklahoma. He had been arrested and convicted for participating in several armed robberies in the Tulsa area. Thousands of Stone County residents attended his funeral in December, 1935. Likewise, hundreds of people turned out for the legal hanging of Roscoe Jackson on the courthouse square in Galena on May 21, 1937.

Life in Galena during the first half of this century was probably much like any county seat town in south-ern Missouri, except Galena had one special attribute. During this period Galena became famous for the world class float trips down the fish-laden and scenic James River. Fishermen could leave Galena on a three day float and arrive at the confluence of the James and White River, take a five-day float down the meandering river to Branson, or an even longer float into Arkansas.

Shortly after the turn of the century, the first camps and fishing lodges began to appear on the river at Galena. Fishermen from throughout the midwest, arriving in trains, on horse drawn hacks, and later by

For a half-century, Galena was famous as the floatfishing capital of the world.
(Photo courtesy of Doal Yocum, a Townsend Godsey photograph.)

The Y-bridge was the third bridge across the James River at Galena. Dewey Short was the speaker at the dedication ceremonies. (Photo courtesy of Mary Lassiter)

automobile visited Galena. The fishing parties, usually with townspeople serving as guides, would fish for bass from long, narrow johnboats and camp on gravel bars along the way. Large parties, sometimes with as many as sixty or seventy people, would make their way over the deep holes and rippling shoals. Guides knew and would point out the many landmarks along the way. Colorful names, each with a history, accompanied each hill, bend in the river, or hole of water: The first day would bring the fishermen past Butler Hole, Gentry Cave, Mack Spring Hollow (where Galena began), Powder Mill Hollow, Tilden Hole, McCord Bend, Rogue Ford, Stone Ford, Mash Hollow (where an obligatory stop for white lightening was normally anticipated), and on to Cape Fair, the stop at the end of the first day. Day number two included Swift Hole, Virgin Bluff, Hoppey Gravel Bar, Winding Bluff, Buttermilk Springs, and finally Crab Tree Hollow. And the journey would normally conclude on the third day with Nolen Hollow, Winding Stairs, Ance Creek, Jackson Creek, and Naked Joe Bald Mountain where the James and White River meet.

Parties ranged from one boat to thirty-five boats. A commissary boat, manned by a cook, normally accompanied the party. This boat, loaded with food and tents, would leave before the fishing party and set up camp for the fishermen while they were still out on the river. Then, the following morning, the cook would be the last to leave the campsite after cleaning and pack-

ing the gear. During the day, he would by-pass the fishermen and have another camp set up for them by nightfall. The johnboats were especially designed for shallow, rippling streams like the James and White River. The long narrow boats sat shallow on the water and were easily controlled by either a paddle or a pole. Because they were usually made from lumber, often from rot resistant cypress, the boats were heavy and leaked. Bailing water was a normal part of any trip. The fishermen, of course, spent their day casting and retrieving their wooden lures, often hundreds of times, in hopes of catching a lunker fish from the rich waters.

In the early 1940's floatfishing on the James and White Rivers declined. World War II took people's attention away from extended vacations, and fuel shortages discouraged travel to remote areas like Galena. After the war, a brief resurgence of floatfishing occurred, but when Table Rock Lake was formed by the completion of the dam on the Stone-Taney County line in 1958, the best waters for floatfishing were destroyed. A long tradition, which made Galena a major vacation spot and brought in outside revenues, ended.

Galena survived because it was the center of government activities in the county. The very lake that destroyed much of its income base for half a century proved to be the impetus for increased and expanded government services. In 1947, when Clyde Robinson was elected to the first of his terms as commissioner on

The motor car ushered in an era of change to Galena and Stone County. Vehicles were shipped to Galena by rail, then sold to county residents.
(Photo courtesy of Ardis Stewart)

the county court, the county budget was $37,000, and the total county payroll totaled seven individuals.

By the early 1960's county residents began to notice an increase in the population of the county, particularly in the southern section. Tourists began arriving to vacation and fish in the lake—followed by newcomers, often senior citizens seeking retirement homes. As a result, two new towns, Kimberling City and Lakeview, were formed. The new residents expected more from local government than was previously available in the county. In particular, the miles of roads under county supervision increased and county offices expanded to provide additional law enforcement, accurate up-to-date assessment of property, and the supervision of voting in the county. The 1992 budget for Stone County provided for over 80 employees with a payroll of $3.7 million.

Galena prospers today because it is the seat of

county government. Building projects have been helpful. In 1986 the fourth bridge across the James River was built to replace the "Y" bridge and reroute traffic around the outskirts of town. But this bridge has fostered the new building of businesses on Highway 13 on the edge of town. A large county garage in which to house and repair county road and bridge equipment has also been built on Highway 13 north of town. Finally, the completion of a new justice center in 1992 across from the courthouse, which contains a jail, sheriff's office, and courtroom facilities, ensures continued employment for many residents.

Galena, a town formed a decade before the county came into existence almost 140 years ago, is destined to remain the county seat of Stone County for many more years.

Robert McGill

The English Village in the Ozarks
Historic Hollister

Deep in the Missouri Ozarks, seven miles "as the crow flies" from the Arkansas state line, is Hollister, a community distinguished by Old English architecture throughout its business district. The instigator of this feature was William H. Johnson, a developer who envisioned an "English Village in the Ozarks." Through his urging, the Old English style was mandated by city ordinance in 1913. How Johnson's vision of an attractive community became a reality is a fascinating tale.

The story begins in 1873 when widowed Malinda Fortner and her grown son Jacob, after a torturous journey by wagon over rough trails from Arkansas, felt they had found their "land of milk and honey." They looked upon the deep pools and shallow rills of a broad creek, smiling in the sunshine and edged by tall grasses. The land had never been turned to the plow. They saw the bluffs to the east and west, protecting the gently sloping valley of Turkey Creek as the stream completed its winding, northward flow to join the White River. For Malinda this was journey's end. This was the site she would homestead.

Records show that a tract of 120 acres became Malinda Fortner's permanent property in 1873 and that another tract of forty acres, adjoining Malinda's to the north and west, belonged to her son, Jacob J. Fortner. The 160 acres would become the heart of Hollister, one of the most unusual little towns in the United States.

Malinda Fortner lived for eight years in her cabin on Turkey Creek "bottom" land. This was long enough for her to learn that gently flowing Turkey Creek could suddenly become a rushing, threatening torrent that reached to the doorway of her little cabin and sometimes surged inside the log walls. After Malinda's death in 1881, her land was purchased by Harden Warren for $150. To avoid flood waters, Warren built a larger log house on higher ground.

Before his mother's death, Jacob Fortner had married and built a cabin on the slope to the west.

The couple and their children lived there until 1882 when they sold their land for $100.00. In 1883, after two changes of ownership of the forty acres in rapid succession, Warren acquired them at one dollar per acre. This, added to the 120 acres from Malinda's estate, made a tract of 160 acres, which he sold in 1891 for $800.

In the 1890's freight wagons came through the Turkey Creek valley en route to Springfield, then growing rapidly as a railhead city. Gobbler's Knob road (today's Taney County Highway BB), a connecting route from northern Arkansas to Springfield, reached Turkey Creek at the Fortner lands. A ferry operated across the White River, just below the mouth of Turkey Creek.

In those years of railroad expansion, traffic to the Turkey Creek Ferry and beyond increased. Wagons came loaded with railroad ties cut from the immense stands of hickory and oak trees in the woodlands, to be hauled northward to a railroad branch at Chadwick. An able-bodied man could cut and square off nine or ten eight-foot lengths in a day, earning twenty cents for each. Two dollars a day was more cash than a man could earn from any other use of the rough Ozark land.

In 1900, land was selling well at $1.20 per acre as prospects for development brightened. Rumors were flying that attracted buyers to the land along Turkey Creek. One rumor was that a railroad would be built to connect northern Arkansas with Kansas City. A portion of the route would follow Turkey Creek, crossing the White River on a bridge near the creek's confluence with the river. Another rumor was that the land was rich in minerals, and many an acre was purchased for mineral rights. The creek valley took on new importance. Although little of value came from the mineral finds, the railroad became a reality.

By 1904 the St. Louis, Iron Mountain and Southern Railway (a branch of the Missouri Pacific) had purchased a right-of-way through what would

Early Hollister was influenced by the railroad. Disembarking passengers dined at the Log Cabin Hotel.
(Right photo courtesy of
Chloe LaRue; below courtesy of Viola Hartman)

Local residents and visitors to the Maine Club enjoyed socializing at the Kite Drug Store, left store in photo.
(Photo courtesy of Chloe LaRue)

become Hollister and the price for the old Fortner lands had risen to $2,500. Even at that price, Reuben F. Kirkham, a store owner at Cedar Valley, believed he could make a profit with a store near the railroad, serving the railroad workers and the growing local population. He purchased the land.

Kirkham arrived with his wife and daughter and built a store adjacent to the railroad right-of-way, near the present day highway railroad overpass in Hollister. He believed business would flourish because trains would stop for passengers, freight, and mail service. He obtained a permit to operate a United States post office, which he named Hollister because the hilly lands reminded him of Hollister, California where he and his family had resided briefly. The official date for the opening of the new post office was June 18, 1904—considered to be Hollister's birthday. Area residents and the railroad workers appreciated the new store's convenience. Kirkham frequently made trips to Springfield to restock with needed items, a round trip of at least five days over a winding, rutted, hilly road.

Other needs of the residents and transients had to be met if the community was to grow. A blacksmith shop was built close to Kirkham's store, and the nucleus of a village had its start. Soon there was another general store nearby. Unfortunately, Kirkham's store was burned to the ground in 1905 when a band of robbers invaded it in the night. In debt, the Kirkham family left the area. Thomas F. Jennings became postmaster and held the appointment until 1914, operating the office in a new store he built.

January 21, 1906 was a great day for Hollister, then grown to a population of 250. The first puffing, noisy locomotive hauled a few cars into town and pulled up at the depot, a boxcar located near the site of today's Ozark Mountain Bank. Almost immediately, tourists became a part of life in the little village of Hollister.

The first tourists were businessmen from St. Louis who would leave their railroad passenger cars at the makeshift boxcar depot. In their city clothes and carrying their gun cases, they contrasted sharply with the townsfolk. The attraction for these vacationers was a sportsmen's club and hunting lodge, known as the Maine Club, located where the College of the Ozarks is now. The St. Louis men had purchased a huge spruce log building which had been the state of Maine Exhibition hall in St. Louis' Forest Park during the Louisiana Purchase Exposition of 1904. The dismantled building was hauled by train to rail's end at Branson, and by wagon across the White River and up the long hill to its new building site.[1]

William H. Johnson, who had a law and real estate business in Forsyth, saw the possibilities of land promotion around Hollister. In 1906, he purchased the old Fortner lands plus adjacent tracts, laid out a business district, and sold lots. Working with him was J.W. Blankinship, a retired professor who had moved with his family into the old Harden Warren house. Land sales boomed.

Johnson's son, William W. Johnson, was a Drury College student in Springfield, but left college to come to Hollister with another Drury student, Rolland B. (Pete) Kite, Jr. They had a frame building erected behind the boxcar depot, facing the dirt street called "Broadway," and opened a drug store, complete with soda fountain. Some of the Maine Club sportsmen brought their wives with them, and the drug store was particularly popular with the younger women. Will recalled in his late years how the young ladies, in their long skirts, would ride into town on muleback. He and Pete enjoyed watching them attempting to mount and dismount, before the young men belatedly offered assistance.

The passenger trains made noon mealtime stops regularly in Hollister. To accommodate them, the Log Cabin Hotel was built about 1907 on the slope to the west of the tracks. It was patronized by train passengers until it burned in 1930.

In 1909, seeking to attract people to the vacant business sites east of the railroad tracks, W.H. Johnson had an inspiration. With cooperation from the railroad administrators, he planned a new street using Old English architectural style. Business buildings would face the railroad. All would be in the same style—tile roofed, walls half-timbered on stucco, with lower walls of stone from Turkey Creek.

There was a problem, however. Existing Hollister business buildings faced the unpaved street Johnson had named Broadway, today the rather narrow avenue between Downing Street and Business 65. It took some persuasion to get the business owners fronting on Broadway to do a "turnabout," but they eventually acquiesced. The new street was named Front Street (now Downing).

The first Old English style building completed on Front Street was the Bank of Hollister, a small structure at the corner of Third.[2] This building and the handsome depot were completed in 1910, and construction began on "Ye English Inn" adjacent to the bank. Although the inn was enlarged to its current size in 1927, the unique curving stairway and fireplace in the lobby were in the original small hotel.

In 1910 Hollister became an incorporated city, and elected Professor Blankinship mayor. Both Will Johnson and Pete Kite had married by then. Will became cashier of the bank; Pete and his bride took over the drugstore business, moving soda fountain and all to a room off the lobby of Ye English Inn in 1912.

The railroad had provided a landscape planner to beautify Hollister, particularly along the "Esplanade" that led to the fine new depot. Since "open range" prevailed, cattle and hogs roaming the dirt streets ate the plantings until the city marshal managed to corral the animals into a pen, against strong opposition from the stock owners, who repeatedly destroyed the pens.

The trains brought tourists aplenty, not just sportsmen. Whole families came from the cities, seeking the natural beauty, and to enjoy swimming and other simple pleasures available in and around Hollister. A tent camp arose along Turkey Creek north of the new buildings, and a big frame building, the "Presbyterian Assembly," was erected atop the eastern bluff. Tourist business increased rapidly in Hollister after the Powersite Dam was completed in 1913, downstream on the White River. Its backwaters formed Lake Taneycomo,

then suitable for both swimming and fishing.

Otto Kohler and his wife, former show people, opened a tourist resort at the south edge of town. As self-proclaimed official Publicity Director, Kohler promoted Hollister far and wide, and was instigator of the Grape Carnival, a major annual event in the 1920's when fruit growing was important in the Hollister environs.

The main highway from Forsyth came through Hollister, crossing Turkey Creek on the first steel bridge in Taney County (the one-lane bridge on Third Street, erected in 1912 and still in use today). Enroute southward, the main highway followed Front Street to Fourth Street and there crossed the railroad tracks, continuing generally along the route of today's Highway 65.

Hollister prospered in spite of periodic floods that inundated the business district. But as the 1930's began, the good times were about to end. The passenger trade on the railroad dwindled as new highways were built for the growing automobile traffic. The Great Depression engulfed the nation and fewer cars arrived. During World War II would-be tourists stayed at home because gasoline was rationed.

The floods that came with spring rains had grown worse with the formation of Lake Taneycomo, as unchecked river waters deepened and widened the lake. Year after year, the business buildings on Front Street were flooded. The peak year of floods was 1945 when, on April 18, the water in Ye English Inn lobby was eight feet, eight inches deep! The Inn closed its doors.

By 1955, only the post office and a grocery operated on Front Street. The inn was a desolate sight. Cedar slabs covered the broken large front windows, and a dirty bit of ecru curtain hung from a second floor window left slightly ajar. The death of the town was predicted and seemed imminent.

But such dire predictions proved false. After Table Rock Dam was completed in 1959, the flood threat ended, and the special qualities of the town drew new investors. A corporation financed by local residents was formed to renovate Ye English Inn, which reopened in 1967 with a street barbecue celebration to mark the event. Soon vacant stores were housing new business ventures. Downing Street, newly renamed, was widened to accommodate the revived traffic flow.

Today the English Village in the Ozarks is alive and thriving. The population growth between 1980 and 1990 was the largest, percentage-wise, of any municipality in Taney County. Many new businesses have opened. The old depot, neglected and only a freight stop for years, was renovated to become Hollister City Hall.

Business operators have made a specialty of antique and craft shops as well as providing services needed by tourists and residents. Because of the Old English theme, begun so many years ago, Downing Street became a registered National Historic District in 1978, and new business buildings are following the established architectural style.

In Hollister, tourists find a relaxing change from the area's concentration of motels, theaters, and bumper-to-bumper traffic. With its architecture and naturally beautiful setting, Hollister remains unique—the English Village in the Ozarks.

Edith McCall

Edith McCall resides in Hollister and is the author of *English Village in the Ozarks, The Story of Hollister, Missouri.*

1 In 1915, after fire destroyed its first building in Forsyth, the School of the Ozarks, presently the College of the Ozarks, purchased the Maine Club building and grounds. Hollister young people attended high school there until the 1920's when high school classes were added to the Hollister public school.

2 The Bank of Hollister served the community until 1931 when the deepening Great Depression forced its closing. The building was not abandoned, but housed the Hollister Post Office until 1960. It has since been enlarged and continues as a place of business.

The charm of English architecture in Hollister continues to please both residents and visitors—as it has for over 80 years.
(Photo courtesy of Viola Hartman)

Hurley

The rippling waters of Spring Creek flow beneath a bridge on the main street of Hurley, Missouri. Spring Creek mill, once an important part of the community, is perched precariously on the east bank of the stream. Its machinery and mill wheel gone, the building is a mere shell, a reminder of days past when farmers for miles around brought corn to be ground into meal, and wheat into flour.

History is a bit hazy as to the identity of the first white settlers in Spring Creek Valley. Most of the early families arrived about 1850 from Kentucky, Tennessee, and Illinois. Many descendants of these pioneers still call Hurley and vicinity home.

In 1861 news of the Civil War reached the small settlement. The Wire, or Telegraph Road, located some two miles northwest of Hurley, was bustling with soldiers of both the Federal and Confederate forces. The war produced hardships. Because local farmers had also gone off to war, the women and children were left behind to tend the fields and livestock. During and even after the war, pioneer settlers experienced many a sleepless night as bands of outlaws, calling themselves bushwhackers, roamed the countryside, plundering and killing at will.

Before the coming of the railroad in 1904, supplies for the Hurley stores were hauled by wagon and team from Marionville, Missouri, the nearest freight center. Mail brought to Hurley in this manner or on horseback from the town of School (later renamed Union City) was delivered as a courtesy rather than in an official capacity.

> ### *Byways*
>
> I love the little country towns
> So quiet and serene,
> With houses nestling small and white
> In shaded lawns of green.
>
> We do not speed, we drift along
> On muted, drowsy wings;
> We loiter by the wild-rose banks;
> We pause at stone-walled springs.
>
> Blue mountain haze, like Galilee,
> Is waiting just out there;
> We feel its cleansing, healing charm
> As answer to a prayer.
>
> Mary Elizabeth Mahnkey

The first commissioned postmaster, E.R. Scott, when asked to send in a name for the post office, suggested Spring Creek. Officials complained that the name was too long. So the post office was called Hurley, either in honor of a postal inspector, or after the fiance of a postal inspector's daughter. No one seems to know which version of the story about Hurley is correct. Town folks simply say, "No matter which story you believe, your stamps cost the same."

After the advent of the railroad, Hurley became a bustling, thriving town. In 1926 Hurley boasted seventeen different business locations, including a canning factory, telephone exchange, and a motor company.

In the 1930's the Great Depression, coupled with a general drought, took its toll of the economy of the small town. As better transportation became available, people began shopping in the larger cities. Hurley's small town merchants could not compete with chain stores and larger outlets. The final blow to the business district came in 1972 when the Missouri Pacific railroad from Springfield to nearby Crane was discontinued.

Today, Hurley has only one general store. However, local activities in the small settlement continue to flourish. The Hurley Community Building provides a meeting place for all occasions. The town boasts an excellent public high school, several churches, and a city park.

Strangers asking directions to Hurley may hear, "Hurley? Oh yes, where Mary Scott Hair lives!" Hurley is proud to claim Mary as its very own. A writer and local historian, her weekly column, "Much in a Basket," has been published in the *Crane Chronicle* for forty-five consecutive years under the pen name of Samanthy.

As this petite, gracious lady sits in her "house by the side of the road," people from all walks of life and far away places find their way to her door. Some seek history of families who lived in Spring Creek Valley long, long ago. Others just stop to rest and "chat a spell." On a warm summer day Mary may be found in her Granny Belle Short's old rocking chair on the screened-in porch. Numerous cats, her constant companions, frolic at her feet. Turtles, birds, and a variety of small animals are regular visitors to her back door, where they are assured a hand-out.

Mary Scott Hair, a lover of people, nature, and animals—and life itself, is always ready to tell about Spring Creek valley and the days when Hurley was a bustling town. Although Mary has no official title she is, by popular acclaim, the First Lady of Hurley, Missouri.

Fern Angus

The Kanakuk Kamps

CARLETON'S SWIMMERS, KUGGAHO CAMP
1932

A group of campers at Camp Kuggaho in 1932 on Lake Taneycomo. The counselor in this photo is Spike White (the tallest individual), who later purchased the camp.
(Photo courtesy of Spike White)

Every summer, 7,000 youngsters—mostly from the midwest but also from distant states and even foreign countries—eagerly look forward to spending one to four weeks at one of the Kanakuk Kamps in Ozark Mountain Country. The camps, located in Taney, Stone, and Barry Counties, emphasize water and team sports, gymnastics, and wilderness adventure—all presented in a Christian atmosphere. Four of today's camps, two on Lake Taneycomo near Branson and two on Table Rock Lake near Lampe, are owned and operated by the White family: Joe, his wife Debbie Jo, and his parents, Spike and Darnell.

The fifth Kanakuk Kamp, Kids Across America, was developed by the Whites in 1991 on Table Rock Lake near Golden in Barry County. This camp provides inner city and mentally handicapped youths the same high quality camping experience that youngsters enjoy at the other camps, but the expenses of the campers are covered by the *I Am Third Foundation*, the not-for-profit organization which owns the camp.

Each of the K-Kamps consists of two units, one for girls and one for boys. A cabin counselor is assigned to each four campers. The counselors and activity directors, who number over a thousand, are Christian athletes drawn from college campuses in the midwest and east.

Camping days are filled with water activities, hiking, and gymnastic and team sports geared to the age and experience of the youngsters, who range in age from seven to eighteen.

The Kanakuk Kamps have a long and enduring history. In the early 1920's, C.L. Ford established Kickapoo, a camp for girls, at the mouth of Bee Creek on Lake Taneycomo downstream from Branson. A few years later, across the lake, he opened Kuggaho, a boys' camp focused on sports. The father of today's camps was W.M. Lantz, Kuggaho's director until the mid-1930's and its owner for some sixteen years.

The boys' camp, renamed Kanakuk after a Kickapoo Indian leader and prophet, was purchased in 1953 by Spike White, the father of the present camp director. Spike had been a camp counselor at Kanakuk during his college years while he studied to become an electrical engineer. When he bought the camp, he was a physical education instructor at Texas A & M University, having returned to school to earn a second master's degree so that he could pursue his deep commitment to working with youngsters in outdoor athletics. With three young sons to support, Spike realized that he would have to maintain his teaching position in Texas, but he and his family came to the Ozarks every summer

Spike and Darnell White, left. Below, their son Joe, daughter-in-law Debbie Jo, and grandchildren. The White family has owned and operated Kanakuk Kamps for nearly forty years.

(Photo courtesy of Spike White)

to run the camp. In 1961, noting that many sisters came along when parents dropped off their sons at Kanakuk, the Whites built Kanakomo, an adjacent camp for girls, and devised a long range plan for the camps' continued growth.

From 1978 through 1990, Kanakuk also ran a week-long "post-season session" which brought three to five hundred inner city youngsters to the Lake Taneycomo camps. Beginning in 1983, a similar program offered camping experiences for seventy to a hundred mentally handicapped youngsters. These programs led to the establishment of the first full season of the Kids Across America operation in 1991. At these camps some

2,000 boys and girls from inner cities across the midwest experience—in a supportive, caring atmosphere—an extended week filled with outdoor sports designed to build self-reliance and cooperation. Sessions also are held for mentally handicapped youngsters.

The *I Am Third Foundation* which funds the Kids Across America camps derives its name from the philosophy which motivates the White family, the Kanakuk Kamps, and the people who are helping fund and operate the Kids Across America camps—the belief that God comes first, then one's neighbor, then one's self.

Kathleen Van Buskirk

The New Towns

Kimberling City
Lakeview/Branson West

Kimberling City: The Town Many People Built

Two trends prompted the development of Kimberling City. First, Table Rock Lake filled with water in 1958, and tourists began visiting the lake and enjoying the beauty and recreational opportunities of the area. And second, in the late 1950's many Americans—especially retirees—were beginning to leave the industrial cities of the north and east for warmer climates and the lower cost of living in the Sunbelt states. Developers noted the trends and began a new town, Kimberling City, to offer a high quality of life to potential new residents.

In 1959 John Q. Hammons of Springfield, who owned property in what is now Kimberling City, registered the name with the State of Missouri and built a new Holiday Inn motel, Kimberling Inn. He named the community-to-be after John Kimberling, a long-time resident of the area who at one time operated a ferry across the White River near where the bridge crosses the lake today. Originally the ferry was a crossing point of the river on the pre-Civil War Wilderness Road between Springfield, Missouri and Berryville, Arkansas when oxen-drawn wagons and freighters traveled the road. Eventually, motor vehicles supplanted animal power and the demands on the ferry became so great that a bridge had to be built across the White River in 1927.

The area immediately around the bridge was already well known to fishermen since the Rogers Motel, a fishing resort, was then in operation on the

The two bridges at Kimberling City just before Table Rock Lake filled. Both bridges still exist but one is under the lake.
(Photo courtesy of Table Rock Lake/Kimberling City Area Chamber of Commerce.)

south side of the river. Float fishermen, too, frequently took their boats from the river there because of the convenience of the highway. When Table Rock Lake was built in the late 1950's, a new, higher bridge was built to link the two sides of the county.

Ironically, when Table Rock Lake filled with water, the first crossings of the lake near Kimberling City had to be taken by ferry because workmen failed to complete the new bridge on time. Army engineers and young soldiers from Ft. Leonard Wood operated the modern ferry for several months until the bridge could be finished.

Residential building in Kimberling City began in 1960 when Hobart Jennings and Mel Taylor, two businessmen from St. Louis, purchased over 600 acres from

John Q. Hammons and began, in partnership with Jim Wolf, to build Kimberling Hills, the major residential area of Kimberling City.

Meanwhile a restaurant and bowling alley, which for many years was the mainstay of the social life of the community and the nucleus of the new shopping center, was built. In 1968 R. Layne Morrow purchased property from Mr. Hammons and extended the shopping center at Kimberling Center.

The city was incorporated in 1973 after heavily debated elections over city boundaries. A first incorporation election took place in May. If the proposition had carried, the city limits would have included roughly the area of the Kimberling Hills subdivision. When that issue failed, a second election held in June established, by a narrow margin, a much larger city limits which curved around the shoreline of Table Rock Lake.

J.B. Norvine was appointed the first mayor until an election could be held. Chester Betts was elected the first mayor and completed one year of his two year term. He was followed by Betty Edgington who, with nine years of service, became the longest-serving mayor. **A later mayor, Ned Locke, retired to Kimberling City from Chicago where, for many years, he hosted children's television shows and was nationally known as the ringmaster for Bozo the Clown.**

The primary duty of the early mayors and city council was to establish basic services for a brand new town, one built where a short time before only grass and trees grew on rocky hillsides. A road department was established so that roads could be built and potholes repaired. The first police chief, deputies, and dispatcher were employed to ensure public protection. A state agency gave the town two trucks which, when the parts were torn apart and reassembled, provided the town's first fire truck for only $800—the cost of transporting the two trucks from Jefferson City. The establishment of the first local ambulance service followed the establishment of the fire department; local volunteers were trained to answer emergency calls for both. The sewage system, after years of planning, was finally installed. The water system was built by an independent district.

But government services do not make a town. And because the town was made up largely of retirees, social activities, especially centered around the bowling alley and country club, have become important. Civic clubs are popular as evidenced by the fact that during the mid-1980's the Lions Club had the state's largest chapter with over 150 members. Several social clubs, including popular square-dancing clubs, provide additional entertainment.

Tourism, too, is important to the town, and the greatest promoter of visitor activities is the Table Rock Lake/Kimberling City Area Chamber of Commerce. The Chamber began early in the history of the town when Fern Scheer, proprietor of the Hillbilly bowl, personally answered requests for information about the town with hand-written responses. In 1977 Kelly Edgington became the first executive director of the Chamber. Presently the Chamber operates from its own building which contains a visitors center, meeting room, and executive offices. Rozella Hamilton is currently the director of the rapidly expanding organization.

Today, Kimberling City is both a residential area with many retired families and a business district that caters to visitors to the lake. In just thirty years, it has become the largest town in Stone County.

Lakeview: One Man's Vision

While Kimberling City is largely a residential town, Lakeview is almost strictly a business community. Lakeview began in 1974 with a handshake between Howard Claybough and Woody Akers. For many years Woody operated a gasoline station, hamburger stand, and convenience store at the intersection of Highway 76 and 13. The store had become an area landmark. Howard, a Chevrolet dealer in Reeds Spring for fifty years, was looking for a new building for his agency. When he asked Woody Akers to sell him three acres of land near his store, Woody responded that he would sell not just the three acres, but the store and surrounding ten acres as well—for $100,000. Negotiations between the two took five minutes. Another ten minutes elapsed while Woody went back into the store and got his personal belongings. When he emerged, Woody handed Howard the key to the store. The following morning the two met at the bank in Reeds Spring, which Howard owned, and legally transacted the exchange. Howard had acquired not only a site for his new Chevrolet agency—but for a new town.

Howard constructed the building for the Chevrolet agency, then decided to put a shopping center on the rest of the ten acres. He placed a grocery store on one end of the center and a branch of his Reeds Spring bank at the other. Various businessmen rented space in between, the first being Lee Michelle who opened a restaurant.

An anomaly of the law caused the town to be incorporated. Howard discovered that branch banks could only be built in incorporated towns, not in the countryside. Therefore before he opened the branch bank, he had a narrow strip along Highways 13 and 76 incorporated in 1974. Howard and Woody named the new town after the scenery at the location, Lakeview. Woody became the first mayor.

In 1985 Howard, who now had been in business for over 60 years, purchased an additional thirteen acres across the highway directly south of his shopping center and began plans for a shopping mall. But before he could begin, Howard needed to lower the intersection by eleven feet to make an approach to the mall. This he accomplished at his own expense. Soon Howard was building the south wing of the mall, with the True-Value Hardware Store, the new supermarket, and his own drugstore as the nucleus. The south wing was quickly followed by the 360 foot long, 60,000 square foot, north-facing wing. Traffic became so con-

Howard Claybough
(Photo by Wayne Johnson)

gested around the mall that the state highway department consented to placing traffic control lights at the intersection, the first traffic lights in the county. Today, the mall is not only completed but filled with businesses, and Howard still tends to business daily.

Other businesses, especially motels, gift shops, and eating establishments that serve the tourist industry, have become established in Lakeview. Fast foods restaurants and franchise establishments help ensure that tourists can be quickly and well fed; and gift shops and other businesses provide services to meet the needs of area residents and visitors alike.

A current local furor exists in Lakeview over the name of the town. In the spring of 1992 the city council officially renamed the town Branson West, despite considerable local opposition. While the new name continues to cause controversy, one thing is certain. This new town, which was once Akers Store, has a very bright future.

Robert McGill

Kirbyville at the Crossroads

Kirbyville as it appeared shortly after the turn of the century. Notice the telephone poles along the highway, indicating telephone service arrived early in this Taney County town.
(Photo courtesy of Chloe LaRue)

The business section of modern-day Kirbyville, located about halfway between Branson and Forsyth on Missouri Highway 76, consists of an old-fashioned general store with a storm door at the front and a post office at the back. Late model cars and road-worn pickups whiz down the hardtop highway. Their drivers, unaware that Kirbyville used to be a prominent commercial center, rarely stop at the "wide spot in the road."

But back in the late 1800s, when eggs were five cents a dozen and present-day Branson was still a cornfield, Kirbyville was a crossroads of commerce.

In 1869, a visionary named Warner laid out the village, calling it Warnersville. He platted three sixty-feet-wide avenues crossed by nine streets. Two years later, William M. Kirby established a post office and renamed the town. Soon dozens of houses, a two-story schoolhouse, a Masonic Lodge, and several businesses lined the streets and avenues of Kirbyville. Merchants named Kintrea and Brazeal, Parnell and Van-Zandt, owned stores there at various times. Other businesses included a hotel, a drug store, two doctors' offices, a livery barn, a blacksmith shop, and a cotton gin.

In no time, Kirbyville became one of Taney County's principal communities, and for good reason: it was an important crossroads for the freight wagons that rumbled along the busy highway between Harrison, Arkansas and Springfield, Missouri.

Long before the Civil War, a major commercial route between Harrison and Springfield had been opened for travel. Freight wagon drivers took the road out of Harrison up to Bear Creek Springs, where they camped for the night.

In the morning, some of the drivers headed west for Berryville. Most of them, however, drove their teams thirteen miles north to Omaha, Arkansas where they crossed into Missouri. The rocky road followed a high ridge between the White River to the east and Turkey and Coon creeks on the west. Then it angled northwest to the freighters' first stop, Kirbyville.

The same route can be followed today. It shares the roadbed of U.S. Highway 65 out of Harrison. Just north of Omaha, the old road—Boone County Highway 23—branches to the right and, as it crosses the Missouri line, becomes Taney County's JJ Highway. JJ passes alongside Murder Rocks, which during the Civil War was a hide-out for Alf Bolin's notorious bushwhacker gang. JJ ends at J Highway, which continues northward to Highway 76 at Kirbyville. Few automobiles, and surely no eighteen-wheelers, travel that route today. But in the nineteenth century, the Harrison-Springfield highway was the period's equivalent of a modern interstate.

When the freighters reached Kirbyville's main thoroughfare, Grand Avenue, the road forked. The drivers usually halted for the night. In the morning, they turned their wagons either northwest toward Hensley's Ferry or northeast to Forsyth.

More than wagons passed through Kirbyville: drovers herded sheep and turkeys to market along that route. The turkey flocks didn't necessarily stop at Kirbyville, however. Wherever they happened to be at sundown, the birds flew into the great hardwood trees along the road and roosted for the night. When they left the next morning, a few of Kirbyville's turkeys sometimes strutted along with them.

Besides its convenience to sheepherders and wagon drivers, Kirbyville also had the good fortune to be located a few miles east of important lead finds—the Silver Moon Mine and the Josie "B" Mine on Wolf's Branch of Turkey Creek. And the town lay just north of the great Layton pinery, a plantation of pine trees where, in 1852, Dr. Augustus S. Layton built the region's first steam-powered sawmill. The mill provided many of Kirbyville's breadwinners with steady employment and furnished consumers south of the White River with a superior grade of pine lumber. For a short time, too, other men found work at a plant that manufactured Schley hay balers.

However, the streets of Kirbyville were not always peaceful. During the reign of the vigilantes known as Bald Knobbers, townfolk witnessed a one-sided duel: a Bald Knobber shot to death an unarmed Anti-Bald Knobber who might have presented evidence against the vigilantes' leader in a murder trial. Grand Avenue also was the arena for a noisy but bloodless standoff between the Bald Knobbers and their antagonists. And then in 1890, a Taney County sheriff and a hired gunslinger went to an Independence Day celebration at Kirbyville, intending to kill Billy Miles, who

was out on bond awaiting trial for the murder of the Bald Knobber's leader. The sheriff found Miles and his brothers at Kirbyville's big spring and fired at them. The Miles brothers shot back, killing the sheriff and his sidekick.

But shortly after the turn of the century, Kirbyville's streets became quiet—too quiet. When the railroad tracks reached Branson, Kirbyville lost its role as a crossroads way station. The freight wagons rumbled right past Kirbyville and took their loads to the train depot. By the end of World War II, the dusty rock road had become a modern, hard-surfaced highway. The once bustling stores gradually went out of business, and the town shrank into a mail stop. Today it's a rare traveler who even bothers to slow down enough to obey the speed limit sign, let alone stop.

Mary Hartman

The VanZandt Cemetery

Strangers have bought the VanZandt place
And I wonder if they know
Of a little plot upon the hill
Where sad white roses grow?
Will they see that way, that solemn way
That leads up to the hill
Where the gate is closed in sorrow
And everything is still?
The old Captain lies here sleeping
In the fields he loved so well
Where melodious tones still echo
From his old farm dinner bell.
We have two darlings lying
Within this sacred sod—
Oh, remember, please, dear strangers,
This acre belongs to God.

Mary Elizabeth Mahnkey

Note: The VanZandt
Cemetery is located near
Kirbyville

Protem

THE TEMPORARY TOWN OF C.C. OWEN

Protem as it appeared shortly after the turn of the century. At the time, Protem was an important trading community on the White River. (Photo courtesy of Kathleen Van Buskirk)

In 1854, a bright young entrepreneur named Christopher C. Owen led a wagon train south out of Benton County, Missouri. After several days, the emigrants reached a big spring on Shoal Creek in southeastern Taney County.

The twenty-five year old C.C., as he was known, called a halt. Six miles farther south were the banks of White River. Crossing the rapid, deep waters that divided Missouri from Arkansas would entail loading wagons one at a time on a rickety ferry. C.C. decided the tired wayfarers should lay over for a few days.

Owen looked around. Besides the spring with its clear, cold water, he discovered a flat area protected from winds by hills on all four sides. Beyond the hills lay acres of unclaimed fertile bottomland. Certain that he had found an ideal location, he convinced his fellow travelers, including two of his brothers and their families, to settle.

C.C. was no stranger to challenges, having always lived on the frontier. He had been born in 1829 in Barren County, Kentucky, son of an educated Scotsman named George W. Owen. When C.C. was thirteen, the Owens moved to Benton County, Missouri where his father opened a tanyard. By 1849, C.C. had married. Along with farming, he operated his own tanyard and a blacksmith shop. During the next few years, he also served as Benton County's assessor and sheriff. In 1854, a restless C.C. talked relatives and friends into heading south toward warmer climates and greener pastures.

The settlers cleared bottomland and planted corn, tobacco, and cotton. The crops thrived, and C.C. built sheds or square-log block buildings so the families could move out of their covered wagons. In time, he replaced the crude shelters with log cabins and plank houses.

Seven years later, the Civil War erupted. C.C. and one brother, William Wilson Owen, returned to Benton County, formed their own companies, and joined McClurg's Union Home Guard Brigade as lieutenants. A few months later, C.C. was promoted to captain. His troops fought skirmishes at Lone Jack, Missouri, in Arkansas, and Indian Territory. Although C.C. escaped injury, his brother William died of wounds.

When the war ended, C.C. returned to Taney County. His other brother, Joel, also returned home from the defeated Confederate Army. Divided loyalties caused a permanent rift; the arguments so alienated the brothers that Joel changed his surname to "Owens."

Despite the schism, C.C. accumulated land until he owned three or four river bottom farms and a fifteen-hundred acre ranch. He continued to build homes and even erected a couple of cotton gins. But C.C. earned his fortune as a trader. Driving his wagon to Springfield, he bought supplies and carted them back to the settlement, selling directly out of the wagon at first. Proceeds financed other trips to Springfield.

C.C. eventually built a retail store and put his wife in charge while he drove the wagon to Springfield for more supplies. He entered politics and held several offices, including a two-year term as state legislator.

In 1875 C.C. established a post office at his store and became postmaster. Two factions had different ideas about naming the town. One Saturday, men from each faction drove their wagons to a meeting. It was to be a showdown; all carried shotguns. C.C., who knew Latin, counseled them: "We're not getting anywhere. Let's call the community 'Protem' from the Latin *pro tempore*, meaning temporary. We can petition the government to change it later." His even-handedness prevailed; the name, however, was never changed.

Peacemaker, postmaster, merchant, politician, builder, and farmer, C.C. soon added another title—doctor. After completing a correspondence course in 1882 and passing the State Board of Health examinations, he become a licensed physician and opened a doctor's office.

That same year, the Springfield & Southern Railroad finished laying tracks from Springfield to Chadwick, Missouri. Goods that had been brought in or shipped out on steamboats landing at the White River port of Forsyth would now be hauled by railroad.

The railhead at Chadwick was a boon to Pro-

tem, which sat at a strategic midpoint on the eighty-five-mile, hilly, rock-rough road from Yellville, Arkansas to Chadwick.

Freight wagons crossed the White River on the Brown or Bradley or Nave ferries, and the drovers camped at least one night near Protem's big spring. Before traveling north to Chadwick, they spent money with the town's flourishing merchants.

Protem became a major trading center. Some said it rivaled Forsyth, the county seat, forty-five miles northwest. As shown in the May 22, 1890 property tax assessment, Protem boasted four dry goods stores, one drug store, two blacksmith shops, a harness shop, a doctor's office, a justice of the peace, and a notary public. It also had a church, Masonic Hall, and one hundred twelve students attending the local school. Fifteen years later, the town's business district had acquired another general store, two millinery shops, a community bank, another blacksmith, a combination garage and ice house, a two-story hotel, and a gristmill. During harvest season, wagons loaded with loose cotton would line up as far as the eye could see along the road leading to the two cotton gins. Baled cotton went by steamship and flatboat to markets in Memphis or by wagon or railway car to St. Louis. Everyone in Protem fared well, especially C.C. Owen.

When C.C. retired, his son, Hiram Franklin, better known as H.F., took over as Protem's entrepreneur. Several clerks held down jobs at the Owen Mercantile, and laborers took home paychecks from the cotton gins. Hired hands worked the family's large ranch, and farmers sharecropped Owen bottomland.

Before long, better roads and highways led out of Taney County. H.F. invested in a couple of Henry Ford's new-fangled trucks, and his freight business found new markets. H.F. bought the farmers' rough timber and shipped it to manufacturers of stave bolts, posts, and crossties. He sold black oak and hard maple to hardwood-flooring manufacturers and oak, maple, wild cherry, and sycamore to furniture factories.

H.F. brought Protem into the twentieth century

when he and four Forsyth businessmen constructed the first crude telephone lines between Protem, Kissee Mills, and Forsyth.

But H.F. died at an early age, and the Owen legacy passed to his nineteen-year-old son, Hobart Franklin Owen. Hobart followed in his grandfather's footsteps when he led a petition drive to incorporate the village. On August 4, 1922, the town's official name became Protem.

Hobart found money easy to come by in the Roaring Twenties. He purchased more trucks, established lumber yards, and trucked finished posts to midwest customers. Then came the Great Depression. It hit Protem like a full load of buckshot.

Cash became so scarce that there were occasions when Hobart couldn't find sufficient change in the register to break a dollar bill. Customers bartered potatoes and cabbages for drill bits or boots, chickens and milk for sugar or coffee. Patrons with nothing to trade asked for credit; Hobart and his wife turned no one away hungry. More than once, Hobart's wife handed an aging man or woman sufficient funds to procure false teeth. When a young couple borrowed money for a marriage license, Hobart tossed in enough for a new dress, a pair of trousers, and a shirt. He loaned another fellow the money to get started in the trucking business. As a consequence, most of the store's assets were tied up in accounts receivable.

But in the late 1930's, with World War II in the offing, the economy started to improve. Cedar posts were in demand, and Hobart's logging trucks made thousands of trips to northern Missouri, Iowa, and Illinois.

Today travelers on Highway 125 south of Protem must cross Bulls Shoals Lake on a ferry.
(Photo courtesy of Kathleen Van Buskirk)

Then the federal government established the Mark Twain National Forest and regulated timber cutting, which put a crimp in the logging business. A few of Hobart's creditors paid him back. Many didn't. Eventually, Hobart threw away charge tickets worth hundreds of thousands of dollars, reached his financial limit, and went broke. He lost the ranch and all his farms, the garage, his trucks, and, most painful of all, the retail establishment. He moved the family to Forsyth and started over. In 1937, he opened an Owen Mercantile and a Chrysler-DeSoto dealership. Owen succeeded, but Protem never recovered.

Today, travelers drive down U.S. Highway 125 on their way to the State of Arkansas' Peel ferry and pass through Protem, Missouri without being aware they're doing so. If they look sharp, they'll see a couple of houses, a graying country store waiting like a tired hitch-hiker beside the highway. There's a block building with an outdoor privy and an abandoned two-story schoolhouse, its shattered windows hidden under a grove of trees. Down the road, a one-lane bridge carries the traveler across Shoal Creek and past a proud cemetery that entombs the bones of old settlers.

The Protem of today serves as little more than a mail drop for a community scattered into the hills by a macabre miscalculation. In the early 1950's, the United States Corps of Engineers dealt the final deathblow when they completed a dam that would tame the White River and create Bull Shoals Lake. The Corps exercised the government's right of eminent domain and built a fill where they calculated that water would back up behind Bull Shoals Dam. Bulldozers leveled Protem, completely distorting century-old landmarks. But the engineers guessed wrong and the Bull Shoals shoreline lies six miles away from Protem. Its seventy-foot depth shrouds family graves, rotting homesteads, and rich bottomland downstream from where C.C. Owen once envisioned, correctly, the tassels of tall corn, the blossoms of bumper cotton crops.

Mary Hartman

Service

When they put away my silken scarf
My beads and thin gold rings
Will they think of my old washtub
My broom and other things?

The little hoe I kept for flowers
The basket for dead leaves:
No one to use them anymore
And so my spirit grieves.

Mary Elizabeth Mahnkey

A Town that Mirrors the Ozarks
Reeds Spring

The Spring at Reeds Spring in the mid-1920's.
Water still flows from the spring today.
(Photo courtesy of Chloe LaRue)

Most first-time visitors to Reeds Spring enter the town from the north. They pass under the railroad viaduct, turn left off highway 248 onto highway 13, and travel south. The small stream of water flowing beside the highway emerges directly from Reeds Spring and becomes Railey Creek as it flows northward and enters the James river near Galena. Visitors then drive past the neatly kept houses and businesses, take a sharp right downtown (often without noticing the source of the spring on their left), and continue southward out of the town and into the heart of the two county tourist area.

In doing so, visitors pass through a town that has mirrored the development of the Ozarks in many ways. While the population of Reeds Spring has remained relatively constant for its first seventy years of existence—the 1930 and 1950 censuses both list the town with a population of 313—the town has changed as residents responded to outside economic influence.

Reeds Spring came to life around the turn of the century when the White River Iron Mountain Rail-road announced in 1902 the building of a railroad, which would pass from Carthage, Missouri through Reeds Spring to Cotter, Arkansas. The railroad would connect Memphis with Topeka. Newspaper accounts of the building of the railroad report that a new town, Reeds Spring, would be built on the rail line.

Some activity existed in Reeds Spring prior to 1900. The focal point for the town was undoubtedly the spring itself. Indians, trappers and early settlers undoubtedly visited the spring as they trapped and hunted on Railey Creek. Settlement in the valley near the spring began immediately after the Civil War when railroads in Missouri extended no further than Rolla, Springfield, and Sedalia. Cattle drovers from Arkansas, Oklahoma, and as far away as Texas herded their cattle to these railheads north and east of Reeds Spring by traveling the Wilderness Road.

Early references in the 1870's are made to two brothers by the name of Reed who arrived at the flowing spring in the late winter and grazed their cattle on the open range until early summer when they moved their herd on to market. The following year the Reed brothers settled permanently by the spring, which was flowing from a hazelnut grove.

With the announcement in 1902 that a railroad would be built through Stone and Taney Counties, Reeds Spring became a boom town. Residents of the small town of Ruth, situated on the Wilderness Road just a couple of miles southeast of Reeds Spring, moved to Reeds Spring when their general store and post office was closed and reopened in the growing town. Two other general stores were opened and, in anticipation of even more growth, a new town plat was recorded with county officials in Galena in 1903.

One of the major engineering feats on the new railroad line was the boring of a quarter-mile tunnel through an Ozark mountain a few hundred yards east of Reeds Spring. The railroad established Camp A

The town of Reeds Spring began when workmen started excavating the railroad tunnel, pictured at left. Shortly thereafter, Dr. L.S. Shumate arrived in town and began a sixty year medical practice.
(Photos courtesy of Chloe LaRue)

at a site near the proposed tunnel and imported a mixture of workmen—Italians, Austrians, and blacks from the South—to drill the tunnel. The workmen, using dynamite and steam drills, started on each end of the tunnel and drilled a 2,000 foot long tunnel, 18 feet high and 24 feet wide through the solid rock. Four years later, when the tunnel ends met, the centers were only a fraction of an inch off center. During the height of construction, the 250 men working at the site could remove ten feet of rock daily; the payroll escalated to $700 per day, and the total project was estimated by the railroad to cost $500,000. Most of the town's life centered around the building of the tunnel.

News of the impending railroad also helped entice young Dr. L.S. Shumate, straight out of Barnes Medical College in St. Louis, to settled in the town in 1902 at the age of 23. In search of a place to establish his medical practice, Doc Shumate rode the train into southwest Missouri as far as Marionville, then took a hack to Galena, where he briefly took up residence with Dr. Forge. A flu epidemic was rampant upon his arrival in Galena. When Mr. Sharpe, from south of Reeds Spring, made the trip to Galena to ask Dr. Forge to look at his child who was sick with malaria, Dr. Forge could

not leave his sick Galena patients. Dr. Shumate agreed to make the call and tended the girl until she recovered several days later. This visit initiated a sixty plus year practice in Reeds Spring. Until he could purchase a horse, Doc Shumate visited patients by walking the rugged trails of the countryside to small cabins in the hills; eventually he purchased a hack and, finally, one of the first cars in Reeds Spring. In 1965 he was honored by the citizens of Reeds Spring for his years of practice, including being present at over 3,000 births.

When the railroad was completed in 1906, the town changed noticeably. A stockyard was built next to the railroad track. Buck Webster built a hotel, later known as the Bush Hotel, across the street from the passenger station to serve visitors, traveling salesmen, and one itinerant dentist. Other businesses included a livery stable, Mr. Brinson's blacksmith shop, and the Swift Bank.

The business of supplying ties to the railroads became the first industry in Reeds Spring. Even before the railroads, ties from Stone County were being floated down the James River to markets in Arkansas and along the Mississippi. The railroad allowed the tie-hackers to market their timbers nearer to home.

The huge red and white oak forests around Reeds Spring and in the massive Roark Valley that extends from Reeds Spring to Branson provided an abundance of trees. Tie-hackers would alternate their activities by cutting a day in the woods and then hauling their ten or twelve ties to the "yards" to be sold. Often the hackers with their loaded horse-drawn wagons waited in lines two or three blocks long before unloading their ties at the tie yards where other workers graded and hand-loaded the ties onto railroad cars. The ties were then shipped to railroad construction sites in the western parts of the United States. In the early 1900's, Reeds Spring proclaimed itself the railroad tie center of the United States. But by 1915 most of the virgin timber had been cut, prices plummeted, and the industry faded quickly.

But fortunately for Reeds Spring, the tomato industry was developing in time to take the place of the tie business. Hundreds of acres of tomatoes were grown on farms around Reeds Spring and several processing plants dotted the hills and hollows of the countryside.

Two canneries existed in the vicinity of Reeds Spring. One of Frank Mease's seven canneries was located just north of Reeds Spring while Bob Emerson's cannery was downtown in a quonset hut near the railroad station. These canneries provided the hub of commercial activities in the summer and early fall when townspeople, in need of spending money for the winter, worked in the fields and canneries.

In the fall of the year, buyers from midwestern grocery wholesalers would arrive at Reeds Spring by rail and travel to the canneries throughout the area to purchase tomatoes. They would arrange for tomatoes to be delivered to boxcars at the Reeds Spring siding and then the buyers, often on the same train with their tomatoes, would depart for another year. Boxcars of tomatoes were shipped from Reeds Spring until Bob Emerson closed the last remaining cannery in1968.

During the 1920's, Reeds Spring changed again when another mode of transportation—motorized vehicles—came into existence. Townspeople purchased the first cars in the area, but soon farmers had the four-wheel vehicles too. People became more mobile, roads were improved, and Reeds Spring became a trading center for the area. Especially in the 1930's, Saturday afternoons became a social occasion when residents from the central part of Stone County came to Reeds Spring to shop or visit with neighbors.

During this period, in 1932, the infamous Bonnie Parker and Clyde Barrow (nationally known as Bonnie and Clyde) took a surprised area resident hostage as he walked to town, blasted their way through a sheriff's blockade south of town, and later released the unharmed man in Arkansas. Today the incident reminds Reeds Spring residents that a thread of violence runs through its history: a murder along the railroad right of way when the railroad was being built, brawls in the streets of the wide-open town in the 1920's, the shotgun killing of the town marshall in 1978, or the murder of a thirty year old man in 1990. In the past thirty years, the town has been the scene of no less than eight murders, suicides, or violent deaths.

After World War II the apparel industry emerged as a major employer in the Ozarks, just in time to supplant the dying tomato canning industry. Again, Reeds Spring was fortunate enough to be the recipient of one of the new factories. In 1945, Reeds Spring Mayor, Frank Judah, and John Workman enticed Tony Hagale to construct the garment factory. The building, which was erected on a site near the railroad where much of the original downtown area had been located, opened with 36 employees. As did most garment factories in the Ozarks, the Hagale factory employed women to operate the clattering sewing machines and whirring cutters on the assembly line. The factory in Reeds Spring, which has employed as many as 250 workers and remains the largest employer in town, began by making overalls and then, depending on the existing contract, coveralls, sleeping bags, khaki pants, and dress slacks.

When Table Rock Dam was completed in 1962, tourism became an important part of the economy of the town. Since many tourists travel on Highway 13 through Reeds Spring, the town is often regarded as the gateway to the tourist industry on Table Rock Lake. For many years, fishermen passed through the town on their way to the lake. In recent years, to cater to the tourist industry, some excellent craftsmen have settled in and around Reeds Spring. The influx of artisans began when the Wilderness Clockworks shop north of town became a gathering point for woodcarvers in the 1960's and 1970's. Carvings are still available through the Clockworks although the only carvers currently calling Reeds Spring home are Alicia Trout and Dave Rausch. Currently, potters dominate the crafts scene. Tom Hess produces terra cotta and Mark Oehler throws pottery at the Omega Pottery Shop. Other potters in the area—Al Lemons, Gloria Warnock, Bruce Thorpe, Dennis Thompson, and Neil Nulton—either market their pottery to retail shops or sell at craft shows. Copperworkers Lee Robertson and Ed Seals prefer creating functional art while Jewelers Ronna Haxby, Jim Day, Greg Becker, and Jeanette Bair fashion copper, silver, and gold rings, broaches, and necklaces. Lori Brown weaves intricate Pine Needle Baskets and the Martins, who are fifth generation basketweavers, create baskets from strips of white oak.

Reeds Spring is one of the centers of education in the county. Truman Powell, a newspaper editor who traveled extensively in Stone County before the turn of the century, reported that in 1883 Reeds Spring consisted of only a log cabin, which was used for a school. The next school, started shortly after the building of the railroad, was a subscription school held in Buck Webster's hotel. But the citizens of Reeds Spring soon built, north of the downtown area, a public school which held eight grades of students. Two successive schools, both eventually razed by fire, were then built on the hill, west of the downtown area. The first school to offer twelve years of education to Reeds Spring youths graduated eight high school seniors in 1927. In 1936 WPA workers completed another new school building near the underpass north of town, a building which at one time or another has housed all grades. Reeds Spring evolved into the dominant school in the central part of the county when school consolidation began taking place in the 1930's, requiring additional classrooms to be added to the schools. In the 1960's the population growth of the area, which began after the building of Table Rock Lake, was reflected in the schools. Since 1960 a near-continuous building program, including the construction of all classrooms in use today, has been instituted, the latest building being the Junior High School completed in 1991. In addition, a multi-county school, the Omar Gibson Vocational Technical School, was constructed in Reeds Spring in 1972.

The outstanding single attraction to Reeds Spring today is the home of Joe Dan Dwyer, which is located on the East side of Highway 13, south of town. Joe Dan was born and raised in a small house on the location of the one in which he now resides. After being injured in a logging accident in the Northwest, he returned to Reeds Spring where he now spends much of his time supervising the construction of improvements to his home and surrounding gardens.

Robert McGill

Skaggs Community Hospital

Skaggs Hospital, on a hill overlooking U. S. Highway 65 and downtown Branson, has been a highly visible landmark since the day it first opened back in January, 1950. What a difference it has made, both to tourists and to the people who live in Ozark Mountain Country.

Without the presence of its emergency room, now rated a Level III Trauma Center, anyone unlucky enough to be injured or become ill while in the area would have to be rushed fifty miles to a Springfield hospital, and nearby residents needing hospitalization would find themselves miles from home and caring friends and relatives.

Hospitals came late and are still scarce in the upper White River region. Even today, few towns in Taney and southern Stone Counties are big enough to support more than one or two doctors.

When the railroad was being built in the early 1900's, and the farming village of Branson began growing into a town, three doctors moved their practice here. J.P. Compton, a long-time country doctor from near Notch, established his office in his new home. Dr. Charles Burdett moved his office and drug store north from Kirbyville. Physician and surgeon Elizabeth McIntyre had her office on the first floor of her building, and let the upstairs be used as a community hall.

In the early decades of this century, the injured or ill usually were cared for in their own homes. A patient needing special care, with no family nearby, was taken to a local boarding house. Before improvement began on the miserable roads in the 1920's, few people in Taney and southern Stone Counties spent their hard-earned dollars on cars; to get to a hospital in Springfield meant a trip by train or a rugged seventy-five mile journey by wagon or buggy. Badly injured or dangerously ill patients might not survive the journey to a hospital.

Automobiles and paved roads, sulfa drugs and penicillin changed medical expectations in the region dramatically during the 1930's and the years of World War II. In 1949, construction of Table Rock Dam was soon to begin and more visitors and new residents were already arriving. Safeway founder M.B. Skaggs, who had grown up in eastern Taney County and was well aware of the area's need for a hospital, told the four doctors then practicing in Branson and Hollister that he would help raise the million dollars such a building would cost by matching any funds the local people could raise.

When the townspeople, enthusiastic but still struggling to modernize businesses, industries, and tourist facilities after the Depression and war years, could not meet Skaggs' challenge, he and his wife Estella paid most of the cost of building a 25-bed hospital. In making the donation, they specified that "no requirements may be made for entry other than the need of care."

From the beginning, most of the directors on the board of Skaggs Hospital have been area doctors. Harry T. Evans, J.M. Threadgill, William C. Magness, and Frank Aubin, the four doctors who made up the first board, underwrote the hospital's operating expenses.

Through most of the 1950's, while Table Rock Dam was being built, having the hospital speeded treatment of frequent on-the-job injuries. As vacationers flocked to enjoy the huge new lake— many buying home sites along its edges—the number of patients being treated in Skaggs' emergency room multiplied quickly. Over the next thirty years, the number of patient beds was increased, first to fifty, then to ninety-nine. A radiology department, intensive care unit, surgery ward, and larger emergency room were added.

In 1984, Skaggs Hospital provided "courtesy cards" for area residents and computerized applicants' physician and insurance information, allowing admissions and other services to be handled with little delay. The number of applications for the courtesy cards soon reached several thousand. Their use also helped the hospital identify and meet the need for satellite walk-in clinics in Kimberling City and Forsyth.

THESE WERE THE FIRST

*One of the first classes of Red
Cross volunteers at Skaggs hospi-
tal, recruited and trained by
Jessie May Hackett.*
(Photo courtesy of Skaggs American Red
Cross Volunteers)

In the 1990's, the hospital is again being enlarged. The emergency room, laboratory, radiology, and same-day surgery sections are being expanded, a state of the art helicopter pad and a two-level parking garage are being constructed, and the original building is being renovated.

As the area's population has grown, hospital services and programs which previously required traveling to Springfield have been added: tomography (CAT scan), same-day surgery, physical therapy, the trauma center, home health services, social services, nuclear medicine, medical equipment stores, pathology and high-tech obstetrical departments, skilled nursing unit, and cardiac and pulmonary rehabilitation. As an adjunct to several of those services, a special bus now provides home-to-hospital service for handicapped or elderly patients who have scheduled appointments at the hospital.

A continuing educational program keeps members of the hospital medical team abreast of changes in medical procedures, and offers health maintenance and first aid training to the community. Through its community wellness program, Skaggs also runs an extensive walking program on several walking courses in the area, developed and monitored by the hospital.

Today there are twenty-three physicians on Skaggs' medical staff, representing family practice, general surgery, orthopedic surgery, ophthalmology, internal medicine, gynecology, radiology, and pathology, as well as five local dentists. In addition, many Springfield specialists are available for consultation and, when a planned clinic building is completed, will see patients in Branson on a regular basis. Some 450 hospital employees work in laboratories and medical services, patient treatment and care, food services, laundry, and hospital maintenance.

Community assistance has always played a vital role in the hospital. The Estella Skaggs Auxiliary, formed before the hospital opened its doors, began with seventy-four women volunteers, an astounding number in a town with fewer than two thousand residents. Through its gift shop and a resale store, the Auxiliary raises thousands of dollars to buy medical equipment for the hospital. The two hundred men and women now in the Auxiliary also act as patient escorts, deliver mail and messages in the hospital, and provide information to visitors.

In 1958, American Red Cross volunteers were

Skaggs Community hospital has provided medical services for over 40 years. The building pictured above has served Branson since 1950. Other building programs have expanded the hospital.
(Photo by Kathleen Van Buskirk)

recruited and trained as aides for the hospital. Red Cross volunteers provide patient comfort services: distributing menus, helping with diet selection, maintaining and distributing library books, combing hair, and assisting with letter writing.

Visitors to Ozark Mountain Country seldom think about the availability of modern medical assistance unless injury or sudden illness occurs. However, over the past four decades quite a few vacationers, along with many residents in the area, have been grateful that qualified, caring medical help was only minutes away.

Kathleen Van Buskirk

The Wire Road

Throughout the nineteenth century, the expanding frontier and westward migration marked the growth of the American nation. For a major portion of that century, Missouri was a jumping off place for expansion. First, the Missouri River led trappers to the beaver pelts of the Rockies; then later in the century Missouri was home to trailheads for major routes to the Pacific Coast.

During the 1840's and 1850's the fertile valleys of Oregon and the gold fields of California beckoned. By the mid 1850's the public brought pressure on the leaders of the country to pass a bill authorizing the Postmaster General to establish a cross country mail and passenger route. A bill to this effect, introduced by Senator William Gwinn of California and Congressman John S. Phelps of Missouri, passed in 1857. Bids were taken, and a contract was awarded John Butterfield of Utica, New York. Twelve months later service began on the cross country venture.

The Butterfield Overland Mail started at Tipton, Missouri in the central part of the state and ran southward, cutting across the northwest corner of Stone County. The route then ran through the southwest and on to San Francisco, California. In building the mail route, the venture established 141 stations and purchased 1200 horses, 600 mules, and over 250 regular coaches, freight wagons, and special mail wagons.

Although Stone County did not have any regularly scheduled stops, two sites were commonly utilized for unscheduled stops. The first was at the Alexander McCullah Settlement, one mile west of Brown's Spring; the second was at the Wesley McCullah Stop, some three miles on down the valley. Large free-flowing springs at both locations provided an abundance of water for both the passengers and the horses. Further down the valley, the Trail crossed Crane Creek, one and a half miles west of Crane, Missouri.

By the time of the Civil War, the Butterfield Trail in the Missouri-Arkansas border area was called the Wire or Telegraph Road because of the communications wire strung along its route from Jefferson Barracks at St. Louis, Missouri to Ft. Smith, Arkansas.

The Butterfield Overland Mail prospered for two and one half years until sectional feelings during the Civil War closed the route; a new central mail route from St. Joseph, Missouri, via Carson City, Nevada and on to San Francisco, California was established.

During the Civil War, soldiers of both the Confederate and the Union armies often camped at the McCullah Settlement and at the McCullah Stop. In fact, a skirmish, one of several in the area, occurred at the McCullah Settlement on August 3, 1861, one week before the Battle of Wilson Creek. Several years later, Wesley McCullah was killed by a band of lawless bushwhackers.

Today, the greater part of the road is on private property and largely inaccessible to travelers. However, vestiges of the Wire Road may be seen at several locations. From Crane, Missouri, take Farm to Market Road No. 110 one and a half miles west to a low water bridge where the Wire Road forded Crane Creek.

A bit of the Wire Road may be seen on farm road M-20, a short distance north of the Pierce-Gold Cemetery. The old road is marked by a row of trees which line the old trail. A short distance up the road north, a dwelling stands on its east side. The old house, built many years ago and aligned to the Wire Road, sits at an angle to the modern road.

In 1991, a contingent of soldiers reenacting the march up the Wire Road to the Battle of Wilson Creek near Springfield, Missouri, passed by the site of the long ago McCullah Settlement. A loud bugle blast rang out, flags waved in the breeze as the make-believe soldiers marched onward. Livestock in the area, grazing peacefully on the lush grass and unaccustomed to all the commotion, took one look, stampeded, and ran for shelter.

Fern Angus

Additional copies of this book may be ordered by sending
$19.95 for the cost of the book
plus $2.50 for shipping and handling
(Missouri residents add $1.05 tax [5.225%]) to
White Oak Press,
P.O. Box 188,
Reeds Spring, MO 65737

or by calling
1-800-356-9315
orders may be made by American Express, VISA, or Master Card
Choice of shipping methods is available.

Orders may be faxed to 1-802-482-3125